Pastors and Public Life

Pastors and Public Life

The Changing Face of American Protestant Clergy

CORWIN E. SMIDT

OXFORD
UNIVERSITY PRESS

OXFORD
UNIVERSITY PRESS

Oxford University Press is a department of the University of Oxford. It furthers
the University's objective of excellence in research, scholarship, and education
by publishing worldwide.Oxford is a registered trade mark of Oxford University
Press in the UK and certain other countries.

Published in the United States of America by Oxford University Press
198 Madison Avenue, New York, NY 10016, United States of America.

Library of Congress Cataloging-in-Publication Data
Cataloging-in-Publication Data is on file at the Library of Congress.
ISBN 978–0–19–045550–7 (pbk) — ISBN 978–0–19–045549–1 (hbk)

1 3 5 7 9 8 6 4 2
Printed by Sheridan, USA

To James Guth, Lyman Kellstedt, John Green, and the late James Penning, professional colleagues, personal friends, and co-researchers on clergy and others facets of American religious and political life. Working with you through the years has brought great joy, personal fulfillment, and scholarly satisfaction.

CONTENTS

LIST OF TABLES

ACKNOWLEDGMENTS

This volume began, in part, as a project while serving as the recipient of the Fulbright-Dow Distinguished Research Chair of the Roosevelt Study Center, Middleburg, The Netherlands. The Roosevelt Center was a congenial host, proving to be stimulating and satisfying environment within which to work, with Middleburg a delightful city within which to live. Special thanks go Cornelus van Minnen, Hans Krabbendam, and Leontine Joosse, all of the Roosevelt Center, for their hospitality and graciousness, and to the Fulbright Scholarship Program which made the experience possible.

ABBREVIATIONS

AOG	Assemblies of God
CRC	Christian Reformed Church
DOC	Disciples of Christ
MCA	Multiple Classification Analysis
RCA	Reformed Church in America
PC USA	Presbyterian Church, USA
SBC	Southern Baptist Convention
UMC	United Methodist Church

Pastors and Public Life

Introduction

The Changing World of Protestant Clergy

Few, if any, analysts would likely dispute the contention that clergy are important leaders within American religious life. After all, most clergy engage in their work at the "grassroots" of American life, seeking to foster and sustain religious vitality among the American people and the congregations they serve. Through their collective efforts, these ministers of the Word and Sacrament help to shape the nature of religious life within American society.

Although clergy are clearly important religious leaders within American society, their significance extends far beyond the religious dimensions of life. Clergy are also important figures within American public life. They are so, in part, because houses of worship stand at the center of American civic life. Gathering to worship is a religious activity, but it is also an important public activity in that, beyond its religious qualities, congregational life brings together relatively diverse individuals for sustained periods of time, frequently on a fairly regular basis. Of course, if relatively few Americans chose to gather together in public worship and participate in congregational life, the public importance of clergy and congregational life would be far less significant.

But, the centrality of religious congregations within American civic life is evident from a couple basic facts. First, the percentage of Americans who report that they are a member of some religious body far surpasses reported membership in any other voluntary association, as approximately two-thirds of the American people report church membership (Cnaan et al. 2006, 124). In fact, nearly as many Americans report church membership as report membership in all other kinds of voluntary associations combined (Smidt et al. 2008, 78)![1] Second, members of religious congregations stand in the center of the matrix intersecting members of voluntary associations within American civic life, as church members join other nonreligious voluntary associations at a higher rate than the population as a whole. As a result, the percentage of church members who report membership in these various types of voluntary associations consistently exceeds the percentage of the unchurched population who report membership in the same such associations (Smidt et al. 2008, ch. 3). Thus, as leaders of religious congregations, clergy also serve as important leaders within American civic life.

Finally, clergy have constituted important actors within American political life as well. Whether one examines their public pronouncements during the Revolutionary War, their championing of benevolent societies emanating during the Second Great Awakening, their involvement in the abolitionist movement of the mid-1800s, their engagement in the Prohibition movement of the early 1900s, their leadership in the civil rights movement of the 1960s, or their endeavors in mobilizing conservative Christians to become more politically engaged in the latter decades of the twentieth century, Protestant ministers have been both important actors and leaders helping to shape the direction and substance of American life culturally and politically throughout the course of its history.

The importance of clergy within American culture stems, in part, from the strategic positions they occupy in American religious and public life. Even taking the most modest estimates of the proportion of Americans who attend religious services on a weekly basis, tens of millions of adult Americans attend worship services on each Sunday led by a pastor who typically leads that congregation on some sustained basis. These houses of worship not only serve as important contexts in which religious worship transpires, but they also constitute locations in which important public deliberations occur (e.g., Coffin 2005; Djupe and Neiheisel 2008), civic skills are acquired (e.g., Verba, Schlozman, and Brady 1995; Djupe and Gilbert 2006), goods and services are provided for the needy (e.g., Cnaan et al. 2006), friendship ties are forged (e.g., Ellison and George 1994; Putnam and Campbell 2010), and the transmission and reinforcement of political attitudes can take place (e.g., Wald et al. 1988, 1990; Gilbert 1989, 1990; Jelen 1993; Welch et al. 1993; Djupe and Gilbert 2009). Given this situation, scholars have long paid considerable attention to the role that ministers play in American public life, seeking to understand the nature and significance of their political orientations and engagement (e.g., Johnson 1966, 1967; Hadden 1969; Quinley 1974; Jelen 1993; Guth et al. 1997; Olson 2000; Crawford and Olson 2001; Djupe and Gilbert 2003; Smidt 2004; Olson, Crawford, and Deckman 2005; Djupe and Gilbert 2009; Olson 2009). These various studies have typically revealed that clergy are indeed important actors within American public life, wielding substantial amounts of influence, particularly within their own religious communities.

However, life is not static in nature. The religious, social, and political environments within which clergy serve their congregants have changed dramatically over the past several decades. Despite the fact that the level of church membership and reports of weekly attendance at religious services have remained relatively stable over the past fifty years (Smidt et al. 2008, 44–45),[2] religion has become increasingly detached from its older social moorings (Roof and McKinney 1987; Hoge, Johnson, and Luidens 1994) and, as a result, it has become much more a matter of personal choice. Rising educational levels and increased geographical mobility have weakened old patterns of relationships between one's particular social and ethnic group membership and the religious affiliations historically associated with that group. At the same time, increased cultural assimilation has diminished many religious differences that were earlier linked to custom and heritage. In the wake of these changes, old loyalties have weakened, enabling new religious identities to emerge. And, as a result, religious life is more fluid today, being driven far more today by personal preferences than was previously the case.

Moreover, the religious marketplace within which clergy function has changed, as the nature of the "demands" related to religious life has shifted. Historically, American cultural life exhibited a more even balance between individualism and communal life (Bellah et al. 2007), but that balancing point has increasingly shifted toward a greater emphasis on individualism, as the old Protestant cultural emphasis on self-denial has weakened and an emphasis on self-fulfillment has become more prevalent. As a result, there are likely to be a larger proportion of parishioners today who embrace their religious faith more for its capacity to help them to attain subjective well-being and resolve their personal problems than for its capacity to provide theological truths and foster faithful living.[3] Accordingly, in their effort to enable congregants to achieve a more satisfying personal life, clergy today may be more likely to place less emphasis on personal sin and the historic doctrines of the faith than clergy several decades ago.

Organizationally, religious life has changed as well. Historically, clergy typically entered the ministry having been brought up as a member of the denomination in which they serve, having graduated from colleges and seminaries of that denomination, and having been licensed by that denomination in order to preach in its pulpits. Nevertheless, there is ample evidence to suggest that denominations do not play the same role in American religious life today as they did several decades ago. This is evident in various ways. Parishioners today are far more likely to move their church membership across denominations than was true several decades ago (Hoge, Johnson, and Luidens 1994; Hout, Greeley, and Wilde 2001). Denominational efforts to launch new congregations are frequently made without identifying the particular denomination with which the congregation is a part—choosing some name that is much more generic in nature (e.g., the New Life Community Church rather than First Baptist Church). In addition, well-established congregations within denominations are also increasingly willing to chart their own courses, as they are "less preoc-cupied with denominational identity and less impressed with denominational delivery systems" (Richey 1994, 89–90)—the net result being that denomina-tional headquarters and staffing have been facing growing financial challenges that have necessitated the elimination of programs and the downsizing of staff. And, finally, the decline of denominational distinctiveness is further evident in terms of licensing for preaching within these denominations, as various denomi-nations have chosen to make collective arrangements that enable clergy to more easily move across denominational boundaries to serve congregations within any of the cooperating denominations.[4]

Finally, the political environment within which clergy function today has also changed in some important ways. First, there is a larger segment of American society today than several decades ago who contend that one's moral convictions should simply be a private matter—with any reference to one's moral convic-tions within public deliberations being viewed as either irrelevant or inappropri-ate (Wuthnow 1999, 22). Whether it is because advocates of the privatization of religion fear that any discussion involving religious values would needlessly divide the body politic in an era of religious pluralism or whether it is because they truly believe such values have no merit in political decision-making, the fact remains that the deeper values and traditions that were once part of the public debate are no longer considered by some segments of the American public to be appropriate considerations within public discussion. As a result, religious beliefs are increasingly treated by many Americans as merely personal opinions best kept to oneself, thereby rendering them irrelevant to civic deliberation (Carter 1993; Casanova 1994).

Second, over the past several decades, an increased level of political polariza-tion has transpired within American politics, as political parties and candidates have become more ideological and have become more willing to adopt extreme positions on a broad set of policy issues (McCarty, Poole, and Rosenthal 2006). Although American public opinion has remained more moderate across a whole range of issues (Fiorina et al. 2005; Baldassarri and Gelman 2008), American voters have also become more polarized in their partisanship, with growing connections evident between and among their ideological orientations, their partisan identifications, and their partisan choices (Abramowitz and Saunders 2006). This growing polarization in American electoral life may well, in turn, affect the extent to which clergy may choose to address civic and political mat-ters publicly—whether from the pulpit or off it.

Finally, many clergy perceive the political environment around them as being more "threatening" than in the past. In late 2013, for example, seven out of ten senior pastors in the United States agreed that "Religious liberty is on the decline in America" (Smietana 2014). One year later, in the wake of some controversy surrounding citizen efforts to overturn a newly passed city ordinance that banned discrimination against LGBT people, the City of Houston, Texas, subpoenaed a number of local pastors, demanding "to see what they preach from the pulpit" related to the topics of homosexuality (Markoe 2014; Metaxas 2014; Stanley 2014). Perhaps in response to growing perceptions of restrictions on religious freedom, there appears to be a growing number of voices, including those of some pastors, who claim that the federal government does not possess the right to punish clergy for what they preach (including the endorsement of political candidates).[5] Not only has the number of clergy participating in "Pulpit Freedom Sunday" grown over the past five years (Kumar 2014), but a "high-profile" commission has called on the IRS to discard a 1954 policy that bans clergy from endorsing political candidates, in part because the current rules are not enforceable (Dart 2013; Smietana 2013).

Yet, despite all these changes, relatively little, if any, effort has been made to assess how American clergy may have actually changed over time—whether in terms of their social characteristics, their theological perspectives, their political attitudes, their norms related to engagement in public life, or their levels of political activism. Much has changed in American life over the past several decades. And, with the changing social and political environment, the growing challenges confronting denominational structures, as well as simply the generational change that has occurred within the ranks of the clergy, patterns that prevailed several decades ago among Protestant clergy may no longer hold true today.

This book then is about contemporary American Protestant clergy and the important changes that have taken place within their ranks. It analyzes the nature of the changes that have occurred among both evangelical and mainline Protestant clergy over the course of the past two decades, and it does so in terms of their social composition, their theological orientations, and their attitudes and behavior related to public life. As such, it constitutes the first published study that systematically examines the changing theological and political characteristics of American clergy over the past several decades, the possible changing nature of the relationship between their theological and political perspectives, and whether such changes among clergy are more evident within the mainline or the evangelical Protestant tradition (or particular denominations within each tradition).

A Brief Overview of Studies on Clergy Involvement in American Politics

Many of the initial studies of clergy and politics were driven largely by an interest in the role that ministers played within the civil rights movement (Olson 2009, 373).[6] These studies focused predominantly on a "new breed" of liberal, activist clergy (Cox 1967; Garrett 1973), generally emphasizing an interplay of various motivating and constraining variables that helped to shape their clerical activism. Overall, these studies did not seek to build theoretical explanations related to clergy involvement in public life; rather, they tended to be largely empirical analyses that advanced, in a more implicit fashion, different explanations in accounting for which clergy became involved in public life and which did not. Simply stated, these competing interpretations focused either (1) on the personal characteristics of those clergy who became politically active, or (2) on the particular contexts within which they ministered.

On the one hand, there were studies that emphasized the contextual role of the particular congregations in which the clergy ministered and served. For example, Campbell and Pettigrew (1959) contended that, if clergy wished to be involved in the movement to achieve racial integration, personal commitment to the cause was not sufficient in that such clergy also needed to enjoy the support of their congregation. Hadden (1969) also emphasized the role of congregations as potential constraining factors related to clerical activism in his analysis of the "gathering storm in the churches," as he sought to document an emerging "clergy-laity gap" that separated more ideologically liberal clergy from their more conservative congregants on matters related to theology and civil rights.

On the other hand, there were also studies of clergy that focused on the attitudinal factors that shaped clergy activism. Benton Johnson (1966, 1967), for example, emphasized how theology shaped political engagement, demonstrating that (at least among the Oregon pastors he studied) theological liberalism was closely linked to liberalism ideologically and Democratic partisanship. In contrast, theologically conservative Protestant clergy located predominantly within more evangelical and fundamentalist denominations largely shunned social and political activity (Koller and Retzer 1980; Nelsen and Baxter 1981). Doctrinally conservative clergy seemingly expressed "an antipathy toward the affairs of this world," believing instead that the salvation and regeneration of individuals would largely solve the problems that confronted American society (Stark et al. 1971, 105). Given this commitment to "miraculous and otherworldly solutions to human problems," theologically conservative pastors supposedly chose not to address social issues in their sermons. Indeed, so rare was their political involvement that some analysts (e.g., Stark et al. 1971) contended that only "sounds of silence" emanated from conservative pastors and attributed this lack of involvement to their "otherworldly" theology.

Thus, scholarly studies of clerical engagement in public life during the 1960s and 1970s largely suggested that their political engagement was generally limited to theological liberals who served within mainline Protestant denominations (Hadden 1969; Quinley 1974) or to black clergy who were involved in the civil rights movement (Morris 1984). And, with regard to such engagement, congregations largely served either as constraining (e.g., liberal pastors of more conservative congregations) or supportive (e.g., black pastors serving black churches) contexts within which such clerical activism might become manifested.

Following this initial wave of studies on the engagement of clergy in American public life, the field largely lay dormant for the next decade or two. It was only with the rise of the Religious Right during the late 1970s and early 1980s that scholars began once again to focus on the political engagement of clergy. Despite the fact that some analysts had contended that doctrinally conservative clergy were committed to "miraculous and otherworldly solutions to human problems," theologically conservative Protestant ministers had become increasingly involved in politics during the late 1970s and during the 1980s, with the apparent changes probably best symbolized by the formation and activity of such groups as the Moral Majority and the Religious Roundtable. No longer did it appear that clerical political activism was solely the domain of theological liberals, as scholars began "to reevaluate the emphasis placed on liberal clergy in the first wave of research" (Olson 2009, 374). Not only were theologically conservative clergy now seemingly at the forefront of political engagement, but once again it appeared that ministers had become a crucial source of political activism.

These substantial changes in clerical political engagement prompted a re-evaluation of the role of theology as a stimulus for involvement in political life (Guth 1983, 1984; Beatty and Walter 1989; Jelen 1993; Guth et al. 1997). One major endeavor that tried to come to terms with the substantial changes taking place was the work of Guth et al. (1997) in the publication of *The Bully Pulpit*. Their study of clergy across eight denominations, including both evangelical and mainline Protestant denominations, advanced the notion of social theology— namely "beliefs connecting theology to public affirms" (Guth et al. 1997, 8). Thus, social theology was posited to serve as an intervening variable that linked the theological viewpoints of clergy with the particular political attitudes they held and the political behavior they exhibited. Two general orientations related to social theology were identified among the clergy studied: a "social justice" orientation and a "moral reform" orientation, with their analysis suggesting that both the theological positions of clergy as well as the social theology associated with those perspectives shaped the political orientations of clergy, and thereby the nature and purpose of their political activism.

The new political activism of Protestant clergy also prompted a renewed examination of the role of contextual factors in shaping such activism (Jelen 1993; Olson 2000; Crawford and Olson 2001; Djupe and Gilbert 2002, 2003). This body of research explored the extent to which contextual factors served to link the political orientations of clergy with the nature and extent of their political activism. These studies, more qualitative in nature and richer in ethnographic detail, went beyond the context of religious tradition and denomination to examine how the local setting might enter into the political calculations of clergy in making their political decisions (e.g., how differences in the nature of the neighborhood in which the house of worship was located might differently affect the political actions of clergy who possessed similar theological view-points and social theological orientations). Scholars who adopted this approach argued that these contextual aspects "are significant indicators of and motivators for political activity" (Djupe and Gilbert 2003, 43) and that the political orientations and activism of clergy are shaped primarily by the ways in which they choose to "respond to the political and social environment in which they live and work" (Djupe and Gilbert 2002, 599).

Over the past decade, however, greater scholarly attention has been given to the extent to which clergy actually do have influence over the political views of their congregants (e.g., Fetzer 2001; Bjarnason and Welch 2004; Smith 2008; Djupe and Gilbert 2009; Nteta and Wallsten 2012; Djupe and Calfano 2014). Certainly most, if not all, of the earlier studies of clergy simply assumed that clergy were elites who, should they choose to do so, exercised significant political influence over their congregants. Some of the more recent research has supported this assumption, while other studies have challenged it. On the one hand, Fetzer (2001) found that pastors within Anabaptist denominations both reinforced and converted the views of their parishioners on issues related to war and peace, and Bjarnason and Welch (2004) found, using data from the Notre Dame Study of Catholic Parish Life, that when priests talked about the issue of capital punishment, such priestly speech had a significant effect on parishioners' attitudes toward the death penalty.[7] Finally, Nteta and Wallsten (2012) found that, in relationship to the issue of immigration reform, the issue preferences of parishioners were shaped, in part, by exposure to the political messages of religious elites.

On the other hand, Smith (2008) using the same data as Bjarnason and Welch (2004) found that priests do exercise political influence over their parishioners, but that such influence was more limited in scope and that its effects were more indirect in nature (i.e., through the shaping of religious attitudes that, in turn, affect political behavior). Moreover, in using their own surveys of clergy and congregational members of two mainline Protestant denominations, Djupe and Gilbert (2009) explored the multifaceted elements of congregational life (e.g., pastors, small groups, social networks) that can shape individual political attitudes and actions. They found that political information flowed plentifully within church life, but discerned little evidence that clergy directly persuaded their parishioners politically. They did find, however, there were indirect effects of clergy speech and that these effects occurred primarily through the stimulation of conversation within congregational life, with such conversation then fostering the majority message in the congregation to be adopted.

Despite the fact that the study by Djupe and Gilbert (2009) took an important step forward in research by pairing surveys of clergy with surveys of the parishioners of some of the pastors surveyed,[8] they may well have underestimated the extent to which clergy may influence the political opinions of their parishioners. This is because they choose to examine the link between clergy political speech and parishioners' political attitudes, even when such clergy noted that they rarely, if ever, addressed a topic,[9] and then did so among any and all parishioners—regardless of their level of worship attendance. In other words, had their focus on the linkage between clergy and parishioners been limited to topics that clergy noted that they had addressed "often" or "very often" within the context of the worshipping community[10] and then examined the influence such messages had among those parishioners who reported that they were in attendance weekly,[11] their assessment of clergy influence might well be much greater than it was—given that they included topics that clergy willingly reported they addressed only "rarely" or "seldom" and then made these assessments that included parishioners who attended church infrequently. Even weekly church attenders might well miss the fact that clergy had publicly addressed some political topic if it had been addressed only rarely by their pastor, but then to include occasional worship attenders in such assessments only further diminishes the likelihood of finding that clergy serve to shape the political views of their parishioners. Nevertheless, even using their particular approach, Djupe and Gilbert (2009, table 2.1) found that, of the five topics that clergy most frequently noted they had addressed in public, between 75 and 96 percent of the parishioners correctly reported that their pastor had addressed the topic—hardly substantiating the statement that "misperception (among congregants) of clergy communication is rampant" (Djupe and Calfano 2014, 28).

In addition, more recent research on clergy has also focused on the particular conditions under which ministers may choose to become engaged in the political process and the constraints under which they operate when they so choose to become engaged (e.g., Djupe and Neiheisel 2008; Calfano 2009; Calfano 2010; Calfano, Oldmixon, and Gray 2014). Scholars have long recognized that pastors operate under particular constraints when addressing political matters or engaging in political behavior. Many of the classic studies of clergy (e.g., Hadden 1969; Quinley 1971) revealed that congregations had a significant impact on clergy political behavior. Clergy whose views on politics diverge from those of their congregants "may feel pressure to remain quiet on political matters," whereas those clergy whose political perspectives are in tune with their congregants might "be encouraged (or at least not be constrained) by members opinions" (Djupe and Gilbert 2003, 101).

Certainly, when contemplating political speech and action, clergy may be rather averse to risking congregational disapproval, particularly if such political behavior is linked to a possible downturn in either membership or parishioner giving (Calfano 2010). For most parishioners, the primary responsibility of clergy is to sustain, if not increase, church membership and to promote the spiritual vitality of the congregation; it is not (primarily) to persuade the congregation to hold the "right" political opinion (Djupe and Calfano 2012, 10).[12]

Consequently, many, if not most, clergy likely avoid any frequent, and explicit, discussion of politics. After all, their primary role is religious and not political (Olson 2009), with political pursuits remaining secondary to religious priorities (Woolfalk 2012, 6). Since many Americans, including many church members, believe that churches should keep out of politics, institutional constraints related to church maintenance and growth "may prevent pastors from making overtly political statements (Woolfalk 2012, 7). Thus, in the end, clergy are far from free to act politically at their own whim, as research has shown that clergy may experience a number of significant, externally imposed, constraints when contemplating engaging in political endeavors.

Nevertheless, despite the presence of such possible constraints, many clergy still choose to become politically engaged. Perhaps it is not too surprising that most clergy note that, when asked about what motivates their political behavior, it is their own theological beliefs that primarily drive their political attitudes and behavior rather than the attitudes of congregation, their denominational leaders, or other clergy (Djupe and Gilbert 2003, 45), with relatively few clergy choosing to acknowledge that the attitudes of their congregations serve as a major force in shaping their political behavior. Finally, when asked whether they have the potential to influence the political beliefs of their congregants, the overwhelming majority of pastors (approximately two-thirds) affirm that they indeed have the potential to do so (see chapter 6).

Furthermore, even granting that congregational constraints may be significant, clergy may be able to overcome these constraints through various means. First, they may choose to engage in more subtle, rather than more explicit or overt, forms of political behavior, making it harder to detect and thereby likely deflecting some potential complaints by congregants. Thus, it is not surprising that clergy are far more likely to engage in cue-giving than more direct forms of political action (Guth et al. 1997, ch. 9).[13]

Moreover, even when engaging in cue-giving, clergy may choose not to directly reveal their particular preferences, but instead veil or frame their messages in particular ways that provide more sympathetic grounds for adopting particular positions on matters of public policy. Indeed, ethnographic research has generally found that clergy messages given during worship services rarely address "political activity or beliefs, such as specific public policies or civic involvement (including voting)," though they may include broader discussions of matters related to morality and social justice (Brewer, Kersch, and Petersen 2003, 125). Similarly, Woolfalk (2012, 12) has found, using data drawn from more than 21,000 sermons posted by more than 2,100 American Christian clergy on a website (SermonCentral.com), that the "vast majority of sermons do not include direct references to political matters," though "many sermons do contain implicitly political content." Moreover, some research has shown that the relative effects of implicit political cues within religious communications are actually greater than those of explicit political cues (Woolfalk 2014).

Second, when confronted with congregants who stand opposed to their political positions, clergy may also choose to adopt particular strategies by which to promote their political agendas and to convey their political positions to congregants. For example, clergy may choose to "diversify" their political cue-giving through the use of adult education study groups or more informal small groups within the congregational organizational structure; likewise, they may choose to "model" to their congregants how to deliberate politically (Djupe and Neiheisel 2008; Djupe and Calfano 2012). In examining how clergy chose to handle the controversial issue of homosexuality and gay rights in response to an Ohio ballot proposal banning gay marriage, Djupe and Neiheisel (2008) found that the personal interests of the clergy drove the amount of discussion given to the topic, whereas the nature of the political divisions within the congregation drove the content of such discussion.

Third, it is also true that, at times, clergy may look to other "reference groups" than that of their own congregation (e.g., elected lay leaders in the congregation, clergy peers, and/or denominational leaders) in order to sustain their political endeavors (Calfano 2009). Certainly, for most clergy who serve congregations, the reference group of greatest import is likely to be the congregation they serve (Calfano 2010, 651). Still, not only local congregations, but denominational superiors and one's professional colleagues can shape career advancement and ministerial success, and clergy political behavior can, at times, be colored by considerations of professional advancement and the desires of the church hierarchy. Consequently, the political behavior of clergy may well be, in part, an outcome of both personal values and the "anticipated reactions and professional sanctions" arising from parish and professional/institutional principals (Calfano et al. 2014, 4).

Furthermore, certain contextual factors may also prompt clergy political action. For example, clergy have been found to become more politically active in order to fill certain leadership gaps within the community (Olson 2000) or "when the congregation's beliefs are underrepresented locally" (Djupe and Calfano 2012, 94). And, despite the constraints that may typically exist when ministers serve congregations that hold far different political positions than that held by the pastor, it is nevertheless possible that, under certain conditions, "congregation-clergy ideological differences may drive greater clergy political activity" (Djupe and Gilbert 2003, 44).

Overall, then, it is likely that clergy do not frequently engage in direct, persuasive efforts, as such efforts may run the risk of alienating a substantial number of their parishioners. Not only do clergy have less credibility with their parishioners when they communicate political, as opposed to religious, messages (Djupe and Calfano 2009), but various cultural norms related to church-state separation may constrain the efficacy of explicit political cues within any religious messages conveyed by clergy in that explicit political appeals may "violate well-accepted standards of limited church involvement in politics" and, as a result, "congregants may resist such cues" (Woolfalk 2014, 7).

On the other hand, when political appeals remain more implicit within religious communications, parishioners may well be more receptive to political cues that, in turn, may unconsciously influence their political behavior. Thus, effective political communications by clergy in relationship to parishioners will likely display a more indirect route of influence (Djupe and Calfano 2014, 170). Just as is true with regard to the mass media, rather than successfully engage in direct persuasion, clergy are more likely able to set agendas, frame interpretations, and prime criteria of evaluations (Djupe and Calfano 2014, 170). Thus, the political influence of clergy is evident much more indirectly through the offering of cues; though these cues may not so much persuade, they do and can play important roles in reinforcing and prioritizing issues and setting political agendas among their congregants.

Time as a Contextual Variable

Despite this more recent research attention on contexts and conditions under which clergy may choose to become engaged in the political process, there is, however, one contextual variable whose effects on clerical political thought and activism has not been analyzed—namely, the contextual variable of time itself. With the passage of time, the contexts (e.g., the cultural, economic, and political contexts) within which clergy perform their ministerial responsibilities can change in that the relative importance of religion within society may have shifted, the status of clergy within society diminished, and the social characteristics of those choosing to enter the ministry modified.

First, over the past several decades, there has been a "softening" in American religious life, as historical barriers to interfaith marriages have diminished and the relative salience of religion has become more "polarized," with far fewer Americans now saying that religion is "somewhat important" their lives (Chaves 2011). As a result, there are far fewer casual members and occasional church attenders who used to swell the ranks of church rolls (Breen 2011).

The social status of clergy has also shifted over time. This shift could well be related to this "softening" of American religious life, but it could be totally independent of it. For example, pervasive and sustained public reports of clergy improprieties could lead to a diminished public stature of clergy even if cultural patterns related to religious affiliation and attendance did not shift. The same would likely be true with regard to various high-profile actions of clergy (e.g., "burning the Koran," organizing demonstrations outside the funerals of gay soldiers, or publicly declaring the date in which Jesus Christ will return to earth). Such actions, given their high public visibility through media coverage, may well have contributed to a decline in public evaluations of clergy as a whole.

Likewise, those who choose to enter the ministry have changed over time. Although the changing social status of clergy may affect the types of people who choose to enter the ministry, significant patterns of change in the pathways to ministry can nevertheless occur without any major changes in the social status of clergy. For example, within most denominations, only males have historically been permitted to become clergy. Now, women are permitted to be ordained as ministers of Word and Sacrament within most denominations. Likewise, increasing numbers of Americans are changing careers in mid-life, and increasing numbers of pastors are entering the ministry later in life. What is unclear, however, is what effects, if any, such changes may have had on the nature and extent of clergy engagement in public life.

Economic conditions also change with the passage of time. Economic growth may characterize one point in time, while economic recession may prevail at another cross-section in time. Just how clergy choose to engage in ministry may well be shaped by such circumstances. Clergy, like others, have only limited amounts of time and energy. One might anticipate, for example, that the time and attention that clergy give to addressing the needs of financially struggling families within their congregations would be far greater during times of economic recession than during times of economic growth. With the increased demands on their time and energy related to addressing such needs during periods of economic downturns, clergy may be less able to devote time and energy to other causes both within and outside their congregation. Thus, under such circumstances, it may be that, with such increased demands on their time and energy, coupled with the increased difficulties of their congregations to address such needs, that larger numbers of clergy may be moved to hold that governments should become more responsible in ameliorating the economic plights of such financially stressed families during these particular periods of time than during periods of economic expansion.

Finally, the political context within which ministry occurs also changes over time. The political context in the immediate aftermath of the collapse of the Soviet Union and the tearing down of the Berlin Wall (the late 1980s) was far different from that only a little more than a decade later in the aftermath of the 9/11 attack on the twin towers of the World Trade Center and the Pentagon. Thus, even if the theological perspectives of clergy do not change over time, how the clergy may choose to interpret their religious understandings and apply them to public life could change with the changing prevailing contextual circumstances at different points in time.

But, even without such cultural, economic, and political changes, time can also shape and color the theological perspectives held by clergy. With the passage of time, theologians may advance different understandings of just how prevailing theological doctrines should be interpreted. The relative emphasis placed on different theological doctrines can also shift with the passage of time, as can perspectives related to how such theological doctrines are to be applied and understood. Likewise, theological understandings related to the role of the church and the role of clergy can shift with the passage of time, along with normative understandings related to what kinds of actions may, or may not, be proper for clergy to do as ministers of the Word and Sacrament.

Thus, one important question not previously addressed by scholars is this: How have Protestant clergy, their social characteristics, their theological and political viewpoints, and their engagement within American public life changed with the passage of time? In other words, how do clergy today differ from their counterparts several decades ago in the ways in which they choose to minister, devote their time and energies to the competing demands of ministry, and in the topics they address from the pulpit? Have their theological perspectives changed over time, and, if so, do we see a convergence or divergence among clergy theologically? And does the same hold true politically? Have Protestant clergy become more polarized politically over the past twenty years? And, to what extent, if at all, has the gap between clergy and the laity they serve diminished with the passage of time? These are the types of questions that this study seeks to address.

The Data Employed

This study is about clergy serving in local churches, and it is based on data collected from clergy from the same seven denominations collected across three points in time over the past two decades—in 1989, 2001, and 2009. It is based on responses to 9,822 surveys from "ordained clergy" who served as the primary pastor responsible for preaching to the congregation in which they ministered.

When a denomination chooses to "ordain" a pastor, they are granting that person the authority or right to "hold office" and to administer the Word and Sacrament. Some traditions ordain a person because they believe that person has been called by God and exhibits particular spiritual gifts tied to the office; other traditions ordain a person because they too believe the person has been called by God but has also obtained some desired specialized knowledge or skills acquired through seminary education that enables that person to speak more knowledgably about the content of the biblical texts.

The data from 1989 were part of a clergy study conducted by means of mailed surveys to pastors across seven Protestant denominations.[14] This study was actually composed of three separate studies conducted with some coordination by six investigators. The first study focused on the Southern Baptist Convention, the Presbyterian Church in the U.S.A., and the Disciples of Christ, and was conducted by James Guth and Helen Lee Turner of Furman University; these surveys were administered in the fall and winter of 1988–89. The Assemblies of God and United Methodist Church surveys were conducted by John Green and Margaret Poloma of the University of Akron, and the studies of the Christian Reformed Church and the Reformed Church in America were conducted by Corwin Smidt and James Penning; both of these studies were conducted during the summer of 1989. The survey instruments varied somewhat, though they contained numerous common items; all surveys were designed to elicit pastors' views of theological, social, and political issues.

The 2001 component of the study was coordinated by the Paul B. Henry Institute for the Study of Christianity and Politics at Calvin College, in which a number of scholars were invited to a planning meeting in the summer of 2000 to discuss a possible study project focusing on clergy. The project was known as the Cooperative Clergy Study Project of 2001. Each participating scholar surveyed clergy from a single denomination, with assignments being made so that each denomination was studied by a scholar who was a member of that denomination or someone very familiar with it. The effort was unprecedented in the breadth of denominations and religious faiths examined,[15] but included in the 2001 study were the same seven denominations studied in 1989. The participants constructed a common questionnaire, including a host of religious and politics questions contained in the 1989 component of the study. After the instrument was forged, the scholar mailed the questionnaire to a random sample of clergy from the appropriate denomination, with the sample size varying from denomination to denomination.[16]

The 2009 component of the study was also coordinated by the Paul B. Henry Institute for the Study of Christianity and Politics at Calvin College. It entailed mailed surveys[17] to randomly selected clergy across ten denominations,[18] including the same seven originally surveyed in 1989 and including another three surveyed in 2001. The survey instrument in 2009 was shorter than the one used in 2001, but the questions that were included were ones that had been asked in 2001 (and, for many questions, ones that had been also asked in 1989).

Thus, we have survey responses from clergy of seven different denominations that span a period of twenty years.[19] Three of these denominations are evangelical Protestant denominations (specifically, the Assemblies of God, the Christian Reformed Church, and the Southern Baptist Convention), while four are mainline Protestant denominations (the Disciples of Christ; the Presbyterian Church in the U.S.A.; the Reformed Church in America; and the United Methodist Church).[20]

The responses of clergy from these seven denominations over time serve as the basis of the analysis in this book. Not surprisingly, the response rates for these denominational surveys have also declined over the past twenty years (see appendix A). Given these lower response rates in 2009 compared to 1989, one might question whether the responses obtained from these 2009 surveys are necessarily representative of the clergy from the particular denominations studied. Fortunately, another survey of mainline Protestant clergy, the Mainline Protestant Clergy Voices Survey, was conducted about the same time as the 2009 Cooperative Clergy Study. This other survey drew upon, and included, many questions contained in our previous clergy surveys, enabling direct comparisons of mainline Protestant clergy across the two studies to see whether the results obtained largely mirror, or deviated considerably from, each other. Given that response rates have diminished over time, being able to make comparisons across these two studies presents the most stringent test for assessing whether the responses obtained in the clergy surveys examined here are necessarily representative of clergy responses in the denominations examined in this volume.[21]

This comparative analysis reveals a remarkable similarity across the two clergy studies in terms of the social, political, and theological characteristics of the mainline Protestant clergy who responded to the surveys of these two different clergy studies. This is true for mainline Protestant clergy as a whole, as well for clergy studied from identical denominations included in the two studies (see appendix B for a presentation of such comparisons). The analysis revealed that the racial and gender composition of those clergy surveyed, as well as their relative age and level of education, are virtually identical across the two studies. Mainline clergy across the two surveys also mirrored each other in terms of the reported ideological orientations and partisan identifications. And, finally, the clergy captured in the two different studies expressed similar theological stands, with the reported theological positions of mainline Protestant clergy being virtually identical across the two studies.

Thus, given that the data used in this study can be viewed as being generally representative of clergy drawn from these seven denominations, this volume focuses on changes among Protestant clergy over time, comparing in part changes evident among evangelical Protestant clergy with changes evident among mainline Protestant clergy. Given that the sample size of clergy across the seven denominations varied by denomination, and that the sample size and response rate of clergy from each denomination also varied by year, it is necessary to weigh the responses obtained from these clergy; this is done in order to prevent differential sample sizes and response rates by denomination across time from unduly shaping the results obtained. Consequently, in order to eliminate the influence of such factors from shaping the final results, the responses of clergy from each denomination were weighted equally (N = 500 responses per denomination) and identically across all three points in time. In other words, such a procedure insures that neither the different initial sample sizes of clergy drawn from these various denominations nor the differential rates of response provided by clergy across these denominations over time shape the patterns of the results obtained. Thus, any reported changes over time reflect differential levels of responses given to the same question—and not differences that may result from different numbers of clergy from different denominations being surveyed or responding at different points in time.

The Outline of the Volume

This study proceeds in the following manner. Chapter 1 of the volume is an analytical chapter focusing on clergy as civic and political actors. Attention is given, first, to those factors that contribute to the public significance of clergy. It then delineates the different roles within which clergy may choose to engage in public life and exhibit such behavior. And, finally, it examines the prominent role that cue-giving, and cue-taking, plays within American political life.

Chapter 2 of the volume begins the analysis of data. The chapter examines the changing composition of those who serve as Protestant clergy as well as changes in the churches they serve. Although the broader contours of the social makeup of clergy remain substantially the same over the past two decades, several major changes are examined: the feminization of the clergy, the aging of the clergy, and the delaying of entry into ministry.

The third chapter addresses the theological changes that have transpired among American Protestant clergy over the past two decades. In particular, the chapter assesses the growing theological orthodoxy expressed by Protestant clergy over this period of time and the growing theological convergence evident between evangelical and mainline Protestant clergy. These broader changes are then analyzed further in terms of gender differences among clergy as well as possible sources of such change within each major religious tradition.

Chapter 4 examines American Protestant clergy in terms of the social theologies they express. Three different topics related to the social theology of clergy are examined: the church and cultural change, the role of religion in contemporary American life, and the nature of politics and the political processes by which to accomplish political goals. The more general social theology of individualism is also analyzed, demonstrating that social theology contributes to differences in political orientations beyond that which occurs by means of theological orthodoxy.

Chapter 5 focuses on change and continuity in the political attitudes held by American Protestant clergy over the past two decades. Specifically, the chapter examines the issue positions of clergy across a number of issues within three broad areas of public policy: social welfare policy, social policy, and foreign policy. In addition, the chapter examines the changing ideological orientations of clergy and how such orientations have become more polarized over time. And, finally, the chapter analyzes the changes in clergy perceptions of how their ideological orientations relate to the ideological perspectives of their congregants—and the extent to which a "clergy-laity" gap may have increased over time.

Chapter 6 examines the norms held by clergy concerning which particular activities may, or may not, be appropriate for clergy to do. Although the issue positions and ideological orientations of pastors reveal something about the political thinking of clergy, such positions reveal little, if anything, about the extent to which clergy believe it appropriate for them to make their positions known publicly. This chapter examines the political norms of clergy and how they may have changed over time, with particular attention being given to those activities that are deemed to be appropriate forms of cue-giving within the worship context itself.

The seventh chapter focuses its attention on congregational life and the major ways in which clergy may seek to shape the political thinking and actions of their congregants. It initially examines the reported political cue-giving behavior of clergy within congregational life, particularly the worship context, and how such behavior has changed over time. Second, the chapter analyzes congregational life as a site for the development of political learning among parishioners and the role of clergy may play in such endeavors.

Chapter 8 focuses on the political activism of clergy. It first analyzes changes in clergy reports about the particular kinds of political issues they have addressed publically and the extent to which political agendas related to social justice and public morality may have shifted time. The second portion of the chapter focuses on the reported involvement of clergy in various forms of political engagement, while the last section of the chapter examines the partisan nature of clergy engagement in politics and how such patterns may have changed over time.

The concluding chapter first summarizes the key findings of the book. It then examines several factors that may serve to diminish the relative importance of clergy within American public life, and it concludes with a discussion of future research related to clergy and American political life.

1

Clergy as Public Actors

Clergy may be counted among the social and political elite of America in that they are, by definition, "in the business of opinion leadership" (Guth et al. 1997, 17). They, like other elites, have highly constrained beliefs systems and are actively involved in advocacy. Although earlier generations of scholars held that a pastor's influence over the opinions and actions of his congregants rested simply on his personality, pastoral skills, and the nature of the congregation served (Vidich and Bensman 1958), later scholarship has emphasized more that clerical influence stems largely from their positions as elites (Guth et al. 1997; Smidt 2004). Indeed, regardless of whether they choose to utilize their influence for political ends, clergy as a whole perceive themselves to have the potential to influence their congregants politically (Djupe and Gilbert 2009, 31–33).

Before beginning our examination of the changes among Protestant clergy related to their engagement in public life, it may be helpful therefore to begin this study with an analytical consideration of clergy as public actors. The chapter will, first of all, examine those factors that contribute to the potential significance of clergy as "opinion leaders." In fact, a variety of factors combine in such a way to position clergy as elites who can exercise, should they choose to do so, significant influence within public life.

Second, the chapter will discuss the public activities of clergy. When clergy choose to engage in public life, they can do so within one of three different roles that they may assume. Some particular actions can only occur through the assumption of one particular role; whereas, for other actions, the same behavior may occur but can transpire through adoption of different roles. Although each of these roles may be a means by which clergy can choose to express themselves politically, the adoption of some roles may well be more influential in terms of their potential effects than the adoption of other such roles. In addition, the chapter will examine the ways in which clergy may choose to become engaged in public life. When clergy choose to engage in public life, they can do so, broadly speaking, either through direct action or more indirectly through cue-giving.

Though direct political action can be important, cue-giving has been the most frequent form of public engagement undertaken by clergy (see, e.g., Guth et al. 1997, ch. 9).

And, finally, the chapter examines the role of cue-giving within democratic political systems. If cue-giving was not significant politically, then analysts could safely ignore the cue-giving activities of clergy. However, research has shown that cue-giving can have important effects politically, and analysts have contended that cue-giving and cue-taking play an important role in democratic life—whether in terms of agenda setting, the framing of issues, or the priming of the criteria for evaluation (Scheufele and Tewksbury 2007).

The Public Significance of Clergy

Why should one even devote any energy and effort to the study of clergy in the first place? Although pastors may be studied simply on the basis of personal interest or as leaders in American religious life, they are also worthy of study in that they occupy unique positions within American public life. This distinctiveness serves not only to differentiate them from others who may serve as intermediaries in American public life, but it also provides clergy with unique and important opportunities to function in such a capacity. This unique nature of their intermediary position stems from various characteristics associated with their position. Specifically, the public significance of clergy stems from (1) the strategic positions they occupy, (2) the distinctive nature of the organizations they lead, (3) the nature of the authority they hold, (4) the resources they possess, and (5) the opportunities they enjoy. Together, these qualities interact to magnify and enhance the potentially significant intermediary positions that clergy occupy within American politics.

The Strategic Position of Clergy

First of all, clergy occupy a strategic position within American public life that stems from particular characteristics of American religious life: the prevalence of religious houses of worship, the large proportions of Americans who claim church memberships, the levels of attendance at worship services, and the frequency with which congregants interact together both within and outside their house of worship.

Congregations constitute the major, and perhaps the most vital, voluntary associational organization in the United States. Not only do churches dot the American landscape, but most such edifices continue to welcome worshippers on a regular basis. Moreover, church membership nearly surpasses reported membership in all other kinds of voluntary associations combined, as anywhere from about three-fifths to two-thirds of Americans report church membership (Cnaan et al. 2006, 124; Smidt et al. 2008, 78).[1] And, though very few voluntary associations meet on a weekly basis, religious congregations typically do so—with many church members choosing to gather together on a weekly or more frequent basis, as nearly two-fifths of Americans report attending worship services weekly.[2]

Moreover, given that friendships are generally forged with those who share similar values, interests, and activities (Verbrugge 1977; Kelly 1979), it is not surprising that congregational life offers fertile ground for forming and sustaining friendships among its various members. And, those who attend church do in fact report larger social networks and more contact with network members than those who do not attend church, even after a controlling statistically for a wide range of covariates (Ellison and George 1994).

The Distinctive Nature of the Organizations They Lead

Moreover, clergy serve as leaders of a distinctive type of voluntary association that further enhances their strategic influence. Certainly some people may deem themselves religious, yet choose not to attend worship services on a regular basis. However, what is important is not simply whether one views oneself to be religious, but whether one's religiousness is sustained by one's social environment (Stark 1996, 164). And, for many, if not most, of those involved in congregational life, churches serve as a moral community that helps to shape their moral thinking and define the nature of their commitment to particular courses of behavior.

The fact that congregations typically serve as a moral community for those who regularly attend worship fundamentally differentiates involvement in congregational life from that of other forms of voluntary associations. Involvement in parent-teacher organizations, literary clubs, or professional associations may serve to promote particular civic values or foster particular civic skills (as may also involvement in congregational life), but most civic associations are highly unlikely to serve, as church congregations do, as the core moral community for its members.

As moral communities, churches promote particular worldviews that advance distinctive perspectives related to such matters as the purpose of life, standards of right and wrong, and the ends of human activity. As moral communities, members of religious congregations hold certain normative expectations of those who choose to be involved within congregational life, and these expectations help to both encourage and constrain different types of behavior related to these beliefs, values, and norms. Higher levels of interaction among group members serve to expose members more fully to the values of the group and enhance the likelihood that group norms will be reinforced in conversation with other groups members (Wald, Owen, and Hill 1990, 200), and active participation within the congregation enhances the capacity of members of the congregation to "punish deviations from collective norms by withdrawing approval from members who stray from acceptable attitudes" or from members who fail to exhibit proscribed forms of behavior (Wald, Owen, and Hill 1988, 533). And, because churches serve as moral communities, the particular values and behavioral norms learned within that context are likely to be relatively salient in the lives of those who participate within the life of the congregation.

The Nature of Authority Clergy Possess

Given that they serve as central figures within these moral communities, clergy play a far more significant role in the life of congregational members than do comparable leaders of other voluntary associations. Thus, it is not simply the prevalence of churches, the level of involvement in congregational life, or the fact that congregations function as moral communities that serve to enhance the significance of clergy as intermediaries in American politics. Rather, it is these factors coupled with the distinctive nature of the authority that clergy possess that further enhances their political significance.

The Protestant Reformation emphasized that the Bible should serve as the final authority on all matters related to religious life. Thus, Protestant clergy possess an additional quality that further enhances their potential significance as intermediaries in American politics—namely, that clergy in most, if not all, Protestant denominations serve as ministers of the Word and Sacrament. As a result, clergy are expected to have the proper theological and biblical training in order to be able to minister to church members. And, in this capacity, Protestant clergy are entrusted with the responsibility to interpret the Bible and its content properly to the "sheep of their flock."

However, given the purposes for which it was written, the Bible does not contain any particular political treatise that outlines and explicates some detailed political philosophy or program of action. Rather, there are various passages within the Bible that relate to politics, some directly and others indirectly, and these passages must be assessed and interpreted in order to ascertain to what extent such passages may be applied to contemporary circumstances. Moreover, these biblical passages can be subject to a variety of interpretations, and parishioners may have difficulty interpreting the political ramifications of their religious beliefs. The net result is that clergy serve "as the primary interpreters of the faith for their congregants, making connections between religious beliefs and everyday life through sermons and other congregational activities" (Djupe and Gilbert 2009, 59).

Given these circumstances, those who attend church may turn to their ministers for some political guidance. And, when they do, clergy are well positioned not only to lead members to opinions that are consonant with church teaching but to opinions that reflect their personal political preferences as well (Lenski 1961; Wald, Owen, and Hill 1988; Djupe and Gilbert 2003, 6). Moreover, given that clergy constitute "professional arbiters of values and absolute truths," their pronouncements related to moral evaluations of what is right and wrong may well "place them in a unique position to shape American political debates" (Olson 2009, 375). Thus, clergy possess a particular kind of authority that leaders of nonreligious organizations are unable to claim.

Accordingly, even when not trying to do so, ministers can influence their congregants through their words and deeds. Laity not only listen to what their pastors have to say, but they frequently turn to them to receive moral guidance on public issues of the day. And those who observe and listen carefully get certain messages about what things they should pay attention to, care about, and act on, and these cues are often not ignored (Wald, Owen, and Hill 1988, 1990; Olson and Crawford 2001). In fact, congregants are generally receptive to the political cues that clergy transmit (Leege, Kellstedt, and Wald 1990; Jelen 2001; Djupe and Gilbert 2009). This is especially true when clergy address certain issues frequently and when they address issues that are salient to their congregations and to society (Djupe and Gilbert 2001).

Pastors can be particularly effective at shaping the views of their congregants when they give legitimate biblical warrants behind their position (Jelen 2001). In fact, congregational members may give greater credence to an issue position expressed by their pastor than they would to a position heard or read in some news medium (Buddenbaum 2001). And, though in many cases pastors may be "preaching to the converted," even under such circumstances, they can still influence their congregations by intensifying their parishioners' partisan attachments and reinforcing their issues preference, which in turn can lead to political activism (Jelen 2001).

The Resources Clergy Possess

In addition to these particular advantages, clergy also typically exhibit several important qualities that enable them potentially to wield political influence. For example, clergy are likely to "engage in more ideological thinking" than those in their congregation (Guth et al. 1997, 103), enabling them to frame issues within broader systems of thought of their particular choosing. As spiritual leaders, clergy are more likely than many of their congregants to be aware of, and concerned by, the moral dimensions of the problems found in the world around them. This moral sensitivity can, in turn, lead to clerical political activism, whether through direct action or cue-giving (Guth et al. 1997).

Moreover, many clergy believe that, because of their positions in society, they "have a special obligation" to be politically informed (Quinley 1974, 64). As a result, clergy may be more attuned to what is being presented in the media than members of their congregations, and they may choose, in turn, to convey such information to their particular congregations. For example, Jelen and Wilcox (1993, 266) have suggested that clergy may serve as a sort of filter in receiving and interpreting political information to their congregations, thereby reflecting the classic "two-step flow of political information." And, as noted earlier, congregational members may give more credence to an issue position stated by their pastor than they would to issue positions heard or read in some news medium (Buddenbaum 2001). Thus, pastors may not only play a vital role in setting the political agendas of their congregants, they may also shape their congregants' views on such issues.

The Opportunities Clergy Enjoy

As political intermediaries, clergy are not only able to draw upon a variety of potentially important resources by which they can try to influence and mobilize others on behalf of their political concerns, but clergy also enjoy ample opportunities—both within and outside the congregation—by which to transmit political messages to their congregants. Clergy, like other Americans, have opportunities to engage in public life through a variety of direct actions.

But, it is the fact that many congregational members gather weekly that enhances the ability of clergy to politicize and mobilize their flocks, by expanding the opportunities they have not only to educate church members politically but also to advance a particular agenda. Through such channels as sermons, congregational prayers, adult education classes, church bulletin announcements, and poster displays, clergy enjoy a variety of opportunities by which to shape and color the attitudes of their parishioners.

The Public Activities of Clergy

Such resources and opportunities would be of limited political importance if clergy did not convey political messages or become engaged in the political arena. But, clergy frequently do become engaged in politics, and when they do, they can assume a number of different roles and convey political messages by a variety of means.

The Public Roles of Clergy

When clergy choose to engage in public life, they can do so by means of adopting one of three different roles. Clergy can adopt any of these three roles at different times and in relationship to different forms of political action. Both direct action and cue-giving, for example, can be done through each of these three roles. Although each of the roles may be a means by which clergy can express their preferences publicly, some roles are likely to be far more significant in terms of their potential effects than other such roles. Hence, it is important to consider the particular roles through which clergy can choose to engage in public life.

Citizen

Sometimes clergy may seek to exert their influence outside their congregation and in roles not directly related to being a pastor. For example, a pastor may seek to persuade other members of one's family politically or influence other citizens by contributing financially to a political campaign. Simply stated, clergy can participate in politics through the role of being an individual citizen. After all, clergy enjoy the same democratic rights as other Americans: they may choose to attend political rallies, join political associations, and cast their ballots at the polls on Election Day. Although such endeavors may not be totally invisible to others, they are largely removed from the public eye. Some clergy activities are largely confined to the role of citizen. For example, casting a ballot on Election Day is done as a citizen, not as a pastor of a local church or chair of a ministerial association. Other actions related to the democratic rights that all Americans possess (e.g., writing a letter of opinion to a local newspaper) can be more visible and more ambiguous as to whether it was done in the capacity as a private citizen or a member of the clergy (depending, in part, on the way in which the letter was signed).[3] In all such citizenship endeavors, the fact that one is a pastor has little bearing on the likelihood of whether such efforts may succeed or fail.

Religious Professional

At other times, clergy may seek to influence the public and foster public engagement through their role as clergy, but outside the context of their particular congregation. Ministers can be political activists by virtue of their role as "religious professionals." Accordingly, one might envision clergy serving as members of civic boards, participating in public ceremonies, or seeking to influence the public position of denominational agencies with which they may be affiliated.

As professionals, clergy associate and interact with their colleagues within regional, state, and national denominational and interdenominational agencies and organizations. As religious leaders, they may collectively issue pastoral letters, statements, or declarations. Likewise, they may work to secure official denominational pronouncements or become involved in lobbying activity. Thus, as members of a particular profession, they may collectively seek to influence and shape the course of political affairs, whether with regard to matters that directly affect their profession (e.g., clergy liability in terms of pastoral counseling) or matters that are shaped by their religious convictions (e.g., speaking out on behalf of the dispossessed).

Pastor of a Local Congregation

Finally, clergy may be political activists as a result of their leadership role in local churches. As noted earlier, the ability of pastors to politicize and mobilize members of "their flock" is enhanced greatly by the fact that many congregants gather weekly. Not only does the relative frequency of gatherings expand the opportunities clergy have to educate church members politically, it also expands their opportunities to advance a particular agenda. And there are various means by which they may choose to do so: sermons, congregational prayers, adult education classes, church bulletin announcements, and even poster displays. If those who attended worship services thought it inappropriate for pastors to address political issues through their communications, such political cue-giving messages could possibly be dismissed. But, given the relatively high esteem with which ministers are held by members of their congregations, any political messages they transmit to their congregants may not only be given a respectful hearing but also enjoy substantial credibility (Wald et al. 1988, 533). Moreover, members of congregations, particularly those who attend regularly, are likely not only to perceive but be receptive to political messages from their pastors (Leege, Kellstedt, and Wald 1990, 45).

Whether or not a minister can shape the views of one's congregants depends upon a variety of factors, including the nature of the congregation, the pastor's personality, and the pastor's skill in dealing with the congregation (Vidich and Bensman 1958, 239). But, recent research has suggested that pastors and local congregations can be important factors in explaining the political attitudes and behaviors of those who attend church. Clergy, in fact, recognize the potential influence they have over their congregations: ministers report that they could exert much political influence over their congregation, should they desire to do so (Guth et al. 1997; Djupe and Gilbert 2001).

And, given the resources and opportunities they enjoy, clergy have the capacity to shape the nature and level of political engagement of many Americans. Thus, it would seem that the attitudes and actions of pastors are likely to hold particular relevance for the ways in which many members of the American electorate come to bring their religious faith to bear in public life. And, it is in this capacity as leaders of their congregations that clergy are likely to exhibit their greatest influence in American public life.

The Nature of Clergy Engagement

Scholars have long noted that clergy engage in public life through two primary means—either through direct action or through verbal cue-giving (e.g., Guth et al. 1997; Djupe and Gilbert 2003, 5–6). Either form of activism provides pastors opportunities to influence members of the congregation as well as those members of the community who look up to them.

Direct Political Action

At times, clergy may themselves be social and political activists (Guth et al. 1997). Some forms of social and political activism on the part of clergy may occur outside the congregational context (e.g., campaigning publicly for a candidate, engaging in protest or civil disobedience activities, or even running for public office). But, at other times, such activism may find expression within the congregation. Clergy may seek to recruit congregational members to join them in activism related to the particular causes they wish to address—whether it is to address hunger, provide housing for the homeless in one's community, or protest local abortion clinics. And, as leaders of their congregation, pastors have a number of means at their disposal to recruit members of their congregation to join them in their social and political endeavors (e.g., forming study groups, forging action groups, or conducting voter registration drives within the church).

Many of the initial classic studies of clergy engagement in public life (e.g., Hadden 1969; Quinley 1974) centered on direct forms of clergy engagement—primarily in terms of protest, civil disobedience, and unconventional behavior rather than in terms of more conventional forms of political action. Such studies typically regarded "pastoral activism" as a single dimension composed of a wide variety of actions that could be undertaken within different contexts—for example, from the pulpit, within the church, and outside the congregation itself.

However, later studies of the mass public suggested that there are different modes of political participation, with different types of individuals "specializing" in these various participatory modes (e.g., "voting," "campaigning," "contacting," "communal activities," and "protesting"). And, subsequent research has revealed that clerical activism also tends to occur in several distinct modes, with different groups of clergy engaging in different modes of participatory behavior, with each mode influenced by distinct constellations of socioeconomic, theological, ideological, and contextual factors (Guth et al. 1997).

Cue-Giving

Although direct political action can be important and rather visible publicly, cue-giving constitutes the most frequent, and probably the most important, and certainly the most subtle, form of political action in which clergy may engage. Cue-giving refers to any communication, however brief, that directs the receiver's attention to civic or political phenomena, with such cue-giving either suggesting particular viewpoints for members to adopt or particular courses of action for them to follow. Cues may be given for different political purposes. Some cues may seek to persuade, others to alter the member's political agenda, and still others to mobilize to action.

Previous research has shown that clergy do engage in these political cue-giving activities, both in and out of the pulpit. For example, pastors frequently deliver weekly sermons from the pulpit in which they provide interpretation of the biblical passages under consideration. In so doing, these clergy may suggest how such passages relate to contemporary life, thereby stimulating further reflection and possibly action among their parishioners listening in the pews. Parishioners for the most part can correctly recall whether or not their pastor had ever addressed various political issues publicly during the past year, with congregants correctly identifying those issues most frequently addressed by their clergy (Djupe and Gilbert 2009, 60–62).[4]

It is should be noted that, though the actual cue-giving within the church service is only one opportunity among a range of opportunities clergy possess to influence their parishioners, it is a particularly important one. Corporate worship is the central act in the church's life. It is the one public activity in which members of the congregation most commonly gather together, and it serves as a central point of congregational life. Moreover, since the Reformation, the primary role of the Protestant clergy has been to exposit the Word of God to the people gathered for worship. Given this relative centrality of the preaching of the Word within the Protestant tradition compared to the relative centrality of the sacraments in the Roman Catholic tradition, the words and actions of

Protestant clergy during the worship service are likely to carry more weight within, than outside, that context. And, as a result, words stated or actions undertaken from the pulpit are viewed differently than words expressed or actions conducted off the pulpit.

Off the pulpit, but within the congregational context, ministers may use other venues by which to convey political cues (e.g., bulletin announcements, church newsletters, or taking a public stand on an issue). And, outside the congregation, clergy may engage in a variety of electoral (e.g., displaying bumper stickers, endorsing a candidates), advocacy (e.g., participating in a rally, writing a letter to the editor of a newspaper), partnership (e.g., joining a civic organization, working on a community taskforce), and gap-filling activities (e.g., joining interfaith programs to feed, clothe, shelter disadvantaged individuals in the community) that can also provide important cues to congregational and community members as to where they may stand on political issues, what they support, and what the nature of their civic and political priorities may be (Olson 2009, 380).

Although clergy may well find it rather challenging to alter the attitudes and positions of their congregants on particular political issues or mobilize them to action, the reason pastors engage in cue-giving activities "is to do just that" (Djupe and Gilbert 2003, 6). Not surprisingly, denominations and their clergy seek to have their members adhere to certain precepts and to view the world in particular ways. Thus, it is easy to understand why clergy would desire to have their congregational members think through their religious faith generally and their particular religious beliefs more specifically in terms of their civic and political implications.

The Role of Cues in Democratic Theory

Democratic theory long posited an attentive, informed, and independent citizenry, where citizens gathered political information, assessed relevant options, and made "rational" decisions based upon such information. However, with the advent of survey research and its capacity to probe the qualities of the mass electorate, early empirical studies of American public opinion challenged these assumptions. Not only was the level of political knowledge within the electorate shockingly low, but independents were less informed politically than partisans. As a result, most research conducted from the 1950s through the 1970s advanced a "minimalist paradigm." Not only did mass publics exhibit "minimal levels" with regard to attention given to, and information about, political matters, they exhibited "minimal stability" in terms of their political preferences and "minimal levels" of constraint between and across issue positions (Sniderman 1993, 219).

More recent scholarly efforts, however, have moved away from this general "litany of minimalism." Instead, scholars have tended to "paint a more optimistic portrait" of the American electorate (Bartels 1996, 196). They have done so largely by changing the focus of analysis. Rather than focusing on the level of political information held by the mass public, they have focused on information processing—the process by which members of the electorate gather, retain, and employ such information.

As a result, "rational" voters are no longer expected to be highly informed politically. Rather, "rational" voters are seen to be economizers. Such rationality of economizing stems from several premises: (1) that political issues are complex, (2) that becoming informed politically requires considerable time and effort, and (3) that citizens experience multiple demands upon their time. Given this situation, mass publics are seen to employ labor-saving devices to reduce the costs of becoming relatively informed politically, and, in so doing, many citizens may sensibly choose to rely upon trusted sources for political information and interpretation—as a means to make decisions that would closely, if not fully, approximate their decisions had they invested sufficient time and energy personally to become more fully informed citizens.

How might such relatively uninformed voters acquire sufficient information to make "rational" choices? One answer which has been advanced has been through the use of "informational shortcuts" (Popkin 1991). Although there are various means by which they can do so, one important means is through the use of cues. As McKelvey and Ordeshook (1986, 934) have argued, "cues provide more than approximations: They provide, under appropriate assumptions, all the information that is required."

Actually, the idea that the mass public seeks shortcuts to gather information, and, as a result, to gather such information indirectly is well rooted in both sociological and political science literature. For example, the two-step flow of communication model, where information is seen to flow from relatively attentive and informed "opinion leaders" to different public audiences who looked to such leaders for guidance (or cues) has had a long established tradition in sociology and communication research (e.g., Berelson, Lazarsfeld, and McPhee 1954). Similarly, political scientists have contended for some time that, within a democratic system, a relatively informed mass public can function with reasonable efficacy through the political cues they receive from more informed elites (Downs 1957; Campbell et al. 1960; Converse 1964).

In fact, pastors are likely to engage in all three forms of cue transmission known to have important political effects: agenda-setting, framing, and priming. Agenda-setting occurs when a pastor chooses to address a particular issue from the pulpit, focuses on a topic in some church education class, or even mentions an issue within a pastoral prayer. By choosing to focus on one issue or topic, as opposed to other such issues/topics, parishioners think about the things addressed by their pastor, while other issues thereby become farther removed from their consciousness.

Framing can occur whenever there is more than one way to think about a subject, and no single dominant attitude exists about a subject (Popkin 1991, 82–83). For example, the issue of AIDS could be framed as reflecting a health issue that needs to be addressed or a moral issue reflecting sexual practices in society. Moreover, the effects of framing are likely to be significant politically in that the particular considerations taken into account when making political decisions are dependent on the manner in which political issues are framed (Iyengar 1987, 16). Ministers frequently engage in framing practices, as biblical passages can be subject to a variety of interpretations.

Pastors are also likely to engage in priming processes. "Priming effects" relate to the criteria by which political leaders and contexts are to be judged. By choosing to focus on certain issues or events, or by choosing to emphasize particular biblical themes or passages, clergy exercise power in affecting evaluation criteria. While agenda-setting affects the perception of which issues are of political importance, priming affects "the weight assigned to specific issues in making political judgments" (Iyengar 1987, 133). Research has shown, for example, that political issues are affected by how prominently an issue is treated by the media. When issues, topics, or events are hardly, if ever, covered in the news media, such matters are rarely primed, and, as a result, are highly unlikely to play a major role in political assessment processes (Krosnick and Brannon 1993, 964). One might thus anticipate that the more a pastor chooses to address a certain issue (or issues), the greater will be the likelihood that congregants will use such an issue (or issues) as bases for the evaluation of political candidates or matters of public policy.

Finally, cue-giving may be important for other reasons as well. Some scholars have contended that certain citizens who exhibit the personal traits and attitudes associated with political participation may nevertheless remain inactive absent some external impetus (Rosenstone and Hansen 1993; Verba, Schlozman, and Brady, 1995). Such individuals may become politically active only as a result of other "triggering" factors: (1) the appearance of some salient issue that either directly or indirectly through political cue-givers motivates their involvement, and/or (2) their active involvement within voluntary groups that foster political skills, provide low-cost political information, and stimulate political interest (Verba, Schlozman, and Brady 1995). And, while most scholarly research has focused on the role of the mass media as the primary political and social cue-giver within the American mass public (Iyengar and Kinder 1987; Iyengar 1991; Dalton, Beck, and Huckfeldt 1998), there is much to be said for the potential of clergy to be important political cue-givers and the local congregation to be a context within which such cues serve to shape political behavior and spur political action.

Within the mass public, those who are more socially engaged are more likely to be politically attentive and sophisticated (Verba, Schlozman, Brady, and Nie 1993; Burns, Schlozman, and Verba, 2001) and more likely to receive and accept political messages from elites (Zaller 1992); so too one might anticipate that those who attend church more often are more likely to be attentive to pronouncements made from the pulpit (political or otherwise) and the pronouncements of other religious elites. Within the mass public, those who are more attentive politically are more likely to structure their political attitudes to correspond to personally relevant political elites (Layman and Carsey 2002); so too one might anticipate that those congregants who are more attentive religiously would be more likely to structure their religious (and related political views) attitudes to stand in alignment with their pastor and other salient religious leaders. Just as the political views of the general population are reinforced and refined through one's social networks (Huckfeldt and Sprague 1995), so too are the political views of congregational members likely to be shaped by the social networks within their congregation. It is probably not too surprising, therefore, that a variety of studies (e.g., Wald et al. 1988, 1990; Gilbert 1993; Jelen 1993) have shown that "church congregations function as contexts for the transmission and reinforcement of political attitudes" (Welch et al. 1993, 244).

Thus, the interplay between political information and influence that occurs among individuals, elites, and social networks within the broader population also occurs within the congregational context. However, given the fact that the social networks within congregational contexts generally exhibit a far greater homogeneous environment in terms of basic values and orientations than social networks forged elsewhere (whether, e.g., in terms of one's neighborhood, one's work, or one's profession), the role of social networks within the congregation are likely to have far stronger effects in shaping the attitudes and behavior of its members than social networks within more heterogeneous contexts. As a result, one might easily argue that in terms of shaping political beliefs and actions, the cues provided by clergy within the context of one's local church might easily rival any influence exhibited by the media, particularly given the high numbers of the church attendees found within the voting population.

Conclusions

Clergy occupy a unique position in American public life that potentially enable them to serve as important "editors, filters, and cue-givers" within American public life. Their unique position stems for the strategic position they occupy,

the distinctive nature of the organizations they lead, the nature of the authority they possess, the resources that they possess, and the opportunities they
enjoy. Substantial numbers of Americans attend church regularly, with ministers
serving as the primary interpreters of the Christian faith for members of their
congregations. Thus, clergy are well positioned to present to their congregants
perspectives that not only embody church teachings but those that reflect their
political perspectives and preferences as well.

Clergy often occupy significant and respected roles within the broader community, and they generally rank among the most highly regarded professions in
terms of their honesty and ethics. These factors also suggest the potential sizable influence held by clergy. It is true that the national rankings of clergy have
dropped in the wake of some of the revelations related to the Catholic priest
sexual abuse scandals. Nevertheless, clergy continue to rank far higher in these
matters than those who occupy most other professions (Jones 2009). Moreover,
those who attend church more regularly generally give clergy much higher ratings of honesty and ethics than those who attend less regularly. As a result, those
who are in the pews are the most likely to accord respect and trust to those
standing in the pulpit.

Third, there is growing recognition that one's social networks (e.g., family,
friends, church, and work acquaintances) are as important agents of both information and influence. As Putnum (2000, 343) has argued:

> We learn about politics through casual conversation. You tell me what
> you've heard and what you think, and what your friends have heard
> and what they think, and I accommodate that new information into
> my mental database as I ponder and revise my position on an issue.
> In a world of civic networks, both formal and informal, our views are
> formed through interchange with friends and neighbors.

Given that church membership is the most common voluntary form of association in the United States today, clergy are likely to be part of many individuals'
social networks and may play a particularly key role in shaping the viewpoints of
others with regard to politics. Many of these individuals gather regularly to hear
what clergy have to say, and as listeners they may be very receptive to the messages that clergy convey. In fact, clergy are well aware of the potential influence
they have over their congregations, acknowledging in recent surveys that they
could exert a great deal of political influence over their congregants if they so
desired (Guth et al. 1997; Djupe and Gilbert 2003).

The resources and opportunities that clergy possess to shape the political
thoughts and actions of their parishioners would have limited political significance were clergy unlikely to convey political messages or choose to engage in

public life, but clergy frequently do become engaged in the political process. When clergy engage in public life, they can do so by adopting one of three different roles: as a private citizen, as part of a larger profession, or as a pastor of a local congregation. It is within this capacity as leaders of their congregations that clergy collectively are likely to exhibit their greatest influence in American public life. And, it is in this role as leaders of their particular congregations that serve as the focus of this study.

Clergy seek to shape the thoughts and actions of their congregants through their words and actions, though the primary means by which they do so is through the use of public speech (Djupe and Gilbert 2003, 93). The particular verbal and behavioral cues that clergy offer may not always achieve their intended purpose, but the major reason why clergy choose to provide cues is simply to shape the opinions of their congregants related to the particular matters addressed (Djupe and Gilbert 2003, 6).

2

The Social Characteristics of Clergy
and the Churches They Serve

Although clergy have long been important actors within American public life, their social standing relative to their congregants, their personal characteristics, and the larger cultural context within which they minister have nevertheless changed over time. Some of these changes have occurred rather slowly; others have been much more rapid and dramatic in nature. And, with these changes have come new challenges as well as new opportunities for those seeking to enter the ordained ministry.

For much of American history, clergy were typically much more highly educated than most other Americans. As late as 1900, only 6 percent of Americans had a high school diploma, and it was not until 1950 that a majority of Americans had even attained that level of educational accomplishment. Yet, throughout that period of time, clergy typically were not only college graduates but were seminary graduates as well. Of course, in some religious traditions, manifesting certain spiritual gifts has been more heavily emphasized than being highly trained in reading scriptural texts in their original language or in the interpretation of those texts—and, as a result, ministers within these traditions have not been generally as highly educated. Nevertheless, despite these differences, throughout much of American history, clergy have generally stood significantly apart from their congregants in terms of their greater levels of educational attainment.

But, today, with the increasing spread of undergraduate and graduate degrees within American society, the level of education among one's congregants has increased considerably in relationship to that of the clergy who lead those congregations. Not only are congregants more highly educated today, but denominations that have long required a seminary degree for ordination are now utilizing increasing numbers of "commissioned lay pastors."[1] Some denominations have long had "lay pastors" serving local congregations (e.g., the United Methodist Church). But, over the past several decades, various

Protestant denominations have created positions that enable lay pastors to serve as ministers of the Word and Sacrament in local congregations in which seminary graduates are unavailable (or unwilling) to serve (Wood 2010). In part, the creation of these new types of clergy offices is a function of necessity, as smaller congregations find it increasingly difficult to financially support full-time, seminary-trained clergy. This has led some critics to contend that the purpose of these lay pastorates is simply to "keep open the doors of as many churches as possible with the denomination's name on them" (Wheeler 2010, 31).

In addition, throughout much of American history, clergy have been drawn from the ranks of male members of society only. Beyond some Holiness and Pentecostal churches, there were hardly any ordained female clergy in the 1930s (Marty 1989, 8).[2] And, even in the aftermath of World War II, the occupational opportunities for women were largely confined to teaching and nursing until well into the latter half of the twentieth century. Only in the 1950s did some of the major denominations begin to permit the ordination of women as members of the clergy.[3] However, these decisions to permit women's ordination were not without conflict, as many clergy (and laity) within such denominations continued to interpret biblical texts as directly prohibiting women from serving as clergy. Even today, many denominations continue to prohibit women from serving in the office, and even within those denominations that do permit ordination women have only slowly begun to enter seminary and seek ordination.

However, it is not simply the social characteristics of clergy that have changed over time; change has also occurred with regard to the social and cultural contexts within which clergy minister. Historically, the strength of American religion has been located more in small towns and rural areas than in its cities. But, with increasing numbers of Americans seeking employment within the more urbanized regions of the country, the population of those living in these small towns and rural areas has been both declining and aging over the past several decades. As a result, many congregations in small towns and rural areas are declining in size, and they are increasingly hard pressed financially to support someone to minister full-time in their midst.

Likewise, the congregational expectations related to the primary responsibilities of clergy may have become less clearly defined over the past century. Although the responsibilities of clergy have probably always been quite varied, the expectations related to being a "member of the cloth" have likely expanded over time. Certainly, within the Protestant tradition, the responsibilities of a pastor have historically been linked to being a minister of the Word and Sacraments. Most congregations today continue to be served by one pastor, and within these more typical contexts, the pastor is expected to be a preacher and a teacher. But, in addition to these expectations, he or she is charged with being responsible for the religious life and spiritual growth of those who are a part of the congregation, for maintaining the vitality and growth of the congregation itself, for protecting the religious heritage of the denomination of which one is a part, for promoting the Christian faith, for applying the tenets of the faith to contemporary life, and for serving as a spiritual counselor to those within the flock. Already in the 1950s, Buzzard (1956) identified six different practitioner roles performed by a typical pastor of a congregation: administrator, organizer, pastor, preacher, priest, and teacher. Not only do each of these different roles make demands in terms of a pastor's time, but they require different skills, with a pastor not necessarily being equally skilled in performing all of these different roles. As a result, clergy and congregations alike have increasingly wrestled with just what is to be the minister's primary and defining function, with many clergy increasingly seeking more specialized ministries within those congregations financially able to sustain "team ministries."

Finally, the social standing of clergy has changed over the past several decades,[4] as clergy struggle to maintain their professional status in relationship to other professions. Certainly, it is true that over the course of the past several decades the financial standing of clergy has declined relative to other professions (Price 2001). But it is not just the financial status of clergy that has declined over the past several decades; so too has their public standing. For years, clergy ranked among the top occupations in terms of their "honesty and ethical standards" (Gallup 1998). But, by 2009, the percentage of American who ranked clergy high in such matters dropped to 50 percent, its lowest percentage in the thirty-two years that Gallup has been making such assessments (Jones 2009). Following the sexual scandals of some relatively prominent televangelists at the time, the perception of the honesty and personal ethics of clergy dipped somewhat in the 1980s, but they soon recovered thereafter. The more recent decline in the public evaluation of clergy may be linked, in part, to some of the revelations of abuse on the part of certain Catholics priests or perhaps even to the growing portion of Americans who are religiously unaffiliated. But, whatever its cause, the social standing of clergy among the American public, even among regular churchgoers, has declined over the past several decades.[5]

Given these social and cultural changes, how has the social composition of Protestant clergy shifted over the past twenty years? Are certain changes in composition more evident within evangelical than within mainline Protestant denominations? Is there a growing convergence or divergence in the social composition of clergy across denominations? These are the questions that this chapter seeks to answer.

The Changing Social Composition
of Protestant Clergy

From one perspective, the social composition of Protestant clergy in America has exhibited considerable patterns of continuity over the past twenty years. Within the seven denominations under study, Protestant clergy have historically been overwhelmingly white, male, married, and rather well educated. And, despite whatever changes may have occurred over the past two decades, there is no denying that Protestant clergy from these same seven denominations continued to be in 2009, just as they were in 1989, overwhelmingly white, male, married, and rather well educated.

As can be seen in table 2.1, Protestant clergy in these sampled denominations remain overwhelmingly white in their racial composition, as only about one in twenty clergy (6 percent) indicated in 2009 that their race was something other than white. Clergy also continue to be overwhelmingly male in terms of gender (88 percent), and almost all (82 percent) also reported that they were married. And, even though some of the denominations under study have typically emphasized gifts for ministry as opposed to an educated clergy and despite the increasing number of denominations utilizing "lay pastors," Protestant clergy in 2009 nevertheless continued to be overwhelming college educated (90 percent) and seminary graduates (79 percent).

Nevertheless, despite these continuities, the data in table 2.1 reveal that important processes of change are also occurring. First, there has been a growing feminization of the clergy. The current predominance of male clergy actually reflects a diminished position from the level they exhibited in 1989, as the proportion of female clergy over the past several decades has nearly tripled (from 4 percent in 1989 to 12 percent in 2009). Regardless of how one chooses to view the propriety and relative speed with which this change has transpired, there is no denying that a growing feminization of Protestant clergy has occurred over the last twenty years.

Second, there has been a substantial "graying of the profession" as well. The proportion of young clergy has diminished and the proportion of older clergy has increased substantially over time. In 1989, nearly one-third of the clergy surveyed were under the age of 40, while only a little more than one-quarter were over 55 years of age. Today, however, relatively few of the clergy (13 percent) are under 40 years of age, and more than two-fifths (43 percent) exceed 55 years of age.[6]

Third, in terms of their marital status, clergy continue to be overwhelmingly married. Nevertheless, important changes have also transpired in the marital status of clergy as well. Most congregants expect their pastor to be of high moral character and be something of a moral model. As a result, for many years, it was unthinkable for a pastor to be divorced (Gaustad 1990, 29). However,

Table 2.1 **The Changing Social Composition of Protestant Clergy, 1989–2009**

	1989 (%)	2001 (%)	2009 (%)
Gender			
Female	4	11	12
Male	96	89	88
Race			
White	x	93	94
Non-white	x	7	6
Age			
Under 40 years	30	14	13
40–55 years	44	57	44
56+ years	27	29	43
Marital status			
Single[a]	x	5	4
Divorced or separated	x	4	3
Divorced, remarried	x	10	12
Married[b]	x	82	82
Education			
High school or less	6	2	2
Some college	9	8	8
College graduate	85	90	90
Seminary training			
None	5	5	3
Bible college	10	9	10
Some seminary	7	7	8
Seminary graduate	53	49	53
Post-seminary graduate work	25	30	26

[a]Includes widowed.
[b]Includes widowed and remarried.
x = not asked.

with divorce becoming increasingly common within American society, so too has the proportion of clergy who have experienced divorce. Although the 1989 survey did not include a marital status question, the data nevertheless reveal that between 2001 and 2009 there was a small increase in the percentage of clergy who report that they have been divorced and remarried. Whereas 10 percent of the clergy surveyed in 2001 reported that they had been divorced and remarried, 12 percent did so in 2009.[7]

And, finally, there has been a changing pathway to entrance into the ranks of the clergy. In particular, there is a growing proportion of clergy who enter the ministry later in life, after working in a different career prior to becoming a pastor. In fact, the average age of those entering seminary rose by more than ten years between 1962 and 2005 (Wheeler, Miller, and Aleshire 2007). Although this pattern of entering the ministry later in life is not directly evident from the data presented in table 2.1, it is reflected, in part, in terms of the declining percentage of clergy who are under the age of 40 years. But, this fact is more clearly shown in the age at which clergy report that they were ordained,[8] as the mean age at ordination rose from 27.5 years of age in 1989, to 30.0 years of age in 2001, and then to 30.6 years of age in 2009 (data not shown).

The Changing Context of Ministry

These changes in the composition of clergy have transpired within a changing context in which ministry occurs. Certainly, the economic, political, and cultural context of American life was different in 2009 from that evident in 1989. And, over the past several decades, the social and religious context within which Protestant clergy serve has also changed in some important ways as well.

The data presented in table 2.2 examines some of the ways in which the social and religious context of ministry has exhibited patterns of both continuity and change over time. Given the relative absence of comparable contextual data across time, the analysis is limited to an examination of the size of the congregations in which clergy serve, the average weekly attendance they report, and the relative size of the community in which the congregation is located.[9]

First, a greater percentage of Protestant clergy serve smaller congregations today than was true twenty years ago. When asked the membership size of the congregations within which they minister, only 9 percent of Protestant clergy in 1989 reported that they served in congregations of fifty members or less, but 15 percent did so in 2009; similarly, the percentage of clergy reporting that they serve congregations of fifty to one hundred members also increased—from 16 percent in 1989 to 22 percent in 2009. In contrast, the percentage of clergy reporting that they served congregations of over five hundred members declined over the same period of time, as did the percentage who served congregations between two hundred and fifty and five hundred members. When examined in terms of average size of the congregations served, the mean level of reported membership of the congregations served declined from 318.9 in 1989, to 302.4 in 2001, to 253.5 in 2009 (data not shown). Clearly, pastors as a whole generally report that they serve smaller congregations today than their counterparts did two decades ago.

Of course, congregational membership and average attendance at Sunday morning worship services are two different things. Not all congregational members are necessarily able to attend each Sunday—whether for health reasons, business travel, vacation travel, or simply visiting grandchildren in some different community. Likewise, some may be attending worship in a congregation on a regular basis without necessarily choosing to become a member of the congregation. Furthermore, different denominations and/or congregations may treat inactive members in different ways—with some religious institutions and/or churches "pruning" their membership lists more readily than others. But, generally speaking, average attendance on a Sunday morning is typically less than what attendance would be were all members of a congregation present that morning.

Although our surveys did not ask clergy to report on their average weekly church attendance in 1989, clergy also reported higher levels of weekly attendance at worship services on Sunday mornings in 2001 than they did in 2009 (see table 2.2). Overall, clergy reports of attendance at Sunday morning worship services declined from an average of 225.1 in 2001 to 188.5 in 2009 (data not shown). Thus, the religious context in which Protestant clergy serve has clearly changed over the past two decades, as clergy from these seven denominations are now serving smaller congregations with fewer in attendance at Sunday morning worship services.

As noted earlier, the strength of American religion has historically been in small towns and rural areas, as there are more congregations per capita in rural and small-town settings than in highly urban, and even suburban, areas (Wuthnow 2013). Hence, the opportunities for serving as a pastor of a congregation are more heavily weighted toward serving in smaller communities, and, as a result, one would expect that a higher percentage of clergy would be found in these smaller-sized communities than in larger, more highly urbanized, settings. In addition, given the relatively short interval of time between 2001 and 2009, one would hardly expect any major change in these rural versus urban patterns of service.

And, in fact, the data presented in table 2.2 reveal no major changes over the past decade in terms of the size of the communities in which clergy engage in their congregational ministries. In both 2001 and 2009, more than half of the Protestant clergy surveyed served congregations in communities with populations of less than 50,000 people. If anything, a greater percentage of clergy serve churches in these smaller communities in 2009 than in 2001, as the percentage of clergy who

Table 2.2 **The Changing Context of Protestant Ministry, 1989–2009**

	1989 (%)	2001 (%)	2009 (%)
Congregational size			
50 or less	9	15	15
51 through 100	16	19	22
101 through 250	34	31	34
251 through 500	25	22	20
501+	16	13	10
Congregational average attendance			
50 or less	x	15	18
51 through 100	x	27	28
101 through 250	x	33	34
251 through 500	x	16	14
501+	x	9	6
Community size			
Rural or small town	x	17	18
Small town	x	25	29
Small city (15,000–50,000)	x	14	15
Medium city (50,000–100,000)	x	10	10
Large city (100,000+)	x	18	13
Suburb	x	16	16

x = not asked.

report that they serve congregations in large cities declined from 18 percent in 2001 to 13 percent in 2009. However, it is unclear whether this drop in percentage of clergy within urban settings reflects real change (e.g., the possibility that a number of small, inner-city, congregations had closed their doors and that fewer pastors thereby could report serving in such settings) or whether it merely reflects a small fluctuation in the percentage of pastors returning questionnaires from such settings across the two periods of time. But, regardless, the data presented in table 2.2 reveal that most Protestant clergy (at least from the seven denominations under study) serve in communities of less than 50,000 people and that, in this sense, their social context of ministry has not changed substantially over the past decade (or two).

Differences among Protestant Clergy

To this point, our analysis has focused on clergy as a whole. In this section of the chapter, the focus shifts to possible changes that may have occurred within particular segments of clergy. Here, we examine differences between male and female clergy, between newly ordained and more "veteran" clergy, as well as differences between evangelical and mainline Protestant clergy.

Female Clergy and Male Clergy

Some of the changes noted earlier in the social composition of clergy (table 2.1) and the context of ministry (table 2.2) may be interrelated. For example, during the past two decades, women may have chosen to enter the ministry at an older age than men—even though males too may be entering the ministry later in life. This may be true for two particular reasons. First, for some women, later entrance into ministry may be a function of the fact that opportunities to serve as a minister of the Word and Sacrament may not have been available earlier in their careers (e.g., the Christian Reformed Church, one of the denominations included in this study, did not open the office to women until 1995). But, for other women, entering the ministry later in life may be related to the fact that family responsibilities may have received greater priority in the earlier decades of their life. Thus, one might anticipate that women clergy overall are more likely to have entered the ministry later in life and to report fewer years in the ministry than male clergy.

Certainly, as can be seen from table 2.3, female clergy have, on the whole, far less ministerial experience than male clergy. In 1989, more than one-half of women reported that they had ten years or less of ministerial experience, while less than one-fifth of men did so. Or, from a different vantage point, less than one-tenth of female clergy reported in 1989 that they had thirty years or more of ministerial experience, but nearly one-quarter of male clergy did so. And, as anticipated, this difference in ministerial experience is primarily a function of the fact that women typically are ordained much later in life than male clergy. For example, in 2009, the average age of women clergy at the time of their ordination was 37.0 years; in contrast, the corresponding average age of male clergy at ordination was 29.3 years (data not shown).

The gender gap in ministerial experience has, to a certain extent, narrowed over the past two decades, as a lower percentage of women clergy in 2009 than in 1989 reported less than ten years of ministerial experience. Nevertheless, the gap continues to remain fairly substantial in nature: women clergy in 2009 were still twice as likely as male clergy to report less than ten years of ministerial experience, and male clergy were nearly four more times as likely as female clergy to report thirty years or more of ministerial experience.

Table 2.3 **Selected Differences between Female and Male Clergy over Time**

	1989 (%)		2001 (%)		2009 (%)	
	Female	*Male*	*Female*	*Male*	*Female*	*Male*
Years in ministry						
1 to 4 years	19	6	15	6	13	6
5 to 9 years	32	13	20	9	22	10
10 through 19 years	27	28	40	30	35	21
20 through 29 years	14	29	23	36	23	36
30+ years	9	24	3	20	8	28
Marital status						
Single, never married[a]	x	x	8	4	4	4
Divorced or separated	x	x	5	3	4	3
Divorced and remarried	x	x	13	10	13	10
Married, never divorced[b]	x	x	74	82	81	82
Seminary education						
None	6	5	5	5	2	3
Bible college	5	11	4	10	5	11
Some seminary	8	7	7	7	8	8
Seminary graduate	81	78	84	78	86	78
Congregational size						
Less than 50 members	16	8	14	19	20	16
50 through 100 members	24	16	17	18	30	21
101 through 250 members	38	34	37	28	33	33
251 through 500 members	19	25	18	20	13	19
501+ members	4	17	15	15	5	11

[a]Includes widowed.
[b]Includes widowed and remarried.
x = not asked.

Of course, the data presented in table 2.3 reveal only the number of years of ministry served by male and female clergy. Another way to capture this fact is simply to examine older clergy members and then inquire about their total years in the ministry. For example, among clergy in 2009 who were 56 years of age or older, female clergy were more than three times as likely as male clergy to report that they had served in the ministry ten years or less: 21 percent versus

6 percent, respectively (data not shown). Clearly women who choose to enter the ministry typically do so at a later age than men. To what extent this gap is likely to diminish over time remains unclear. Certainly institutional barriers to entrance into the ordained ministry for women have diminished over time, providing increased opportunities for women to enter the ministry earlier in life. Nevertheless, traditional role responsibilities related to child rearing may continue to prompt a greater proportion of women than men to delay seminary training and ordination to ministry until later in life.

The marital experiences of female clergy also tend to set them somewhat apart from male clergy as a whole, as the former exhibit slightly different martial patterns than the latter. As shown in table 2.3, female clergy are more likely than their male counterparts to report that they are either currently divorced/separated or previously divorced and now remarried than their male counterparts. Whereas slightly more than one in six (17–18 percent) female clergy reported either currently being divorced/separated or having previously been divorced, only about one in eight male clergy (13 percent) did so.

Female clergy also tend to be somewhat more highly educated than their male counterparts, as they are more likely than their male counterparts to report being seminary graduates; this is true for each point in time over the past two decades. Moreover, as can be seen from table 2.3, the percentage of women clergy who are seminary graduates has increased over the past twenty years, while the percentage of male clergy who are seminary graduates has not changed. Thus, it would appear that women are not becoming ordained through special educational processes associated with the office of "commissioned lay pastors." Rather, they have typically obtained a conventional seminary education prior to entering the ministry. Of course, some of these differences in educational attainment between male and female clergy may be related to the denominations in which such clergy serve and the proportion of female clergy found within each of them—as some denominations more typically require an educated clergy than other denominations. Nevertheless, given the denominations under study here, female clergy are generally more likely than male clergy to be seminary graduates.

Female clergy are also somewhat more likely than their male counterparts to serve smaller congregations. A majority of female clergy in 2009 (50.2 percent)[10] reported that they served congregations of one hundred members or less, while less than two-fifths of male clergy (37 percent) did so. In contrast, nearly one-third of male clergy (30 percent) reported in 2009 that they served congregations of more than two hundred fifty members, but less than one-fifth of female clergy (18 percent) so reported.

Of course, this disparity in serving larger congregations may be a function of the different levels of ministerial experience exhibited by males and females, as more experienced clergy tend to serve larger congregations. And, as was shown above, women clergy tend to exhibit less ministerial experience overall than male clergy. However, even when one compares male and female clergy with similar levels of ministerial experience, female clergy generally report that they serve smaller congregations than their male counterparts. In 2009, for example, the mean membership size of the congregations served by female clergy with less than ten years of ministerial experience was 151.5 members, while it was 168.2 members for male clergy with such limited experience (data not shown). Moreover, this gender disparity in the size of congregation served was even greater for those with the most years of ministerial experience, as the mean membership size of congregations served by female clergy with twenty or more years of ministerial experience was 166.6 members compared to 267.0 members for male clergy (data not shown). Thus, not only do women typically enter the ministry later in life than male clergy, but they typically serve smaller congregations than their male counterparts with similar levels of ministerial experience.

Newly Ordained Clergy and "Veteran" Clergy

It was noted earlier, there has also been a substantial "graying of the profession" over the past several decades. However, it is also true that increasing numbers of clergy are now beginning their ministry later in life, after having worked in another profession prior to entering the ministry. In part, some of the "graying of the profession" may be related to the growing feminization of the clergy, as women clergy frequently enter seminary later in life than male clergy. But, regardless of its basis, it is far from clear to what extent those who choose to enter the ministry today exhibit similar characteristics as those who chose to enter the ministry in years past. Are the pathways of recruitment to ministry then similar to, or different from, the pathways evident several decades ago? To what extent do the social characteristics of the more newly ordained Protestant clergy reflect, or diverge from, that of their more veteran counterparts? These questions are addressed in table 2.4, which compares the social characteristics of those clergy who have been ordained in the office for less than ten years with those who have served in the office for a decade or longer.

The data reveal that, though there is a fair amount of continuity in the social characteristics of newly ordained clergy over the past twenty years, there are also some important changes that have transpired as well. Not surprisingly, given what we have seen earlier, the ranks of newly ordained clergy have changed substantially in terms of gender composition. Given the seven

Table 2.4 **The Social Characteristics of Newly Ordained and More Veteran Protestant Clergy over Time**

	1989 (%)		2001 (%)		2009 (%)	
	New	*Veteran*	*New*	*Veteran*	*New*	*Veteran*
Gender						
Female	13	3	23	9	23	10
Male	87	97	77	91	77	90
Race						
White	x	x	94	95	97	95
Non-white	x	x	6	5	3	5
Age						
Under 40 years	69	19	46	7	46	6
40–55 years	25	47	44	60	35	46
56+ years	6	34	11	33	19	49
Marital status						
Single[a]	x	x	4	5	4	4
Divorced, separated	x	x	4	4	3	3
Divorced, remarried	x	x	12	10	9	13
Married[b]	x	x	80	81	84	81
Education						
High school or less	10	9	3	2	3	2
Some college	13	13	9	7	10	7
College graduate	78	78	89	91	87	91
Seminary training						
None	6	4	8	4	7	2
Bible college	15	15	9	10	7	11
Some seminary	10	9	11	6	16	6
Seminary graduate	69	72	72	80	71	81

[a]Includes single, never married, and widowed.
[b]Includes widowed and remarried.
x = not asked.

denominations under study, only a little more than one-eighth (13 percent) of all newly ordained clergy were women in 1989. But, two decades later almost one-quarter (23 percent) of all newly ordained clergy were women.

Although the ranks of newly ordained clergy have exhibited greater gender diversity over time, the same cannot be said with regard to the racial composition of newly ordained clergy. In fact, given the seven denominations under study, newly ordained clergy were more homogeneously white in racial composition in 2009 than they were in 2001. And though the percentage of non-whites among clergy who have been ordained for ten or more years remained constant over that same span of time, it will not be long before the percentage of non-whites among more veteran clergy will drop within these particular denominations as well.

Newly ordained clergy are also entering the ministry much later in life. In 1989, more than two-thirds of all newly ordained clergy were under 40 years of age, but, by 2009, less than half were. In contrast, only 6 percent of all newly ordained clergy were 56 years of age or older in 1989, but that percentage increased to 19 percent two decades later. Clearly, part of the "graying of the profession" relates to the fact that far greater numbers of clergy are now entering the ministry later in life than was true several decades ago.

In contrast, far greater continuity is evident in terms of the marital status of newly ordained clergy. In 1989, the overwhelming majority of newly ordained clergy (80 percent) were married, and the same was true in 2009 (84 percent). However, a smaller percentage of newly ordained clergy reported in 2009 than in 2001 that they had been divorced at some point in their life (12 percent in 2009 versus 16 percent in 2001).

Finally, there are also marginal changes related to the educational training of newly ordained clergy over the past two decades. Newly ordained clergy today are far more likely to report today that they are college graduates than did newly ordained clergy in 1989. Similarly, a far higher percentage of newly ordained clergy today have had at least some seminary training than was true two decades ago—though the actual percentage of seminary graduates has only increased slightly over the same period of time. In other words, higher percentages of newly ordained clergy today indicate that they have had some seminary training, though they were not seminary graduates, than in 1989, while fewer newly ordained clergy entered the ranks of ministry through Bible college training now than several decades ago.

Thus, overall, much of the social composition of newly ordained clergy today continues to mirror that of newly ordained clergy several decades earlier. Nevertheless, though the major social sources of clergy recruitment have remained predominantly the same, important changes are also evident. Newly ordained clergy today are, as a group, more feminine, somewhat whiter, older, and somewhat more highly educated than was true with regard to newly ordained clergy twenty years ago.

Evangelical Clergy and Mainline Clergy

Just as there are important differences between male and female clergy and between newly ordained and more veteran clergy, so too there are important differences between evangelical and mainline Protestant clergy. And, as shown in table 2.5, evangelical and mainline Protestant clergy exhibit both a fair number of similarities but also some important differences in terms of their socio-demographic characteristics.

First, within the particular denominations under study, evangelical and mainline Protestant clergy differ in terms of their gender composition. In 2009, only about one in forty clergy within the three evangelical denominations under study were female, but nearly one in five within the mainline denominations were. Moreover, while the percentage of female clergy within mainline Protestant denominations more than tripled over the past two decades (from 6 percent in 1989 to 19 percent in 2009), the percentage of female clergy within the three evangelical denominations remained basically the same over that identical period of time.

In contrast, the racial composition of evangelical and mainline Protestant clergy has remained rather similar and stable over time. Non-white clergy constituted slightly more than 6 percent of clergy within both religious traditions in 2009—basically the same percentage evident for both traditions in 2001 (the 1989 survey did not include a racial question).

The "graying of Protestant clergy" is clearly evident among both evangelical and mainline Protestant clergy. Within both religious traditions, the percentage of clergy under the age of 40 has declined substantially between 1989 and 2009, while the percentage over the age of 55 has increased over the same period of time. However, the rate at which this has been occurring varies by religious tradition, as mainline Protestant clergy, as a whole, have become much "grayer" than their evangelical counterparts. In fact, by 2009, nearly one-half of the mainline Protestant clergy (48 percent) reported that they were over 55 years of age; in contrast, slightly more than one-third of evangelical Protestant clergy did so (37 percent).

Evangelical and mainline Protestant pastors also differ in terms of their marital status. Clergy within mainline Protestant denominations are far more likely than their evangelical counterparts to report that they are single, currently divorced or separated, or previously divorced and now remarried, with mainline

Table 2.5 **The Social Characteristics of Evangelical and Mainline Protestant Clergy over Time**

	1989 (%)		2001 (%)		2009 (%)	
	Evangelical	Mainline	Evangelical	Mainline	Evangelical	Mainline
Gender						
Female	2	6	3	18	2	19
Male	98	94	97	82	98	81
Race						
White	x	x	91	93	94	94
Non-white	x	x	9	7	6	6
Age						
Under 40 years	32	27	17	11	16	11
40–55 years	43	46	56	58	47	42
56+ years	25	27	27	32	37	48
Marital status						
Single[a]	x	x	2	6	1	5
Divorced, separated	x	x	1	6	*	5
Divorced, remarried	x	x	3	15	3	19
Married[b]	x	x	93	73	95	72
Education						
High school or less	13	1	5	1	3	1
Some college	17	4	13	3	12	4
College graduate	71	95	82	96	85	94
Seminary training						
None	8	2	8	3	4	2
Bible college	23	1	21	1	23	1
Some seminary	9	5	9	5	8	7
Seminary graduate	59	92	62	92	66	89
Community size						
Rural or small town	x	x	21	14	17	18

(continued)

Table 2.5 (Continued)

	1989 (%)		2001 (%)		2009 (%)	
	Evangelical	Mainline	Evangelical	Mainline	Evangelical	Mainline
Small town	x	x	24	25	30	29
Small city (15,000–50,000)	x	x	13	15	15	15
Medium city (50,000–100,000)	x	x	10	10	10	9
Large city (100,000+)	x	x	17	19	14	12
Suburb	x	x	14	17	14	17

ªIncludes single, never married, and widowed.
ᵇIncludes widowed and remarried.
x = not asked.
ˊless than 1 percent.

Protestant clergy being five-to-six times more likely than evangelical Protestant clergy to report such. And these differences in marital patterns between clergy of the two traditions remained rather stable over the ten years examined.

Mainline Protestant clergy also tend to be more highly educated than their evangelical counterparts. This is true in terms of both the percentage who report that they are college graduates and the percentage of clergy who report that they are seminary graduates. Nearly all mainline Protestant clergy report that they are college graduates (approximately 95 percent do so), and only slightly less report that they are seminary graduates (around 90 percent). In contrast, the percentage of college and seminary graduates of evangelical Protestant clergy falls substantially below that of mainline Protestant clergy.

However, as can been seen from table 2.5, this educational gap between evangelical and mainline Protestant clergy is narrowing—both in terms of college education and in terms of seminary education. In 1989, only 71 percent of evangelical Protestant clergy reported that they were college graduates, but 85 percent did so in 2009. In fact, among evangelical Protestant clergy under the age of 40, the percentage of college graduates has actually increased to 88 percent (data not shown). The gap in seminary education has also narrowed somewhat between evangelical and mainline Protestant clergy, though a rather substantial gap remains. The percentage of seminary graduates within the ranks of evangelical Protestant clergy has increased from 59 percent in 1989 to 66 percent in

2009. And, over the same period of time, the percentage of seminary graduates among mainline Protestant clergy has actually declined slightly (from 92 percent to 89 percent). This decline is due, in part, to the fact that the percentage of mainline Protestant clergy who report that they have had only "some seminary" education has slowly increased over that period of time—perhaps reflecting the rise of "commissioned lay ministers" within the ranks of mainline Protestant churches.

Overall, as might be expected, non-seminary graduates in both religious traditions generally serve smaller congregations than their counterparts who are seminary graduates. In 2009, 65 percent of the non-seminary graduates among evangelical clergy served congregations with a hundred members or less, while only about 30 percent of evangelical and mainline Protestant seminary graduates served in congregations of a hundred or less (data not shown). And, not surprisingly, this pattern of clergy with seminary degrees serving larger congregations, while those without such education primarily serving smaller congregations, has prevailed over the past two decades (data not shown).

Likewise, the size of the communities within which evangelical and mainline Protestant clergy serve their congregations is quite similar. Relatively similar percentages of clergy across the two traditions report that they served congregations in rural communities, small towns, small and medium-sized cities, and in large cities or the suburbs of such large cities. Thus, the context of ministry for both evangelical and mainline Protestant clergy is fairly similar—as least in terms of the relative distribution of the different types of communities within which their congregations are located.

Yet, despite the relative similarity in the size of the communities within which evangelical and mainline Protestant clergy conduct their ministries, evangelical clergy are more likely than mainline clergy to serve congregations of a hundred members or less. For example, as can be seen from table 2.6, more than two-fifths of evangelical Protestant clergy in 2009 served congregations of a hundred members or less, while only one-third of mainline Protestant clergy did so (43 percent versus 33 percent, respectively). Moreover, this pattern has been evident over the past several decades, as a larger percentage of evangelical than mainline Protestant clergy has consistently reported serving such relatively small congregations.

Although this pattern has been consistently evident, the percentage of clergy from both traditions who serve congregations of a hundred members or less has substantially increased over the past two decades. Among evangelical Protestant clergy, only 30 percent reported in 1989 that they served congregations of a hundred members or less, but 43 percent did so in 2009. Among

Table 2.6 **The Changing Context of Ministry for Evangelical and Mainline Protestant Clergy**

	1989 (%)		2001 (%)		2009 (%)	
	Evangelical	*Mainline*	*Evangelical*	*Mainline*	*Evangelical*	*Mainline*
Congregational size						
Less than 50 members	13	6	25	8	20	10
50 through 100 members	17	16	22	17	22	23
101 through 250 members	29	37	24	37	27	38
251 through 500 members	22	27	20	23	20	20
501+ members	20	14	10	16	11	9

mainline Protestant clergy, the percentage of clergy who reported that they ministered in congregations of a hundred members or less jumped from 22 percent in 1989 to 33 percent in 2009. Moreover, within both religious traditions, this increase in the percentage of clergy serving relatively small congregations has occurred largely at the expense of larger congregations, as a smaller percentage of clergy reported in 2009 than in 1989 that they serve congregations of 251 members or more.

This decline in membership (as well as average weekly attendance at worship services) has occurred within all types of communities. As shown in table 2.7, Protestant clergy across these seven denominations, regardless of the size of the community in which they minister, report both a decline in membership size and worship attendance over the eight-year interval of time between 2001 and 2009. In other words, it did not matter whether the congregations were located in small towns, small or mid-sized cities, larger cities, or even the suburbs— clergy consistently reported a decline in membership and attendance between 2001 and 2009. The only exception to this pattern of decline in membership and weekly worship attendance relates to congregational membership size within rural communities—where there was a slight increase in the mean number of congregational members from 2001 to 2009. Otherwise, the pattern is consistent across all sizes of communities—with both the mean number of congregational members as well as the mean level of worship attendance having declined in magnitude between 2001 and 2009.

Nevertheless, as can also be seen from table 2.7, there are some important differences in these patterns related to whether these congregations are within the evangelical and mainline Protestant traditions. First, within evangelical congregations, the average weekly level of worship attendance much more closely mirrors

Table 2.7 **Mean Number of Members and Average Attendance by Size of Community over Time Controlling for Religious Tradition**

Community size	2001		2009	
	Members	*Average attendance*	*Members*	*Average attendance*
All				
Rural	132.4	113.2	137.2	108.1
Small town	219.2	171.1	208.7	157.3
Small city (15,000)	295.2	213.0	256.1	184.6
Medium city (15,000–100,000)	407.8	295.0	271.8	208.1
Large city (100,000+)	385.4	280.7	303.1	223.3
Suburb	470.4	342.1	409.6	297.4
Evangelical Protestant				
Rural	110.3	112.3	148.2	134.3
Small town	197.5	197.8	200.4	183.4
Small city (15,000)	259.7	255.0	251.9	238.7
Medium city (15,000–100,000)	307.4	318.0	292.4	256.9
Large city (100,000+)	312.5	329.2	324.9	312.8
Suburb	329.7	403.9	451.9	368.6
Mainline Protestant				
Rural	158.4	114.2	129.7	90.2
Small town	236.0	150.9	215.1	137.2
Small city (15,000)	318.3	185.6	239.5	141.8
Medium city (15,000–100,000)	487.2	276.7	255.2	169.3
Large (100,000+)	438.5	245.9	270.5	160.9
Suburb	562.6	301.5	383.7	253.5

the average congregational membership—with average weekly attendance even exceeding membership size among evangelical congregations within rural and small town communities in 2001. In contrast, within mainline Protestant congregations, clergy report that the average weekly worship attendance within their congregations lags substantially behind the membership size of their congregations.

The pattern of change in reported average congregational membership size across different-sized communities varies somewhat by religious tradition. Evangelical clergy within rural, small town, large city, and suburban settings actually reported somewhat larger average membership sizes for the congregations they served in 2009 than they did within such settings in 2001. In contrast, mainline Protestant clergy in 2009 consistently reported both smaller membership levels and lower worship attendance levels than did mainline Protestant clergy in 2001—regardless of the size of the communities in which their congregations were located.

Nevertheless, despite such appearances of membership gains among evangelical congregations, the reported average weekly worship attendance reported by both evangelical and mainline Protestant clergy declined between 2001 and 2009—and this was true regardless of the size of the community within which such congregations were located (with, as noted previously, the only exception occurring among evangelical congregations in rural congregations). Thus, despite the fact that the mean level of membership within small-town evangelical congregations jumped from 197.5 members in 2001 to 200.4 members in 2009, the reported average weekly worship attendance nevertheless declined over the same period of time—from an average of 200.4 to an average of 183.4 worshippers in attendance on Sunday mornings. Similar patterns of decline in worship attendance among evangelical congregations can be found for each community size within which evangelical congregations exhibited membership gains over the same period of time.

Yet, despite this consistency in declining worship attendance, the magnitude of the decline in average worship attendance between 2001 and 2009 was, overall, substantially greater within mainline than evangelical Protestant congregations. When the mean score for the average weekly worship attendance in 2009 is subtracted from the corresponding mean score for average weekly worship attendance in 2001, differences are far greater for mainline than evangelical Protestant churches. And, as a result, the gap between membership and attendance remained far smaller for evangelical than for mainline Protestant congregations. However, the decline in average membership was far greater than the decline in average worship attendance. And, as a result, average levels of worship attendance on Sunday mornings within mainline Protestant congregations more closely mirrors their membership levels in 2009 than they did in 2001.

Conclusions

From certain perspectives, the social composition of Protestant clergy in America looks largely the same today as it did twenty years within the seven denominations under study. Clergy within these denominations have been historically white, male, married, and rather well educated. And, in 2009 as in 1989, the clergy from these denominations were overwhelmingly white, male, married, and rather well educated.

Still important changes are occurring in the social composition of Protestant clergy. There is a growing feminization of the clergy, particularly within the mainline Protestant denominations, while there has been a small, but rather steady, presence of female clergy within the evangelical Protestant tradition. But, between 1989 and 2001, the proportion of female clergy nearly tripled within mainline Protestant churches. And, though this feminization of mainline Protestant clergy continued between 2001 and 2009, its growth subsided substantially over that period of time.

Meanwhile, there has also been a graying of the profession; clergy are, as a whole, far older today than twenty years ago. This graying of the profession is occurring within both evangelical and mainline Protestant denominations, though it is somewhat more prevalent among mainline, than evangelical, Protestant clergy.

In part, this graying of the professional is the result of a growth in the delay of ordination, as increasing numbers of clergy are entering seminary later in life. And, to a certain extent, this is also a function of the feminization of clergy, as many women focus on childrearing responsibilities initially and then choose to enter seminary later in life once their children have grown. Nevertheless, though the feminization of the clergy is part of the explanation for the graying of the profession, it is not the complete explanation, as many men are also entering ministry later in life as well.

In addition, the social context of ministry is also changing. Given that there are more congregations per capita in rural and small-town settings than in more urban areas, the majority of clergy serve in rural and small-town settings. However, these rural and small-town settings are losing population to the larger, more urban, settings, and this has contributed to an aging of such rural populations as well. As a result, one may anticipate that the membership size and average attendance of congregations within such smaller settings may be declining.

And, in fact, over the past decade, clergy from such settings report a drop in both church membership and average weekly attendance. Nevertheless, these declines have occurred across all types of communities. And though such loss in membership and attendees has been greater in mainline Protestant churches, evangelical Protestant churches are not immune to such changes. The losses are simply less, overall, for evangelical than for mainline Protestant churches.

The Theological Orientations
of American Protestant Clergy

In many ways, theological reflection rests at the center of clergy life. This is particularly true within the Protestant tradition of the Christian faith, as it has historically emphasized the preaching of the Word as the central hallmark of ministry. Interest in theological matters may prompt some, perhaps many, to enter the ranks of clergy. But, once they enter seminary,[1] theological education clearly constitutes a central component in their training regardless of the particular seminary they may attend. And, once ordained, those pastors who serve congregations are typically called upon to deliver a sermon on a weekly basis—sermons that are to provide theological reflection on the passages of scripture from which the message is drawn. Moreover, congregants look to their pastors for guidance and answers to their particular theological questions. So, in many ways, theology lies at the center of the life of those who serve as clergy.

Given this situation, one might anticipate that the theological perspectives of clergy would shape the ways clergy go about conducting their ministry, as their theological understanding would likely shape their worldviews and their behavior both on and off the pulpit. Hence, in our effort to understand the changing attitudes and behavior of Protestant clergy over the past two decades, we begin within an analysis of their changing theological orientations over that period of time.

Change and Continuity in Theological Beliefs

The three clergy surveys conducted over the past two decades contained a number of theological statements that were used to assess the theological stance of the ministers from the seven denominations surveyed. As noted in the introduction, the study in 1989 was actually composed of a series of denominational surveys that employed similar, but not totally identical, questionnaires. As a result, some items addressing certain theological matters were asked of clergy across all seven denominations; while other theological beliefs were examined in only five, or three, or two of the seven denominations. Consequently, relatively few common items tapping theological beliefs were asked of all clergy in 1989.[2]

Despite this situation, the 1989 study did contain a number of common items across all denominations that addressed different kinds of theological matters. These included elements of the Apostle's Creed (e.g., "Jesus was born of a virgin"), eschatology (e.g., "Jesus will return bodily to earth one day"), the nature of biblical authority (e.g., "the Bible is the inerrant Word of God"), the distinctive nature of the Christian faith (e.g., "there is no other way to salvation but through belief in Jesus Christ"), and later surveys also addressed matters related to dispensationalism[3] (e.g., "modern-day Israel is a special nation blessed by God") and universalism[4] (e.g., "all major religions are equally good and true").

Table 3.1 presents the change and continuity in theological beliefs among Protestant clergy over the past two decades as reflected by the responses of the clergy from the seven denominations under study. As a whole, American Protestant clergy in 1989 overwhelmingly subscribed to long-standing beliefs of the Christian faith. For example, approximately, three-quarters of Protestant clergy in 1989 held that Jesus was born of a virgin, that the devil actually exists, and that there is no other way to salvation but through belief in Jesus Christ,

Table 3.1 **Continuity and Changes in Theological Beliefs among American Protestant Clergy, 1989–2009**

Agree	*1989 (%)*	*2001 (%)*	*2009 (%)*
Jesus was born of a virgin	75	79	85
There is no other way to salvation but through belief in Jesus Christ	79	74	78
The Devil actually exists	75	76	80
Adam and Eve were real people	54	59	67
The Bible is the inerrant Word of God, both in matters of faith and in historic, geographical, and other secular matters	44	50	57
Jesus will return bodily to earth one day	x	84	83
Modern-day Israel is a special nation blessed by God	x	35	40
All great religions are equally true	x	7	7

x = not asked.

while slightly more than half of the clergy in 1989 held that Adam and Eve were real people.

On the other hand, less than one-half of the clergy in 1989 (44 percent) expressed agreement that the Bible constitutes the inerrant Word of God. At first glance, this may seem somewhat surprising, as Protestants historically have emphasized the authority of scripture. In fact, it was the issue of the relative importance of the authority of scripture versus that of the Pope and church tradition that prompted the Protestant Reformation and advanced the notion of *sola scriptura*. However, inerrancy reflects a relatively new view of biblical authority that stands in contrast to an older, infallible view of biblical authority. Those who subscribe to an infallible view of scripture believe that the Bible is the inspired Word of God and that it is true in all that it teaches. From this perspective, scripture is infallible in that it does not deceive humans concerning matters of salvation. It isn't that scripture does not contain information about history, geography, science, or astronomy; rather, the nature of the information provided is governed by the purpose of God's revelation.

In contrast, the inerrancy position is more stringent than the infallibility position. The inerrancy position posits that the Bible, at least in terms of the original documents, is totally without error in all its statements whether they relate to religious faith, historical events, or natural occurrences. Accordingly, biblical inerrantists would be prone to stress that the account of creation in Genesis 1 is a true account religiously—and scientifically. Although many inerrantists would recognize that the term "day" discussed in the account does not necessarily refer to a twenty-four-hour span of time (as the account is poetic and God is eternal and exists outside the dimension of time), such inerrantists might still well insist: (1) that the creation sequence is true in terms of the natural history of matter, and (2) that many, if not most, scientific accounts of the origins of the universe can be harmonized with the account of Genesis 1. On the other hand, those who adhere to the infallibility of scripture would stress the revelational truths contained in the Genesis account of creation relate to God being the creator of the universe and people being created in the image of God rather than to any general "scientific" statements concerning the specific, sequential nature of that process. Given these different views of biblical authority, it may not be all that surprising that only 44 percent of the clergy surveyed in 1989 subscribed to biblical inerrancy (though many additional clergy would likely have subscribed to biblical infallibility).

Nevertheless, given this starting point in 1989, several shifts in the expressed theological positions of Protestant clergy have occurred over the past twenty years. For the most part, the patterns suggest a great deal of continuity in adherence to the particular theological beliefs examined. But, to the extent that change is evident, it is one that moves in a more theologically conservative, than a theologically liberal, direction. For example, the percentage of Protestant clergy who expressed agreement with belief in the virgin birth jumped from 75 percent in 1989 to 85 percent in 2009. Likewise, over the course of the twenty years analyzed, belief in the devil increased from 75 percent to 80 percent, belief in a literal Adam and Eve jumped from 54 percent to 67 percent, and belief in the inerrancy of the Bible increased from 44 percent to 57 percent. Thus, the only belief for which there was no major shift in increased subscription occurred with regard to whether there is no other way to salvation but through Jesus Christ: 79 percent of Protestant clergy reported agreement with the statement in 1989, and 78 percent did so in 2009.

The other three theological belief items found in table 3.1 were asked only in 2001 and 2009. But the patterns of aggregate change associated with these three beliefs also reflect the same patterns just described. Subscription to the belief in the bodily return of Jesus to earth one day is not only widespread among Protestant clergy, but adherence to this belief has not changed over the course of the first decade of the twenty-first century: 84 percent of Protestant clergy from the seven denominations reported they believed such in 2001 and 83 percent did so in 2009.

On the other hand, there was some increase among clergy between 2001 and 2009 in the percentage who agreed that "Israel was a special nation blessed by God." Much of Christian theology has long emphasized that the New Testament church has now become the "New Israel." But, dispensationalists, in contrast, generally argue that God's promises to Israel were unconditional in nature and therefore are still binding, with both Israel and the church existing in special relationship to God. Given this latter dispensational perspective, our surveys asked clergy whether they agreed that Israel was a special nation blessed by God, with a little more than one-third (35 percent) so agreeing in 2001 and two-fifths (40 percent) doing so in 2009.

Finally, almost all Protestant clergy in both 2001 and 2009 refused to subscribe to any notion that "all great religions are equally true," as only 7 percent of the Protestant clergy from the seven denominations surveyed agreed with the statement in both 2001 and 2009. Given that clergy are people who have chosen to serve in the work and ministry of the Christian church, perhaps this is not surprising. Still, there are Christian universalists, including some pastors, who hold to the doctrine of universal salvation—contending that the life and death (and the physical resurrection) of Jesus has provided salvation for all. Perhaps, for some Christian universalists, the end result is that "all great religions are equally true." On the other hand, given that Christian universalists typically hold that such universal salvation is effected by the grace of God through the specific work of Jesus Christ, it might be that even many such universalists would not necessarily subscribe to the equivalency of all major religions. But, whatever may be the reasons, relatively few Protestant clergy are willing to subscribe to any notion that "all great religions are equally good and true."

The Changing Levels of Theological Orthodoxy

Of course, it is one thing to argue that an understanding of the theological perspectives of clergy is central to any understanding of the worldviews and behavior of clergy. But, it is another thing to try to isolate the particular theological contentions that should be considered as central or crucial in ascertaining their perspectives. A variety of theological understandings exist, covering a host of different topics. What then should serve as the focus of scholarly attention in seeking to understand the nature of the change that might be occurring within the ranks of clergy today?

Certainly one prominent strand of scholarly research on the theological perspectives of clergy has focused on the level of theological orthodoxy that clergy exhibit. Of course, just what constitutes theological orthodoxy can be a matter of scholarly dispute (e.g., Stark and Foster 1970), but the notion of theological orthodoxy is generally understood to reflect the level of adherence to established beliefs or doctrines of the Christian faith as formulated in the early ecumenical creeds and confessions.

The linkages between the "orthodox" theology of clergy and social and political variables are well documented (Johnson 1967; Hadden 1969; Jeffries and Tygart 1974; Quinley 1974; Guth et al. 1997; and Johnson 1998). This is especially true for one's stands on political issues, one's ideological orientation, one's partisan identification, and one's voting behavior. Pastors who exhibit a strong adherence to traditional doctrines like the existence of the Devil and the centrality of Jesus' role in salvation, for example, have been found to be more conservative and Republican than their brethren less committed to these positions (see, e.g., Guth et al. 1997, 123).

What then are the core components of Christian orthodoxy that survey questions should tap when studying clergy? No scholarly consensus has emerged as to which specific beliefs related to the historic creeds should be addressed when seeking to examine theological orthodoxy. Moreover, in this study, any measure of theological orthodoxy is limited not only by the requirement that identical theological questions need to have been asked across all seven denominational surveys at one cross-section in time, but that they were also used over the course of all three clergy surveys. Given these limitations, our measure of theological orthodoxy is based on responses to four specific theological statements:

1. There is no other way to salvation but through belief in Jesus Christ.
2. The devil actually exists.
3. Jesus was born of a virgin.
4. Adam and Eve were real people.

Perhaps some explanation is in order concerning the choice of the items included in this index of theological orthodoxy. As noted earlier, only a very limited number of common theological questions were contained within the various denominational surveys conducted in 1989, creating only a limited pool of possible common theological items for the measure of theological orthodoxy. And, given that it is better to have more, rather than fewer, items when constructing an attitudinal index (Johnson and Reynolds 2008, 112–13), it was deemed preferable to have a four-variable, rather than a three-variable, measure of theological orthodoxy.

Given this situation, if there was to be a four-variable measure of theological orthodoxy, the choice was limited to either using an item related to Adam and Eve or an item related to biblical inerrancy.[5] Although one may question whether the inclusion of the item related to Adam and Eve is appropriate, it a far better measure for capturing theological orthodoxy than is the inerrancy item. Certainly, it is true that the belief in a literal Adam and Eve is not included within the historic confessions of the Christian faith. Nevertheless, it is also true that a belief in a literal Adam and Eve has been commonly held throughout the past two millennia by Christian clergy and laity alike.

Moreover, a belief in a literal Adam and Eve is a better measure for capturing theological orthodoxy than the alternative option of using adherence to biblical inerrancy. Certainly adherence to biblical authority may constitute an important component of theological orthodoxy. But subscription to biblical authority is far different from adherence to the more specific notion of biblical inerrancy, a view of biblical authority that was largely formulated in the late 1800s in response to challenges to historic interpretations of the Bible mounted by German higher criticism of textual material (Marsden 1980, 113–15). Given its relatively recent formulation, adherence to biblical inerrancy cannot really be viewed as reflecting adherence to a historic understanding of the Christian faith. Consequently, the inclusion of the Adam and Eve item within the theological orthodoxy index was deemed a far better approach to the assessment of theological orthodoxy than inclusion of a measure tapping biblical inerrancy within such an index.

Now, if the four items do indeed measure the same underlying concept of theological orthodoxy, then all four items should be highly correlated together.

In other words, the correlation between belief in a literal Adam and Eve with the other measures of theological orthodoxy should not be markedly different from the correlations found between and among the other three measures of theological orthodoxy. And, in fact, the inter-item correlations of the four orthodoxy measures are rather similar, and very high, in magnitude (see table 3.2), demonstrating that the belief in a literal Adam and Even is strongly associated with the other three, more conventional, measures of theological orthodoxy.[6]

Consequently, responses to these four items were used to measure theological orthodoxy and were then coded in the following manner. Agreement with a statement was coded as a value of +1, disagreement coded as a score of −1, and uncertainty as a score of 0, with the resulting measure of theological orthodoxy ranging from a value of −4 (disagreement with all four statements) to a value of 4 (agreement with all four statements). Thus, any resultant negative score with the overall index reveals that the respondent disagreed more than agreed with the four statements, whereas a score of 0 reflects a balance between agreement and disagreement with the items, and a positive score

Table 3.2 **Inter-item Correlations among Component Measures of Theological Orthodoxy over Time**

	Virgin birth	Jesus only way	Devil	Adam and Eve
1989				
Virgin birth	x	.723	.811	.735
Jesus only way		x	.732	.689
Devil			x	.757
Adam and Eve				x
2001				
Virgin birth	x	.749	.833	.726
Jesus only way		x	.758	.720
Devil			x	.763
Adam and Eve				x
2009				
Virgin birth	x	.792	.836	.744
Jesus only way		x	.798	.743
Devil			x	.763
Adam and Eve				x

reveals greater agreement than disagreement with the four statements. These
scores were then recoded in the following manner: all negative scores were
recoded as "low" in theological orthodoxy, with clergy who expressed agreement with all four items being scored as "high" in theological orthodoxy, and
with all remaining scores coded as "medium" in terms of their level of theological orthodoxy.

Table 3.3 presents both the raw distribution and the recoded distribution on
the four-item index of theological orthodoxy. Several conclusions can be drawn
from the data. First, it is clear that clergy fall across the full spectrum of possible
responses, as each potential score has a certain percentage of clergy associated
with it. Second, a majority of clergy, regardless of the year in which the survey
was conducted, gave responses that reflected full agreement with each of the
four items contained in the index. And, finally, and more substantively important, one can observe that clergy, as a whole, have become more theologically
orthodox over the past two decades: whereas 54 percent of the clergy from the

Table 3.3 **The Changing Level of Theological Orthodoxy**
among Protestant Clergy, 1989–2009

	1989 (%)	2001 (%)	2009 (%)
Four-item orthodoxy measure			
−4	6.5	6.0	6.1
−3	4.0	3.2	3.3
−2	5.5	4.8	3.4
−1	4.3	3.5	3.0
0	6.1	7.7	5.3
1	4.2	3.4	2.7
2	9.4	8.7	8.4
3	5.8	6.8	5.6
4	54.2	55.8	62.1
Four-item orthodoxy measure (recoded)			
Low	20.3	17.5	15.9
Medium	25.5	26.7	22.1
High	54.2	55.8	62.1

seven denominations surveyed could be classified as high in theological ortho-doxy in 1989, 62 percent could be so classified in 2009.

Just how valid then is this index in terms of capturing the level of theological orthodoxy of American Protestant clergy? One way to assess the validity of our orthodoxy measure is to examine whether it exhibits expected patterns of empirical relationships with other variables linked to theological orthodoxy. In other words, does the measure exhibit qualities that should be evident empirically if the measure truly captures the con-cept it is employed to reflect. For example, clergy were asked in 2001 and 2009 about their level of agreement with the statement "Jesus will return bodily to earth one day." Because this item was not included in the 1989 surveys, it could not be included in the theological orthodoxy index that seeks to assess change in theological orthodoxy across the twenty-year span in time. But, this item can now be used to assess the validity of our measure of theological orthodoxy given that the "second coming of Jesus" is a long-standing doctrine of the church.[7] Consequently, if the four-item index of orthodoxy is a valid measure of theological orthodoxy, then the "second coming" item should be highly correlated with the orthodoxy index in both 2001 and 2009.

In addition, it has been argued that subscription to biblical inerrancy does not constitute an element of historic Christian orthodoxy. Consequently, responses to the "second coming" statement should be more highly related to theological orthodoxy than responses to the biblical inerrancy statement. Of course, responses to biblical inerrancy may still be rather strongly related to theological orthodoxy, but if biblical inerrancy is not a component element of theological orthodoxy, then clergy who are highly orthodox should be more likely to subscribe to the "second coming" statement than to the biblical iner-rancy statement.

If these two expectations hold, then one can have greater confidence that the four-item index does indeed capture and measure what it seeks to reflect—namely, one's level of theological orthodoxy. How then do these two items relate to the constructed measure of theological orthodoxy?

Table 3.4 addresses this question. First, as shown in the table, virtually all (99 percent) of those who were classified as high in theological orthodoxy by our four-item measure agreed that Jesus would return to earth one day. In con-trast, only three-quarters to five-sixths (depending on the year of the survey) of the highly orthodox indicated that they subscribed to biblical inerrancy. Furthermore, those classified as exhibiting medium levels of theological ortho-doxy were also far more likely to hold to a second coming of Jesus to earth than they were to subscribe to biblical inerrancy.[8] Consequently, we can also conclude

Table 3.4 **Validation of Level of Theological Orthodoxy Measure**

Agree	Level of Theological Orthodoxy		
	Low (%)	Medium (%)	High (%)
The inerrancy of the Bible			
1989	1	11	75
2001	2	18	80
2009	2	20	84
Jesus will return to earth			
1989	x	x	x
2001	40	79	99
2009	23	73	99

x = not asked.

that our measure of theological orthodoxy is a valid, as well as a highly reliable, measure of theological orthodoxy.[9]

Differences in Theological Perspectives

Having established that this measure of theological orthodoxy is both highly reliable and valid, the question arises as to whether the increase in theological orthodoxy among Protestant clergy over the past twenty years is a function of increased theological orthodoxy among clergy within a couple of the denominations surveyed or largely evident across each of the denominations examined. Hence, table 3.5 examines the percentage of clergy reporting agreement with all four component items of the measure within each of the seven denominations surveyed across each of the three surveys.

First, as evident from the data presented, clergy across the seven denominations clearly exhibited different levels of agreement with the four component items of the measure of theological orthodoxy. For example, nearly all clergy from the Assemblies of God (AOG) in 1989 (98 percent) expressed agreement with all four items, while only 15 percent of the clergy from the Disciples of Christ (DOC) did so. Thus, there are substantial denominational differences among Protestant clergy in terms of the extent to which they willingly express agreement with the four component items of our measure of theological orthodoxy.

Second, the data also reveal that there is a general increase in the level of agreement with these four items among clergy across almost all of the denominations surveyed. Clergy in only two of the denominations (the AOG and the Christian Reformed Church, CRC) exhibit a decline in theological orthodoxy over the past two decades, but these declines were very small in magnitude and occurred within denominations that were already highly orthodox theologically. Far more substantial increases in theological orthodoxy were evident among clergy in the other five denominations examined. Most of these increases in theological orthodoxy were 10 percent or greater in magnitude. Clergy from the Southern Baptist Convention (SBC), who were relatively high in theological orthodoxy in 1989, became even more theologically orthodox. Of course, a substantial part of this increase may be more a "function of subtraction" than a replacement of older, less theologically orthodox pastors with newer, more theological orthodoxy clergy. Given the particular theological battles within the denomination during the 1980s and 1990s and the subsequent departure of some clergy and churches from the denomination into the Cooperative Baptist Fellowship, the remaining clergy within the SBC have thereby simply become, as a whole, more theologically homogeneous.

However, such departures of clergy from the denomination cannot directly account for the double-digit increases in theological orthodoxy found within the Reformed Church in America (RCA), the United Methodist Church (UMC), or the DOC. In these instances, it is far more likely that the increase in theological orthodoxy is more a function of newly ordained, and more theologically orthodox, clergy replacing older, less orthodox clergy. Finally, although clergy within the Presbyterian Church in the U.S.A. (PCUSA) exhibited only a 7 percent increase in theologically orthodox clergy within their ranks, even this small increase in orthodoxy is remarkable given that the denomination has also experienced, over the past several decades, an exit of many more theologically conservative congregations and clergy into newly formed denominations or "emerging denominations" (e.g., the Evangelical Presbyterian Church).

Finally, the data reveal a growing, though modest, convergence in theological orthodoxy among Protestant clergy over the past twenty years. The percentage

Table 3.5 **Level of Theological Orthodoxy by Denomination over Time (% High Orthodoxy)**

Year	Denomination						
	AOG	*SBC*	*CRC*	*RCA*	*UMC*	*PC USA*	*DOC*
1989	98	82	85	47	33	19	15
2001	93	90	85	54	28	22	19
2009	97	96	82	58	48	26	28

difference in theological orthodoxy across the seven denominations was 83 percent in 1989, but it decreased to 74 percent in 2001, and then declined further to
71 percent in 2009. Thus, over the past two decades, clergy across the spectrum
of American Protestant denominations have exhibited a modest level of convergence in their level of theological orthodoxy.

What difference, if any, then does it make for a pastor to be more highly
orthodox theologically? Here, the relationship between one's level of theological
orthodoxy and the holding of other theological and religious perspectives will
be briefly analyzed as a way to substantiate its utility as a measure in capturing
important theological differences among clergy. In later chapters, the relationship between theological orthodoxy and various social and political attitudes
and behavior will be examined.

As evident in table 3.6, the level of theological orthodoxy expressed by
clergy is highly related to a variety of theological and religious attitudes. For
example, those who are more theologically orthodox are more likely than those
who are less orthodox to agree that "there are clear and absolute standards for
what is right and wrong," with nearly all clergy high in theological orthodoxy
(95 percent) agreeing with the statement and only about one-quarter of clergy
low in theological orthodoxy (27 percent) doing so. In addition, those who are
more theologically orthodox are more likely than those who are less orthodox
to hold that "Islam encourages violence more than other major religions" and
that "modern-day Israel is a special nation blessed by God."

Table 3.6 **Religious Positions by Level of Theological Orthodoxy, 2009**

	Level of Theological Orthodoxy			
Agree	*Low (%)*	*Medium (%)*	*High (%)*	*r*
Modern-day Israel is a special nation	9	19	51	.47
Islam encourages violence	11	25	67	.50
There are clear standards of right and wrong	27	62	95	.66
All clergy positions should be open to women	99	96	62	−.44
All clergy positions should be open to practicing homosexuals	82	31	2	−.76
Evolution is the best explanation	69	24	4	−.70
All great religions equally true	30	7	1	−.62

Even larger differences are evident, however, between those low and those high in theological orthodoxy when one examines responses to whether "all clergy positions should be open to practicing homosexuals." In fact, one would be hard pressed to find some other relationship in which such stark differences would be similarly present. Nearly all clergy low in orthodoxy (82 percent) agreed with the statement, but virtually none of the clergy high in orthodoxy (2 percent) did so, with the relationship exhibiting the strongest correlation ($r = -.76$) in terms of the eleven relationships examined in the table. Major differences between clergy who are high and low in theological orthodoxy are also evident in terms of whether such clergy consider evolution to be "the best explanation for the origins of human life," whether "feminist theology provides valuable insights," whether "all great religions of the world are equally good and true," and whether "liberation theology gets at the heart of the gospel," with those low in theological orthodoxy being much more likely to agree with these statements than those high in theological orthodoxy.

Those who are less theologically orthodox are also more likely than those who are more orthodox to hold that "all clergy positions should be open to women." Virtually all of the least orthodox (99 percent) agreed with the statement. Yet, even though highly orthodoxy clergy were less likely to agree with that position, nearly two-thirds (62 percent) of the most orthodox theologically expressed agreement.

Finally, in comparison to the other relationships examined in table 3.6, the weakest relationship found is that between level of theological orthodoxy and whether "social justice gets at the heart of the gospel." Nearly all those clergy low in theological orthodoxy agreed with the statement, but almost half of those clergy high in orthodoxy did so as well. Still, even in this instance, the magnitude of the correlation coefficient remains relatively strong ($r = -.35$).

Thus, the data presented in table 3.6 reveal that the level of theological orthodoxy expressed by Protestant clergy is strongly related to the positions they adopt on a host of other theological and religious beliefs. Even the weakest relationship still exhibited a rather robust correlation coefficient, and even the smallest percentage difference found in the table between those low and those high in theological orthodoxy was a difference of 29 percent—with many relationships exhibiting differences of 60 percent or more.

The Changing Social Location of Theological Orthodoxy

Having demonstrated that there has been an increase in theological orthodoxy among American Protestant clergy over the past two decades and that

differences in theological orthodoxy are associated with differences in a variety
of other theological perspectives, the question now becomes whether there are
particular segments of clergy within which this growth in theological orthodoxy
is more pronounced? In other words, do we find greater increases in theological
orthodoxy more among certain, rather than other, kinds of clergy? Or has this
increase in theological orthodoxy been generally uniform across all clergy?

Table 3.7 assesses differences in levels of theological orthodoxy in terms of
the socio-demographic characteristics of the clergy in order to ascertain where
such changes in theological orthodoxy have been most pronounced. First of all,
major differences exist between male and female clergy in terms of the extent to
which they express high levels of theological orthodoxy, with male clergy being
far more likely than female clergy to exhibit high levels of theological orthodoxy.
In 2009, for example, 67 percent of male clergy expressed agreement with all four
items of the index, while only 28 percent of female clergy did so. And, though
both male and female clergy over the two-decade period exhibited a growth in
the percentage who could be classified as high in theological orthodoxy, the percentage increase was far greater among male than female clergy—with the net
result being that gender differences in levels of high theological orthodoxy were
even greater in 2009 than they had been in 1989.

In 1989, the largest percentage of those exhibiting the highest level of theological orthodoxy was found among the youngest clergy—those less than
40 years of age (with 58 percent being classified as high in terms of theological
orthodoxy). In contrast, the lowest level of theological orthodoxy that year was
found among middle-aged clergy (40 to 55 years of age), with a little more than
one-half being classified as high in theological orthodoxy. The oldest clergy then
fell between the other two age groups—though closer in their level of orthodoxy
to the youngest than to the middle-aged clergy. However, in 2001, it is the oldest
clergy who were the least orthodox, as those clergy who were between the ages
of 40 and 55 in 1989 were now, twelve years later, located primarily within the
56+ age category. Likewise, in 2009, it was the middle-aged category of clergy
who exhibited the highest level of theological orthodoxy (67 percent did so), as
twenty years later, the youngest cohort of clergy in 1989 now largely fell within
the middle-aged category.

All of this suggests it is not so much age per se that shapes the level of theological orthodoxy of clergy as it is when clergy first entered the ministry. In other
words, what largely shapes the theological perspectives of clergy is the particular
theological education that clergy received in seminary, along with the particular formative experiences they may have had prior to, and during, their seminary training. Hence, table 3.7 also examines the level of theological orthodoxy
expressed by clergy in terms of the decade in which such clergy were ordained
into the ministry. And, while the level of theological orthodoxy expressed by

Table 3.7 **The Changing Level of Theological Orthodoxy by Socio-Demographic Factors, 1989–2009**

High in Orthodoxy	1989 (%)	2001 (%)	2009 (%)
Gender			
Female	23	21	28
Male	56	61	67
Age			
Under 40	58	65	62
40–55	51	58	67
56+	56	51	58
Date of ordination			
Prior to the 1960s	49	y	y
1960s	45	51	56
1970s	53	60	61
1980s	50	59	65
1990s	x	52	64
2000s	x	y	59
Marital status			
Single	x	36	36
Divorced or separated	x	24	33
Divorced, remarried	x	35	39
Married	x	62	68
Seminary education			
None	80	80	90
Bible college	97	96	98
Some seminary	77	75	76
Seminary graduate	50	50	58
Post-seminary education	34	47	49
Religious tradition			
Evangelical Protestant	88	89	92
Mainline Protestant	29	31	40

x = not applicable.
y = too few respondents for meaningful results.

each cohort of seminary graduates increases over time, it is also evident that it is those clergy ordained in the 1960s who consistently exhibited the lowest level of theological orthodoxy across all three points in time.

Moreover, newly ordained clergy (i.e., those with less than ten years of ministerial experience) differ in terms of their level of theological orthodoxy, depending upon whether they were relatively young in age or chose to enter the ministry later in life. For example, among evangelical Protestants in 2009, 86 percent of newly ordained clergy under the age of 40 years were highly orthodox theologically, but 97 percent of newly ordained clergy 40 years of age or older were (data not shown). The same pattern holds true among mainline Protestant clergy in 2009: among newly ordained mainline Protestant clergy under 40 years of age, 28 percent were highly orthodox theologically, but the corresponding percentage found among newly ordained clergy 40 years of age or older was 50 percent (data not shown). It appears therefore that those who enter the ministry later in time tend, on the whole, to exhibit more theologically conservative stands with regard to the historic tenets of the Christian faith.

In addition, marital status is also significantly related to differences in levels of theological orthodoxy, as high levels of theological orthodoxy are far less evident among those clergy who are single, separated, or who have experienced divorce than it is among those clergy who are married and have never been divorced. Moreover, despite increases in high levels of theological orthodoxy within most marital categories between 2001 and 2009, the level of differences in theological orthodoxy found across the marital categories remained relatively the same across those two periods of time.

Education also shapes the likelihood whether clergy will express a high level of theological orthodoxy, as those with the least seminary education (i.e., those who never attended seminary, attended a Bible college, or only had some seminary education) are the most likely to express high levels of theological orthodoxy, while those who have had seminary education beyond their divinity degree are the least likely to do so, with seminary graduates falling between the two other categories. However, though the rank ordering of theological orthodoxy in terms of seminary education remained the same across all three points in time, the greatest increase in theological orthodoxy occurred within the ranks of the most highly educated clergy—namely, among seminary graduates and among those who have had some postgraduate seminary training.

Finally, table 3.7 examines differences in levels of theological orthodoxy in terms of the religious tradition with which the clergy were affiliated. Nearly nine in ten evangelical Protestant clergy in 1989 (89 percent) could be classified as high in theological orthodoxy, while less than one-third of mainline Protestant clergy could be so classified (29 percent). Two decades later, approximately the same percentage of evangelical Protestant clergy continued to exhibit high levels of theological orthodoxy, while the extent to which mainline Protestant clergy exhibited high levels of theological orthodoxy grew from less than one-third in 1989 to two-fifths in 2009. Thus, the greatest level of growth in theological orthodoxy over the course of the two decades has occurred among mainline Protestant clergy.

Given the patterns evident in table 3.7, one may ask just how these variables may interact to shape adherence to orthodox theological interpretations. Gender, marital status, and religious tradition have all been found to be strongly related to the probability of clergy exhibiting high levels of theological orthodoxy. Is it then religious tradition, gender, or marital status that serves primarily to shape these theological perspectives?

Table 3.8 begins to address this question, by examining the level of theological orthodoxy by marital status controlling for the clergy's gender. As the data reveal, the percentage of male clergy who are married, never divorced, and who agree with all four theological items of our orthodoxy index far exceeds the percentage found among comparable female clergy. The same is true with regard to male clergy who are single, separated, or divorced; they too exhibit higher levels of theological orthodoxy than their female counterparts.

However, the marital status and gender of clergy tend to "interact" together, as marital status has a relatively weak impact among women, but a far greater impact among male clergy. The percentages of married, never divorced, female clergy who exhibit high levels of theological orthodoxy across each of the two points in time tend to be only slightly higher than that found for female clergy who are single, separated, or have been divorced. In contrast, among male clergy, there are far more substantial differences in theological orthodoxy between those male clergy who are married and never divorced, and those male clergy who are single, separated, or have been divorced.

Table 3.8 **Theological Orthodoxy by Marital Status Controlling for Gender, 1989–2009**

High in orthodoxy	1989 (%)	2001 (%)	2009 (%)
Female			
Single, separated, divorced	x	18	24
Married, never divorced	x	24	30
Male			
Single, separated, divorced	x	38	43
Married, never divorced	x	65	71

How then does gender interact with religious tradition affiliation? Is it gender or religious tradition that shapes such high levels of theological orthodoxy? As shown in table 3.9, it is religious tradition that largely does so. Women within the ranks of evangelical Protestant clergy are highly orthodox theologically—with more than four-fifths being high in theological orthodoxy across each of the three points in time. Their mainline Protestant counterparts, however, exhibit far different patterns of adherence to theological orthodoxy. Despite a growing level of theological orthodoxy within their ranks, only 22 percent of mainline clergywomen could be classified as high in theological orthodoxy in 2009, while 86 percent of evangelical clergywomen could be so classified. Thus, gender has some impact within both the evangelical and mainline Protestant tradition, but it has a far greater impact within the mainline Protestant tradition. Consequently, it is religious tradition more so than gender that shapes the likelihood of clergy exhibiting high levels of theological orthodoxy.

At the same time, however, important differences still exist between male and female clergy, regardless of their level of theological orthodoxy. As shown earlier, male clergy are far more likely than female clergy to express high levels of theological orthodoxy, and one's level of theological orthodoxy shapes the responses of clergy to a host of other theological matters. Still, even among those clergy who exhibit high levels of theological orthodoxy, there are substantial differences in the theological positions expressed by male and female clergy. Table 3.10 examines the influence gender has on a number of theological positions adopted by clergy, controlling for their expressed level of orthodoxy. For the purposes of this analysis, the table simply presents the resultant relationships for six theological items, including the two items that exhibited the strongest correlations in table 3.6 as well as the two that exhibited the weakest correlations. In addition, the table also includes the two theological items related to feminist theology and liberation theology, as various commentators and scholars (e.g., Anderson 1979;

Table 3.9 **Theological Orthodoxy by Gender Controlling for Religious Tradition, 1989–2009**

High in orthodoxy	1989 (%)	2001 (%)	2009 (%)
Evangelical Protestant			
Female	96	83	86
Male	88	90	92
Mainline Protestant			
Female	8	14	22
Male	30	35	44

Table 3.10 **Theological Positions by Gender Controlling for Theological Orthodoxy (% Agreeing)**

| | Level of theological orthodoxy | | | | | |
| | Low | | Medium | | High | |
	Female	Male	Female	Male	Female	Male
Church should place less emphasis on individual sanctification						
1989	61	48	36	24	9	8
2001	57	45	20	14	7	4
2009	70	55	37	22	18	8
Social justice is at the heart of the gospel						
2001	83	77	85	69	43	48
2009	99	86	83	67	64	44
Liberation theology gets at the heart of the gospel						
2001	82	75	64	43	28	12
2009	92	78	82	49	33	12
Feminist theology provides valuable insights						
2001	91	82	64	44	25	10
2009	96	88	69	59	38	12
Evolution is the best explanation						
2001	66	70	30	25	2	4
2009	73	80	47	39	7	5
All clergy positions should be open to practicing homosexuals						
2001	82	75	64	43	28	12
2009	92	78	82	49	33	12

Nesbitt 1997, 165–73) have noted that many female clergy have been drawn to liberation theologies that seek "to inspire and empower marginalized groups to engage in sociopolitical conflict" in order to achieve a "more equitable distribution of resources" (Nesbitt 1997, 161).

As can be seen from table 3.10, substantial[10] differences emerge between male and female clergy even when they exhibit the same level of theological orthodoxy. Only in a few instances does one find an exception to this pattern. Otherwise, gender differences in theological perspective prevail within each of the three levels of theological orthodoxy. Thus, it is not only orthodoxy that shapes the stances clergy adopt on various other matters of theological thinking: gender also serves as a major contributor to differences in theological perspectives, with women clergy typically placing less emphasis than male clergy on individual sanctification and a greater emphasis on social justice, and with women clergy being more sympathetic than their male counterparts toward liberation and feminist theology as well as the opening of all clergy positions to practicing homosexuals.

Likewise, as noted earlier, evangelical clergy are also more likely than mainline Protestant clergy to exhibit high levels of theological orthodoxy. And just as was the case for gender, so too one finds that, even when controlling for theological orthodoxy, there still are substantial differences in the theological positions adopted by clergy across the two traditions (see table 3.11). Using the same items found in table 3.10, one finds that, within each level of orthodoxy expressed by clergy, mainline Protestant clergy are typically far more likely than their evangelical counterparts to adopt more "liberal" stances on theological matters.[11] For example, those mainline Protestant clergy who exhibited high levels of theological orthodoxy in 2009 were far more likely than their theologically orthodox evangelical brethren to agree that the social gospel is at the heart of the gospel and to express appreciation for liberation theology and feminist theology.

However, when one compares table 3.11 with table 3.10, one can discern that there are fewer instances in which major differences are evident between evangelical and mainline clergy than those previously found between clergymen and clergywomen. This is particularly the case among those clergy who exhibit high levels of theological orthodoxy, as highly orthodox evangelical and mainline Protestant clergy do not differ substantially in terms of whether less emphasis should be placed on individual sanctification, whether evolution is the best explanation, or whether all clergy positions should be open to practicing homosexuals. Nevertheless, in many instances, substantial differences still emerge between evangelical and mainline Protestant clergy, and these differences hold across time even when one controls for the level of theological orthodoxy that clergy express. Hence, it would appear that certain "cultural differences" prevail between the two different religious traditions of American Protestantism that lead those clergy expressing similar levels of theological orthodoxy to hold somewhat different perspectives on various other theological matters. Whether these "cultural differences" are a function of different content in theological education, their particular professional and friendship networks, or something else is unclear. But, regardless, simply knowing the level of theological orthodoxy expressed by clergy is not sufficient to explain the particular

Table 3.11 **Theological Positions by Religious Tradition Controlling for Theological Orthodoxy (% Agreeing)**

| | *Level of theological orthodoxy* | | | | | |
| | *Low* | | *Medium* | | *High* | |
	Evangelical	*Mainline*	*Evangelical*	*Mainline*	*Evangelical*	*Mainline*
Church should place less emphasis on individual sanctification						
1989	47	49	33	23	9	7
2001	39	49	11	14	4	5
2009	50	61	17	26	7	11
Social justice is at the heart of the gospel						
2001	58	80	49	51	42	46
2009	63	90	59	71	39	56
Liberation theology gets at the heart of the gospel						
2001	83	77	31	46	9	20
2009	100	82	41	57	9	21
Feminist theology provides valuable insights						
2001	92	85	30	47	6	22
2009	100	90	50	62	8	23
Evolution is the best explanation						
2001	83	69	14	26	3	5
2009	63	78	42	40	3	8
All clergy positions should be open to practicing homosexuals						
2001	50	70	3	19	2	3
2009	63	82	10	35	*	3

* less than 1 percent.

positions that they adopt on various other theological matters, as the religious tradition of these pastors frequently serves to shape such responses as well.[12]

The Changing Sources of Theological Diversity

Of course, the preceding analysis of the social location of theological orthodoxy has been based on a limited number of variables. Although helpful to sorting out the relative importance these variables have in shaping variation in theological orthodoxy, it does not take into account more than three variables simultaneously. Other factors beyond the variables included in the analysis might also shape differences in levels of theological orthodoxy. Hence, it is necessary to engage in some form of multivariate analysis. Therefore, in order to control for the relative effects of various social variables on theological orthodoxy, a Multiple Classification Analysis (MCA) was conducted. MCA accommodates the use of categorical variables in multivariate analysis and avoids the necessity of using dummy variables.[13] Thus, one distinct advantage of using MCA in multivariate analyses is that it can provide a single summary beta value for a categorical variable as a whole[14] with the magnitude of the beta value revealing the relative strength of the relationship between the independent and dependent variables once the effects of the remaining variables in the analysis have been taken into account. The beta values for each of the independent variables are presented in table 3.12 along with the resulting value of R-squared which represents the total amount of variance in the dependent variable (in this case, theological orthodoxy) explained by the independent variables contained in the analysis.

The top portion of table 3.12 examines the relative importance of five different variables available across each of the three points in time. The lower half of the table examines a larger number of variables that may shape the level of theological orthodoxy exhibited by clergy, but because several of these variables used in this fuller battery were not available in the 1989 survey, analysis in the lower portion of the table is limited to just the 2001 and 2009 surveys.

Five variables are examined in the upper portion of the table: gender, age, the extent of seminary education, the size of the congregation served, and the religious tradition of which the clergy is a part. Several notable patterns can be discerned by the changes evident in the beta coefficients over time. First, in 1989, religious tradition is by far the most important of the five variables examined in accounting for variation in the theological orthodoxy of the pastors surveyed (with a beta value of .52). Ranking next in importance is the extent of one's seminary education (beta = .14), followed by whether the clergyperson is a male or female (beta = .12).

Over time, however, the relative importance of religious tradition declines (as mainline Protestant clergy have become more orthodox), and the importance of gender increases in importance as an explanatory factor. In addition, it should be noted that, given these changes, the five variables are able to explain less variation in theological orthodoxy in 2009 (with the five-variable model explaining 30 percent of the variance in theological orthodoxy) than in 1989 (with the same five variables explaining 41 percent of the such variance).

Table 3.12 **Explaining Theological Orthodoxy**

	1989	2001	2009
Gender	.11	.19	.21
Age	.05	.09	.06
Seminary education	.15	.12	.11
Congregational size	.10	.05	.07
Religious tradition	.52	.44	.41
R^2	.41	.32	.30
Gender	x	.19	.21
Age	x	.09	.06
Seminary education	x	.10	.09
Congregational size	x	.03	.06
Religious tradition	x	.44	.42
Race	x	.02	.08
Marital status	x	.03	.04
Type of community	x	.07	.16
R^2	x	.33	.33

The lower portion of table 3.12 examines the relative effects of eight variables—the five same variables previously analyzed in the upper portion of the table, plus the race and marital status of the clergy as well as the type of community in which these clergy served their congregation. Despite the inclusion of these three additional variables, religious tradition continues to be, by far, the most important explanatory factor in accounting for differences in theological orthodoxy among Protestant clergy. The inclusion of the three additional variables does nothing to reduce the relative importance of the clergy's gender or religious tradition in either 2001 or 2009. By 2001, gender (beta = .19) emerges as a clear frontrunner in terms of relative importance behind religious tradition (beta = .44), and remains so again in 2009. In addition, by 2009, the type of community in which the congregation is located also moves ahead of seminary education and age in relative importance, as type of community (beta = −.16) ranks third in relative importance in 2009. Nevertheless, despite the inclusion of these three additional variables in the analysis, this eight-variable model hardly explains any more total variance than the five-variable model (as revealed by their respective values of R^2). Most likely the inability of the three additional variables to explain additional variance in orthodoxy is due to the importance of religious tradition in accounting for such variation: once you know the religious tradition of the pastor, you have the most basic factor shaping expressions of theological orthodoxy.

Nevertheless, even with the eight-variable model, it is clear that foundations undergirding theological orthodoxy are somewhat shifting over time. As theological orthodoxy has increased among mainline Protestant clergy, religious tradition is becoming less important as a factor accounting for variation in theological orthodoxy among clergy, and gender has become more important. Whether such trends continue in the future remains to be seen, but it is highly unlikely that substantial changes will occur in the short run in terms of these factors shaping theological orthodoxy.

Conclusions

At the core of clergy reflection and thinking are theological matters. This chapter initially examined change and continuity among clergy in terms of their theological perspectives related to historic understandings of the Christian faith (e.g., elements of the Apostle's Creed), eschatology, the nature of biblical authority, dispensationalism, and universalism. However, while there are a variety of theological perspectives that can be examined, substantial scholarly attention has been given to the matter of theological orthodoxy, in that orthodoxy relates to the historic understandings of the Christian faith.

This chapter, therefore, has given considerable attention to changing levels of theological orthodoxy evident among American Protestant clergy over the past two decades. It has assessed a particular measure of theological orthodoxy based upon the relative appropriateness and availability of questions employed in the denominational surveys across each of the three different cross-sections in time in which they were conducted. Given these particular constraints, a four-item index of theological orthodoxy was constructed. Various assessments were made related to the validity of the constructed measure, with the resulting patterns indicating that the constructed measure of theological orthodoxy constitutes a reliable and valid measure of theological orthodoxy.

Given this measure of theological orthodoxy, different segments of American Protestant clergy exhibit different levels of theological orthodoxy. Male clergy are far more likely than female clergy to exhibit high levels of theological orthodoxy, with the marital status of clergy interacting with gender to shape adherence to theological orthodoxy. Male clergy, regardless of their marital status, are more theological orthodox than female clergy exhibiting the same marital status. Marital status has rather minimal effects on the level of theological orthodoxy exhibited among female pastors, but it has much stronger effects on the level of theological orthodoxy expressed by male clergy.

The particular era in which clergy were theologically trained proved to be far more important than either age or years in ministry in shaping one's level of theological orthodoxy—suggesting it is more the particular theological training one receives than one's particular stage in life that shapes responses to the questions tapping theological orthodoxy, as younger pastors are not always, as a group, more theologically liberal than older pastors. In particular, it was those clergy who were ordained into the ministry during the decade of the 1960s who exhibited the lowest level of theological orthodoxy.

Likewise, both the kind of education obtained and the level of education attained serve to shape responses to questions tapping theological orthodoxy. Those clergy whose routes to ministry were outside the walls of seminary education were the most theological orthodox, while those clergy who were engaged in seminary education beyond their divinity degree were the least so. And, finally, and perhaps not surprisingly, one's religious tradition serves to shape responses to questions measuring theological orthodoxy, as evangelical Protestant clergy exhibited far higher levels of theological orthodoxy than did mainline Protestant clergy.

However, not only do different segments of American Protestant clergy exhibit different levels of theological orthodoxy, but the analysis has revealed that there has been a growth in theological orthodoxy among American Protestant clergy over the past twenty years. This growth has occurred largely within mainline Protestant denominations, as clergy in evangelical Protestant denominations, given their already relatively high levels of theological orthodoxy twenty years ago, have exhibited patterns of relative stability in relationship to theological orthodoxy. Moreover, this growth in theological orthodoxy has occurred within mainline Protestant denominations despite the growing feminization of the clergy within those denominations, as female clergy exhibit far lower levels of theological orthodoxy than male clergy. Hence, the increased growth in theological orthodoxy within mainline Protestant denominations is due, in large part, to the increased levels of theological orthodoxy exhibited by male clergy within those denominations.

Finally, when one engages in multivariate analysis to account for differences in theological orthodoxy, it is clear that the most important variable explaining differences in theological orthodoxy relates to the particular religious tradition with which the pastor is affiliated. Religious tradition served as the most important explanatory variable regardless of the year in which the survey was conducted. However, it is also clear that, with the growing levels of theological orthodoxy within mainline Protestant denominations over the past two decades, the relative importance of religious tradition as an explanatory variable has declined over time, while the relative importance of gender has increased in accounting for differences in theological orthodoxy among Protestant clergy. The extent to which one has had a seminary education, generally ranks third in relative importance, though with the increasing levels of theological orthodoxy exhibited by seminary graduates, the magnitude of the effects of seminary training has also declined in its ability to account for differences in theological orthodoxy among Protestant clergy.

4

The Social Theologies of American Protestant Clergy

Of course, theological perspectives are not limited to matters related to historic tenets of the Christian faith. There are theologies related salvation and redemption (soteriology), the nature of the church (ecclesiology), and "the final days" (eschatology). There are also theologies that are written from the perspectives of the underprivileged and downtrodden (e.g., liberation theology) and from distinctive group experiences (e.g., "black theology" or "feminist theology").

An important focus of this study, however, is on changes related to the nature and level of public engagement among Protestant clergy over the past two decades. But, just where one stands on historic interpretations of the Christian faith (orthodoxy) may not reveal much, if anything, about where such clergy stand on how the church, and Christians more generally, should relate to its cultural context, including its social and political life. Rather, these considerations pertain to the domain of what has been variously labeled as social, political, or public theology, which for ease of discussion will simply be labeled here as "social theology."

Social theologies can be quite varied in nature, as different social theologies have emerged over the course of the history of the Christian church. But, regardless of their differences, all social theologies make some assessment of the value and importance of the empirical world and contemporary life, as well as possible prospects for social reform in the light of theological understandings related to such matters as human nature, the nature and purpose of government, and the direction of human history. In addition, social theologies often identify and prioritize those aspects of human life that require attention (e.g., structural conditions, individual morality), and they can propose a vision for change and suggest general strategies for effecting change, some of which may involve political activity (Gray 2008, 222).

This chapter examines the perspectives of Protestant clergy related to social theology and how such perspectives may have changed over time. The chapter is organized into two sections. The first section examines three different topics related to the social theology of Protestant clergy: (1) possible changes in how American Protestant clergy view the church and cultural change, (2) possible changes in the manner by which Protestant clergy view the role of religion in contemporary American life, and (3) possible changes in how clergy understand the nature of politics and the process by which to accomplish political goals.

The second portion of the chapter creates a composite measure of social theology that taps differences along an individualism-communitarian continuum (which is simply noted, for stylistic purposes, as tapping individualism). This section of the chapter then analyzes the extent to which adherence to individualism as a social theology may have changed over time, and it seeks to discern the extent to which such social theologies contribute to an understanding of the political perspectives of Protestant clergy beyond that which is known through the particular level of theological orthodoxy they may express.

The Social Theology of Protestant Clergy over Time

The church does not exist in a social vacuum; rather, it is found within a myriad of different social settings and cultural contexts. Hence, throughout the centuries, a continuing issue for Christians and the church has been the matter of how each should relate to the particular cultural context within which they find themselves situated. In other words, just how should the church as a body of believers and Christians as individuals seek to embody the gospel socially within the broader culture in which they are located?

The Church and Cultural Change

Perhaps no theological concept relates more specifically to social theology than the concept of "The Kingdom of God." After all, the term "kingdom" has clear social and political overtones. However, theologians have differed over just what constitutes the nature of this kingdom and when it is to be fully realized. For the most part, however, the Christian church understands the Kingdom of God in terms of "now, but not yet." On the one hand, the kingdom currently exists in the world in that, in fulfillment of Old Testament promises, the kingdom has come and a new covenant has been established. On the other hand, the Kingdom of God is not yet fully realized; its final manifestation and consummation lie in the future. Nevertheless, though the Kingdom of God will never be fully realized until the Second Coming of Jesus Christ, the question remains as to just how, in the interim, that Kingdom of God may be more fully (though never completely) realized within one's particular cultural context?

How then is the church to work in order to more fully realize the Kingdom of God in the present? Is cultural change best accomplished through individual spiritual renewal and revival or through structural reforms? Of course, both may be important and serve to complement each other. But should one approach be more heavily emphasized than the other? And, does political engagement detract from the primary mission of the church or does it flow naturally from its efforts to more fully secure social justice?

Over the years, two different, potentially opposing, positions have emerged within the Christian faith. The first perspective, individualism, starts with the guiding assumption that the fundamental mission of the Church is that of "saving souls for Christ." Within this individualistic framework of understanding, the primary emphasis is placed on personal salvation, a status obtained through spiritual regeneration and personal moral reform (Jelen 1993, 43–44). Given the Fall and the inherent sinful nature of humankind, this perspective sees efforts to transform the social and political order through structural reform as never fully accomplishing their intended purposes. Rather, social reform is best accomplished through individual regeneration, with the function of the state being primarily one of restraining evil. However, despite the fact that governments may be able to restrain some of the social manifestations of evil, they cannot eradicate its root causes, as these causes reside outside its control—within human nature itself and the "demonic forces" that are loose in our fallen world. Not surprisingly, therefore, individualists are far from optimistic that structural changes in the institutions of society will necessarily achieve much of the greater common good that proponents typically anticipate from such changes.

Other clergy, however, subscribe to a more communitarian social theology. Communitarianism holds that "the primary mission of the Church is to transform the social order progressively to conform to Judeo-Christian ideals for a just society," believing that such changes will ultimately achieve "widespread social reconciliation across barriers of culture, race, religion, gender, and lifestyle" (Gray 2008, 222).

Adherents of a communitarian perspective contend that the state functions not only to hold back sin, but to enable members of society to accomplish more in their life together and fare better than would occur were individuals simply to live on their own. Even though the world is fallen, communitarians argue that things are not as hopeless as individualistic perspectives would suggest. Rather, God sent Jesus Christ to redeem all things (individuals, social life, and natural life, including the environment and animal life)—and to reconcile everything to Himself and each other.

It is true that the state is, in part, an instrument to restrain evil. But the duties of the state also include securing and administering justice. And securing justice involves more than just punishing wrongdoers and addressing the proximate causes of injustice. Neither is it the task of government to compel everything that is right or moral nor to punish everything that is wrong or immoral.[1] Rather, it is to seek justice.

This pursuit of justice is not equivalent to pursuing morality per se (Monsma 1984, 47). While governments may seek to deter certain behavior (e.g., killing one's neighbor) through laws threatening violators with imprisonment or even death, or seek to encourage other kinds of behavior through various incentives, governments are far less able to shape human thoughts and desires. Governments might be able to stop an individual from acting out the hatred within his or her heart, but they are far less able to eradicate the hatred itself.[2] Because morality is a matter of the heart, no one can be forced to be moral. Rather, governments can deal only with outward actions, and "justice is a matter of overt acts, and that is what government can and should control" (Monsma 1984, 47).

Historically, communitarian perspectives were clearly evident in the early efforts of liberal Protestant theologians to address various intellectual and socio-logical challenges confronting the church and American society in the late nine-teenth century. Intellectually, these challenges related to the teachings of Charles Darwin and the contentions advanced by German higher criticism of the Bible; sociologically, these challenges related to the growing social changes and mala-dies associated with growing industrialization, urbanization, and the increasing religious pluralism.

As a result of the intellectual challenges, there arose within Protestantism a new "liberal" theology which sought to reconcile the Word of God with mod-ern, scientific contentions. This effort at accommodation was achieved in vari-ous ways. First, rather than emphasizing the particular revelation of God in Jesus Christ, these liberals emphasized the general revelation of God in nature and history—thereby downplaying the supernatural and distinctive aspects of the Christian tradition. Rather than adopting a divine stance toward the biblical texts, these liberals adopted a more naturalistic stance toward scripture by view-ing it as wisdom literature containing eternal truths. And, rather than empha-sizing God's transcendent nature, this liberal element taught immanence, the presence of God in the midst of the world.

In response to the sociological challenges, a strong "social gospel" element emerged within American Protestantism that rejected revivalism as the basis of social reform. Rather than stressing the need for spiritual conversion, advocates of this social gospel stressed education, ethics, and social change. For advocates of this social gospel, the human condition was not so much the result of human depravity as the result of human deprivation. Reflecting the generally optimistic mood of the times, advocates of the social gospel tended to adopt a more optimistic view of human nature in that sin was something that either education could mitigate or social reform prevent (Hoge 1976, 21).

Although communitarianism has ties to this earlier theological liberalism and the social gospel perspective, its contemporary manifestations are linked far more closely to various intellectual and social developments that occurred after World War II. Generally speaking, contemporary communitarianism emerged during the 1960s as a "more inclusive and sociologically informed successor to the social gospel" that had begun to develop largely in response to "the social upheavals produced by the social rights movement and the Vietnam Wars" and from the emergence of what are known as liberation and the "death of God" theologies (Gray 2008, 223). Subsequently, contemporary communitarians have continued to emphasize peace and justice. But, today, these emphases are largely seen in terms of their focus on issues related to minority rights (including those of homosexuals and women), poverty and homelessness, environmental degradation, and greater international cooperation.

Of course, subscription to these more individualist and communitarian perspectives need not be mutually exclusive. After all, the biblical instruction "to feed my sheep" has both spiritual and physical overtones to it. Thus, there likely are many clergy who believe that church must both cultivate a personal faith in Jesus Christ among those both within and outside the church[3] and work communally for social justice as well.[4] Nevertheless, these two positions (i.e., cultivating faith and working for justice) can stand somewhat "in tension" with each other, as to focus time and energy on the one may come at the expense of focusing time and energy on the other.[5]

Clergy Views on Church and Cultural Change

To what extent, then, are these different individual and communitarian perspectives expressed by Protestant clergy today? And, how, if at all, have they changed over time? These questions are addressed, in part, by the data presented in table 4.1, which displays responses provided to the relevant items across each of the three surveys. Several of the items presented in the table directly assess whether clergy view the church's primary mission largely in terms of evangelism, individual salvation, and helping individuals live a more Christian and moral life. Once again, however, the initial core items used in 1989 are augmented by additional questions posed in the 2001 and 2009 surveys, with these additional items endeavoring to assess whether clergy view social justice as being "at the heart of the gospel" and whether they think the theological perspectives of

Table 4.1 **The Views of Clergy Related to the Church and Cultural Change, 1989–2009**

Agree	*1989 (%)*	*2001 (%)*	*2009 (%)*
Individualism-communitarianism			
If enough people brought to Christ	42	48	47
Church should place less emphasis on sanctification	21	15	20
Social justice is at the heart of the gospel	x	52	57
Many ideas of liberation theology get at heart	x	32	34
Feminist theology provides values insights	x	33	36
Economic life			
Free enterprise only system compatible	23	16	20
Christianity requires a substantial redistribution of wealth	x	x	35
The mission of the church			
Politics detracts from the church's primary mission	x	x	16

liberation theology and feminist theology provide valuable insights about the gospel message.

Clearly, as is evident from table 4.1, a sizable proportion of Protestant clergy subscribe to notions that reflect an individualistic social theology. For example, more than two-fifths of the clergy in 1989 agreed that "if enough people were brought to Christ, social ills would take care of themselves," with the percentage of clergy agreeing with the statement having grown slightly over the past two decades.

Moreover, an overwhelming majority of clergy (roughly four-fifths) reject the notion that "the church should place less emphasis on individual sanctification and more on transforming the social order." In other words, even though most clergy may believe that "social justice is at the heart of the gospel" (discussed later), such clergy are still rather reluctant to shift the emphasis of their ministry to a greater emphasis on "transforming the social order." Nor have their opinions really shifted over time: only about one-fifth of Protestant clergy agreed that the church should place a greater emphasis on transforming the social order in 1989 and a similar proportion continued to do so two decades later.

In addition to these two items, there are several items in table 4.1 that are more directly linked to a communitarian social theology: (1) that "social justice is at the heart of the gospel," (2) that "many ideas of liberation theology get at the heart of the gospel,"[6] and (3) that "feminist theology provides valuable insights about being a Christian."[7] These three items were not included in the 1989 clergy surveys but were asked in the 2001 and 2009 surveys.

Even though a substantial number of clergy subscribe to positions that may be viewed as reflecting an individualistic social theology, a substantial number of clergy also report agreement with positions reflecting a more communitarian social theology. For example, a majority of clergy in both 2001 and 2009 agreed that "social justice is at the heart of the gospel." A bare majority (52 percent) did so in 2001, but eight years later approximately three-fifths did so (57 percent). Far fewer clergy, however, expressed agreement that either liberation theology reflected the heart of the gospel or that feminist theology provided valuable theological insights, as only about one-third of Protestant clergy reported agreement with each statement in both 2001 and 2009.

Several other items asked in our clergy surveys addressed matters of economics, though they also relate to matters of "church and cultural change." One question was asked across all three surveys, while the other was asked only in 2009. The former assessed clergy positions related to free enterprise and whether or not they agreed that "free enterprise is the only (economic) system compatible with Christianity," while the latter asked clergy whether they agreed that "Christianity requires a substantial redistribution of wealth." Less than one-quarter of the Protestant clergy surveyed in 1989 agreed that free enterprise was the only economic system compatible with Christianity, and this proportion declined to less than one-fifth of Protestant clergy by 2009. In fact, a far greater percentage of clergy indicated in 2009 that "Christianity requires a substantial redistribution of wealth" than stood in agreement that the free enterprise was the only economic system compatible with Christianity (35 percent versus 20 percent, respectively).

Finally, when asked in 2009 whether involvement in politics detracted from the church's primary mission,[8] relatively few clergy responded that it did (16 percent). In contrast, nearly two-thirds (63 percent) indicated that there was a need for the church to be involved in public affairs in order to remain faithful to its mission (data not shown).[9] Thus, overall, there are nearly four times as many clergy who believe the church, in order to remain faithful to its mission, needs to remain involved in political affairs than believe that such involvement detracts from the church's primary mission.

Clergy Views on the Role of Religion in Public Life

Of course, views related to the role of the church in effecting cultural change reveal little, if anything, about how clergy view the role of religion in American public life. Although commentators frequently treat public life as being synonymous with political life (Cochran 1990, 51), the former entails far more than the latter. Political life is less encompassing than public life, as political life is aimed at "influencing the selection of governmental personnel and/or the actions they take," while civic life reflects "publicly spirited collective action," non-remunerative in nature, that is not guided, at least directly, "by some desire to shape public policy" (Campbell 2004, 7).

The role of religion in public life can have both potentially beneficial and potentially detrimental effects.[10] These different potential consequences were actually recognized by the framers of the American constitution, as the two-pronged nature of the religion clause of the First Amendment reflects this recognition.[11] The establishment clause of the First Amendment prohibits any establishment of religion that would privilege one church over another, as doing so may not only lead to political problems but also to possible religious conflict and, at times, even violence.[12] Furthermore, the state is not in a position to determine religious truth, and the establishment of any religion privileges that particular religious expression as being the "correct" expression of religious faith. Finally, the framers of the constitution feared the concentration of political power, given that any concentration of power potentially threatened individual liberty. In the words of Lord Acton "power tends to corrupt, and absolute power tends to corrupt absolutely." Consequently, by not creating some established church, the framers sought to prevent certain detrimental effects that potentially could be associated with a concentration of institutional power within an established church—a power that, in turn, could threaten the religious freedom of others within the life of the polity.

On the other hand, the framers were charting new territories politically by engaging in a bold experiment to create a republic in which the people both governed and enjoyed personal liberty. However, to succeed, such a democratic republic required that its citizens exhibit moral constraint and behavior, as only a moral people, who exhibited honesty, honored their commitments, and willingly obeyed the law (and were not compelled to do so through the coercive power of the state) could insure that such a democratic republic would stand. But, from whence did such personal characteristics and moral propensities arise? For the framers, it arose primarily from the religious faith of the people. The particular religion or denominational expression of that religion was less crucial than the fact that religion needed to be thoroughly rooted in the lives of the people of a democratic republic. Hence, the free exercise clause of the First Amendment was advanced not only to foster the flourishing of religion but also to enable it to be more firmly rooted in the lives of the citizens of the land (as the effects of religion in one's life would be stronger when each person was free to embrace the religion of one's choice).[13]

Most contemporary debates about the role of religion in American public life involve considerations related to (1) the relative benefit of religion's role in public life, (2) the role of religion in the founding and maintenance of our system of government, (3) the extent to which, as well as the manner by which, religious institutions, organizations, and individuals should be involved in political life, and (4) the growth of religious pluralism within American society. Our surveys addressed matters related to the first three topics, but did not directly inquire about views related to religious pluralism. Moreover, almost all inquiries related to the role of religion in American public life were asked in 2001 and 2009, with certain questions being asked only in 2001 and others only in 2009. Hence, although we can say a fair amount about clergy perspectives related to religion in American public life, our ability to assess change in these perspectives is rather limited (see table 4.2, with responses organized around the three topics addressed).

The first two items in the table relate to the overall contribution of religion to American civic and political life. Almost all Protestant clergy hold that religion has beneficial effects in terms of American civic life. When asked in 2001

Table 4.2 **The Views of Clergy Related to the Role of Religion in Public Life, 1989–2009**

Agree	1989 (%)	2001 (%)	2009 (%)
The relative benefits of religion in public life			
Has positive effect on American social and civic life	x	87	x
Has positive effect on American political life	x	65	x
Role in founding and maintaining our government			
United States founded as a Christian nation	x	54	54
Religious freedom in the United States threatened	x	63	62
Civil liberties threatened by those imposing religion x	x	35	x
Religion threatens to divide our country	x	x	28

(continued)

Table 4.2 (Continued)

Agree	1989 (%)	2001 (%)	2009 (%)
Religious involvement in political life			
Churches should not try to lobby	x	27	22
My denomination needs to be more involved	x	43	42
Some clergy have gone too far	x	37	49
Religious people should withdraw from politics	x	7	8
Organized religious groups should stay out of politics	x	x	10

whether religion has positive effects on American social and civic life, nearly all of the Protestant clergy surveyed (87 percent) reported it did, though fewer clergy believed these positive effects necessarily extend to American political life. Still, most Protestant clergy (65 percent) generally perceive religion to have positive benefits for American political life as well.

The second group of items examined relate to the role of religion in the founding and maintenance of democratic life in the American context. Here we see initially that a majority of the Protestant clergy, though only a bare majority (54 percent), hold that "the United States was founded as a Christian nation," with responses to this item not changing in the aggregate between 2001 and 2009.[14]

Many Protestant clergy also perceive clear threats to religious freedom within contemporary American society and political life. Just what serves as the basis of these threats (e.g., whether it is the growth of groups opposed to religion, the increasing religious diversity within American society, or recent court decisions) is unclear. But regardless of the particular source, more than three-fifths of the Protestant clergy surveyed in 2001 (63 percent) held that religious freedom in the United States was threatened, with a similar percentage (62 percent) continuing to express that same viewpoint in 2009.[15]

However, other clergy perceive the reverse—that religion is threatening American political life. More than one-third of the clergy surveyed in 2001 (35 percent) expressed the belief that "civil liberties are threatened by those imposing religion," though when phrased somewhat differently eight years later, only about one-quarter of the clergy (28 percent) thought that religion threatened to divide the country politically.

When evaluating the role of religion in American political life, clergy generally differentiate between and among the involvement of religious leaders, religious groups, religious institutions, and religious people in their evaluations. Clergy are far more supportive of certain, rather than other, forms of religious involvement in politics. For example, despite the fact that substantial numbers of pastors reported that religion was threatening the civil liberties of Americans or threatening to divide the country, far fewer clergy surveyed in those years held that "religious people should withdraw from politics" (7 percent in 2001 and again in 2009). Thus, not all clergy who perceive religion as threatening politically necessarily want religious people to withdraw from political life. In fact, among those clergy in 2009 who held that religion was threatening to divide the country politically, only 14 percent contended that religious people should stay out of politics (data not shown). Thus, despite the fact that many Protestant clergy see certain dangers related to the involvement of religious people in political life, very few clergy are inclined to contend that religious people should stay out of politics. Moreover, this support for religious engagement in politics does not stop there, as clergy are also supportive of organized religious groups being engaged in the political arena (with only 10 percent of the clergy in 2009 agreeing with the statement that "organized religious groups of all kinds should stay out of politics").

However, a somewhat greater percentage of clergy held that churches should not try to lobby (27 percent and 22 percent, in 2001 and 2009, respectively). Pastors therefore are seemingly more concerned about churches as institutions becoming involved in the political process than religious people doing so either individually or through organized religious groups. Yet, clergy are not overly concerned about churches as institutions becoming politically involved either, as an even greater proportion (slightly more than two-fifths) contended that "my denomination needs to be more involved politically" than held that churches should not try to lobby. However, clergy seemingly do not perceive their denomination's lobby efforts as political involvement. This can be inferred from the fact that, even among those clergy who indicated that they wished their denomination to be less involved politically, only two out of five (40 percent) agreed with the statement that churches should not try to lobby (data not shown).

Clergy Views on the Nature of Political Life

How then do clergy view the nature of politics and the manner by which one should engage in the political process? Questions related to these matters were only included in our 2001 and 2009 surveys, and far fewer items were asked related to this topic than the previous ones addressed. As a result, our examination of this matter is far more restricted in its scope of analysis. Nevertheless, it is still possible to provide some important insights into how clergy view the nature of politics and how such perspectives may have shifted over time.

Overall, as revealed in table 4.3, almost all clergy in 2009 (slightly more than three-quarters) believed that there are clear and absolute standards for what is right and wrong. But, this belief in the presence of absolute moral standards does not necessarily translate into holding absolute positions related to political issues. Thus, when asked whether there is only one Christian position on most matters of public policy, only about one-fifth of the clergy so agreed in both 2001 and 2009. And, even among those clergy who agreed that there were absolute standards, only 26 percent expressed agreement that there was only one Christian position on particular policy issues (data not shown).

Nevertheless, though clergy acknowledge that more than one Christian position can be adopted on most issues, they seemingly are reluctant to compromise on issues when principles are at stake. When asked whether it is better in politics "to compromise and achieve something than to stick to one's principles even at the risk of achieving little," only about one-third of the clergy expressed agreement, with the percentage expressing agreement declining between 2001 and 2009 (from 35 to 30 percent). And, among those clergy who hold that there are clear and absolute moral standards, there is general reluctance to compromise politically, as a majority (55 percent in 2009) within their ranks express the preference to stick to one's principles rather than compromise politically (data not shown).

Now some scholars, particularly Gilligan (1982), have argued that women possess different moral tendencies than men, contending that men think more in terms of rules, while women are more inclined to think of morality through the lens of personal relationships, making women thereby more hesitant than men to judge others.[16] And, it is Gilligan's theory that provides a basis for the expectation that "clergywomen offer a different approach to ministry" than that offered by clergymen (Robbins 1998, 76).

Table 4.3 **The Views of Clergy Related to the Nature of Political Life, 1989–2009**

Agree	1989 (%)	2001 (%)	2009 (%)
On most issues, only one Christian position	x	20	21
Better to compromise	x	35	30
There are clear and absolute standards	x	x	77

Questions related to the morality of particular human actions are matters that clergy, at least occasionally if not more frequently, address in relationship with their parishioners. Do clergywomen then respond differently than clergymen in terms of their level of agreement with the statement that "there are clear and absolute standards for what is right and wrong?" And, the answer is clearly "yes." As shown in table 4.4, twice as many clergymen (82 percent) expressed agreement with the statement as clergywomen (41 percent).

What then contributes to these particular gender differences in relative or absolute standards of morality? To a certain extent, it may be a function of age differences, with younger adults being more likely to embrace notions of moral relativism than older adults. However, it may be a function of different life experiences, as the proportion of clergywomen who have experienced divorce is greater than that for clergymen, and the experience of divorce can, at times, bring into question whether absolute standards hold with regard to the lifetime commitment many frequently vow at the time of their marriage. Finally, perhaps such differences are a function of differences in levels of theological orthodoxy exhibited by female and male clergy, as those who express higher levels of orthodoxy are more likely to express agreement with the idea that there are absolute standards of morality (data not shown).

Table 4.4 therefore also examines the possible contributing factors for these different perceptions of moral standards expressed by clergywomen and clergymen. First, there are certainly some age differences among female pastors related to these standards of morality, as older female clergy are far more likely than younger female clergy to hold that there are absolute moral standards. However, among male clergy, no such age differences are evident.

Likewise, having gone through a divorce also contributes to some of the gender differences evident in these differences in absolute standards of morality, as those who have experienced divorce or separation in their marriages are less likely to acknowledge absolute standards of right and wrong. But, once again, these differences in lifetime experiences appear to have a far greater effect among clergywomen than among their male counterparts, and female clergy, regardless of their marital status, are still far more reluctant than male clergy to contend that such standards exist.

Rather, it is primarily (though not solely) one's level of theological orthodoxy that shapes such views of morality. Gender differences in notions of morality prevail regardless of one's level of theological orthodoxy, but such differences are considerably smaller among those who exhibit high levels of theological orthodoxy. Moreover, even though female clergy high in theological orthodoxy are somewhat less likely than their male counterparts to subscribe to absolute standards of morality, nearly all (84 percent) female clergy do so.

Table 4.4 **Differences among Clergy on Views Related to Absolute Moral Standards, 2009**

Agreeing Absolute Moral Standards	Female (%)	Male (%)
All	41	82
Age		
Under 35	32	80
35 to 55	38	84
56+	49	81
Marital status		
Single	*	66
Have been or currently are separated or divorced	32	79
Married, never divorced	42	83
Theological orthodoxy		
Low	14	33
Medium	39	66
High	84	95

* Too few cases for meaningful results ($N = 7$).

Hence, to the extent that clergywomen offer a different approach to ministry than that offered by clergymen, it is likely to be more a function of differences related to theological orthodoxy than something based on gender differences in childhood socialization. Still, not all gender differences can be explained by one's level of theological orthodoxy, as such differences continued to prevail even when controlling for those theological differences. Consequently, though differences in levels of theological orthodoxy help to account for some of these important gender differences related to standards of morality, it does not fully account for all such differences.

Exploring Changing Social Theologies over Time

As noted earlier in this chapter, many of these perspectives related to social theology have been incorporated into a broader, more encompassing, framework of understanding that embodies various ideas related to individualism and communitarianism. Hence, in exploring the social theology of clergy, it would be helpful to have some summary measure tapping this framework of understanding in order to ascertain just where many clergy stand in relationship to it and the extent to which clergy may have shifted in their views on this matter over time—just as was done with regard to a measure of theological orthodoxy.

Of all the items analyzed in the first three tables of this chapter, only three items were asked of clergy from all seven denominations across all three points in time.[17] These three items were: (1) whether social ills would largely disappear if enough people were brought to Christ, (2) whether the church should place less emphasis on sanctification, and (3) whether free enterprise is the only economic system compatible with Christianity.

Fortunately, however, these three items appear to assess the same underlying concept—namely, one's social theology in relationship to where one stands along an individualism-communitarian orientation. Certainly, the third item is not directly theological in nature. Nevertheless, given that the free enterprise system values individual initiative and individual responsibility, the item can be viewed as assessing an individualism-communalism orientation in relationship to economic life. In other words, one might anticipate that individualists in terms of social theology would be individualists within the narrower domain of economic life as well. Nevertheless, the question remains whether these three items empirically constitute a relatively valid measure tapping individualistic[18] social theology. The three items were therefore factor analyzed, with the results revealing that the three items loaded on a single factor for each of the three survey years.[19] As a result, the three items were first combined into a simple index[20] and then examined in terms of the measure's relationship to various criterion measures. The analysis revealed that the constructed measure was a valid one, as the measure's relationship to the criterion variables reflected the theoretical expectations that would be associated with a measure of individualism.[21]

What percentages of Protestant clergy, then, generally adhere to this particular expression of social theology? And, what patterns of change, if any, have occurred over the past several decades in the distributions of such orientations?

These questions are addressed in table 4.5. Given the seven denominations surveyed, a far higher percentage of Protestant clergy scored low on the individualism measure than scored high, as roughly two-fifths of Protestant clergy exhibited low levels of individualism as a social theology while roughly one-quarter exhibited high levels. Moreover, over the past two decades, little change has occurred in the distribution of individualism among Protestant clergy. There was, however, some shift in the distribution between 1989 and 2001 (with a decline in the percentage scoring low on the measure and an increase in the percentage falling in the medium category), but the distribution on the measure found in 2009 largely mirrors the pattern found in 1989.

Table 4.5 **The Distribution of the Social Theology of Individualism over Time**

Individualism	1989 (%)	2001 (%)	2009 (%)
Low	43	36	40
Medium	33	39	34
High	24	25	26
Total	100	101	100

Individualism as a social theology is related to, but distinct from, theological orthodoxy. The correlation coefficient between the two variables was .47 in 1989 (data not shown), with the relationship between the two variables remaining virtually the same over time. Hardly any clergy who scored low in theological orthodoxy, scored high in individualism (with 2 percent doing so in 1989, 3 percent in 2001, and 1 percent in 2009), but, among those who scored high in theological orthodoxy, more than one-third (38 percent in 1989, 39 percent in 2001, and 37 percent in 2009) did so (data not shown).

Does the social theology of individualism, then, add anything in an explanatory capacity for understanding the political perspectives of clergy beyond what might be explained by differences in the levels of theological orthodoxy exhibited by clergy? In other words, is it also important to consider the social theology of clergy, as well as their theological orthodoxy, when seeking to understand the nature of clergy engagement in American political life?

Of course, it is not fully possible here to examine how social theology and theological orthodoxy interact in relationship to all matters related to political life. But, certainly two important variables that serve to shape how Americans act and think politically are their ideological orientations and their partisan identifications. Hence, in table 4.6, the ideological orientations and partisan identifications of clergy are examined in relationship to their adherence to individualism as a social theology, while controlling for their level of theological orthodoxy.

Clearly, as shown in table 4.6, both theological orthodoxy and the social theology of individuals contribute to clergy differences in ideological orientations and partisan identifications. First of all, for each level of theological orthodoxy examined, regardless of the particular year of the survey, the percentage of clergy who self-classify themselves as political liberals as well as Democrats in their partisan identifications declines as one moves from lower to higher levels of adherence to individualism as a social theology. For example, among those clergy in 1989 who were low in theological orthodoxy, the percentage of clergy who classify themselves as political liberals declines monotonically from 82 percent to 39 percent

Table 4.6 **The Effects of Individualism on Political Orientations Controlling for Theological Orthodoxy, 1989–2009**

Level of theological orthodoxy	*Level of individualism (%)*		
	Low	*Medium*	*High*
1989			
Low			
Liberal	82	57	39
Democratic Partisan Id.	84	62	50
Medium			
% Liberal	54	29	15
% Democratic Partisan Id.	63	38	22
High			
% Liberal	21	5	2
% Democratic Partisan Id.	23	12	11
2001			
Low			
% Liberal	89	71	47
% Democratic Partisan Id.	90	67	56
Medium			
% Liberal	52	28	14
% Democratic Partisan Id.	62	42	24
High			
% Liberal	15	4	2
% Democratic Partisan Id.	20	9	8
2009			
Low			
% Liberal	92	72	17
% Democratic Partisan Id.	93	86	17
Medium			
% Liberal	65	34	7
% Democratic Partisan Id.	71	44	20
High			
% Liberal	17	6	2
% Democratic Partisan Id.	24	11	5

as one moves from the lowest to the highest levels of adherence to individualism as a social theology.

Likewise, within each category of individualism, across all three clergy surveys, the percentage of clergy who label themselves as political liberals and as Democrats, monotonically declines as one moves from lower to higher levels of theological orthodoxy. Thus, both theological orthodoxy and the social theology of individualism serve to shape the ideological orientations and partisan identifications of Protestant clergy. This was true in 1989 and continued to be true in 2009.

Conclusions

This chapter has examined the social theologies of American Protestant clergy. Initially, the chapter focused on the perceptions of clergy related to the church and cultural change, the role of religion in American public life, and their views related to political life, and how such perceptions may have changed over time. Many of the initial items examined, however, were contained in surveys conducted at only one point in time, diminishing the ability to assess change over time using this larger battery of survey items.

Still, when examining their perspectives related to social theology as expressed by Protestant clergy, one is struck by the rather nuanced view of public life held by clergy. First, of all, most clergy agree that the church needs to be involved in public affairs in order for it to remain faithful to its mission, with relatively few clergy contending that such involvement in politics detracts from the church's primary mission. Fewer clergy, though a majority nonetheless, hold that social justice stands at the center of the gospel message. But even with this emphasis on social justice, only a little more than one-third hold that the Christian faith, regardless of context, requires a substantial redistribution of wealth. Even fewer, and declining numbers, contend that free enterprise is the only economic system compatible with the Christian faith. A rather stable, and large, proportion of clergy (roughly four-fifths) reject the notion that the church should place greater emphasis on transforming the social order and less emphasis on individual sanctification. And, finally, a growing number of Protestant clergy, now nearly a majority, believe that simply bringing enough people to faith in Christ would, by itself, solve contemporary social problems.

Protestant clergy also perceive religion to have positive benefits for American public life. However, they are far more willing to ascribe beneficial effects to religion within American civic, than political, life. Still nearly two-thirds of the clergy hold that religion has positive effects even with regard to American political life. Nevertheless, many Protestant clergy (roughly three-fifths) currently perceive clear threats to religious freedom within American society and political life, though about a third perceive the reverse—namely, that religion is threatening American political life.

Still, when evaluating the role of religion in American political life, clergy do not "paint the political landscape with one color," as clergy differentiate between and among the political involvement of religious institutions, religious groups, religious leaders, and religious people in their evaluations. Relatively few (less than one-tenth) clergy held that religious people should withdraw from politics, and only one-tenth thought that organized religious groups should stay out of politics. Nor were clergy overly concerned about churches as institutions being involved politically, as only about one-quarter held that churches should not engage in lobbying efforts. In fact, a slightly high percentage of clergy held that their denomination should be more involved politically than contended that churches should not try to lobby.

Finally, although clergy overwhelmingly believe that there are clear and absolute moral standards concerning matters of right and wrong, they are nevertheless hesitant to contend that there is necessarily only one Christian position related to most political issues. But, despite this recognition, many clergy are reluctant to compromise on issues when principles are at stake—even at the risk of achieving little politically.

Because many of the social theology items examined were asked in surveys conducted at only one or two points in time, the ability to assess change over time using a larger battery of survey items was rather limited. Consequently, the issue of how the social theologies of American Protestant clergy may have changed over time was addressed by creating a composite measure that captured individualist-communitarian orientations. Although this social theology is related to one's level of theological orthodoxy, they are analytically distinct and their distributions have differed over time. Whereas theological orthodoxy has increased among American Protestant clergy over the past two decades, relatively little change has occurred in the distribution of individualism as a social theology over the same span of time.

More importantly, however, both theological orthodoxy and the particular social theology expressed by clergy (as related to their views along an individualism-communitarianism continuum) have served to shape the political views and orientations of clergy across time. The ideological orientations and partisan identifications of clergy are clearly related to the level of theological orthodoxy as well as the level of individualism expressed by clergy, regardless of the year in which the survey was conducted. Hence, knowing the social theology of clergy, as well as their level of theological orthodoxy, contributes to our understanding of the political inclinations and dispositions of American Protestant clergy.

5

The Positions of Clergy
on Contemporary Issues
of Public Life

Religious faith does more than simply address questions related to the meaning of life or the role of the church in society. It also addresses practical issues of daily life—what is right and wrong behavior, what should be valued, and how people should relate to one another. And, given that political life in democratic societies involves people choosing to arrange their lives together, including what policies, goals, and values they wish to have promoted, it is inevitable that religious faith and politics will intersect—as religious beliefs will likely inform political beliefs, and religious values are likely to shape political values. Of course, the extent to which one's religious faith will shape one's stance on a particular issue is likely to vary—both in terms of the specific issues under consideration and in terms of the particular positions that equally religious individuals choose to adopt on an issue. This is because one's religious perspective may be more relevant to certain issues than to other such issues and because the particular religious values and beliefs held by similarly religious individuals may vary, moving them to different directions politically.

This chapter focuses on the change and continuity in the political attitudes held by American Protestant clergy over the past two decades. Specifically, the chapter examines the issue positions of clergy across a number of issues within three broad areas of public policy: social welfare policy, social issues, and foreign policy. It analyzes the attitudes of clergy toward such issues as abortion, homosexuality, affirmative action, health care, and the war in Iraq, and reveals the waxing and waning of stands on particular issues, and whether, given the growth in theological orthodoxy among Protestant clergy, there is a growing convergence in their political issue positions as well.

Second, the chapter examines the ideological self-classifications of clergy. It analyzes how those orientations have changed over time, the changing relationship between the ideological orientations of clergy and their stands on political issues, and what factors help to account for the ideological self-classifications they adopt.

And, finally, the chapter examines the extent to which clergy report holding issue positions that align with, or depart from, those generally held by members of the congregations they serve. Nearly a half century ago, Hadden (1969) analyzed differences in the political stances between clergy and laity within a number of major Protestant denominations, and he found the gap to be rather substantial. Given these differences in perspectives, Hadden anticipated what he labeled "a gathering storm" within American Protestant churches. And, since that time, there have been major conflicts with many denominations and various denominational splits. Of course, there is no direct way of knowing the extent to which these clergy-laity gaps in political perspectives may have led to these particular denominational disputes. But, in the abstract at least, such differences serve as potential bases for discontent within both congregations and denominations. As a result, this chapter will also examine reported differences between the political positions of clergy and those of the congregations they serve and the extent to which such differences may have narrowed or increased over the past two decades.

The Issue Positions of American Protestant Clergy over Time

In the immediate aftermath of World War II, Americans largely struggled with the same set of political issues that had dominated American politics prior to the war, namely, social welfare issues and the policies of the New Deal that endeavored to address the economic consequences of the Great Depression. Though the specific policies varied in terms of what each sought to address, the political dispute over these policies typically centered on one major question: "What was the proper role of government, notably the national government, in providing for the general welfare of the citizenry?" (Carmines and Layman 1997, 91) Generally speaking, Democrats were far more committed than Republicans to the idea that the federal government should take an active role in managing the economy and providing for the general welfare, whereas Republicans generally stood in far greater opposition than Democrats to the federal government doing so.

However, it did not take long before a new set of highly salient issues began to emerge in American politics—issues that many have lumped together under the label "social issues." Beginning in the late 1940s and culminating in the 1960s, controversies related to equal rights for blacks emerged, with issues related to race becoming a powerful and divisive issue in American politics. But, soon thereafter, this conflict became extended to other social and cultural issues, such as the treatment of gays, the role of women, and "the right" to an abortion.

Finally, the 1960s saw the (re)emergence of another set of issues—namely, just what should be America's role in the new international order. The anti-Vietnam War movement that emerged in the 1960s brought into question the extent to which, and the conditions under which, American military intervention should be utilized as a means to advance American foreign policy goals. As a result, the relative unity of Americans on matters of foreign policy which had previously existed, first in the aftermath of Pearl Harbor and then during the initial years of the Cold War era with its fight against communism, gave way to much more divided positions on American foreign policy as new foreign policy issues emerged related to different regions of the world.

Thus, over the course of the past half century, issues related to American politics can largely be divided into three issue domains: social welfare issues, social and cultural issues, and foreign policy issues. And, consequently, these three policy domains will be used to organize the examination of the issue positions of clergy.

Social Welfare Issues

Most, if not all, of the major religious faiths hold that their adherents should demonstrate charity toward the poor. Yet, issues related to the generation and distribution of wealth constitute some of the most fundamental and enduring political issues in any society (Wilson 2009, 191). And, given the presence of competing visions of justice related to the distribution of wealth, the positions of clergy as to how the poor may best be served and poverty best addressed may well vary both among clergy and across political issues.

The three clergy surveys have sought, in part, to assess clergy positions on political issues of the day, though relatively few questions related to the role of the federal government in addressing social welfare needs have been asked across the three clergy surveys. The questions that were asked are presented in table 5.1.

Despite the limitations related to the number of questions asked, several important conclusions about clergy positions on such matters can be drawn from the data analyzed. First, a substantial proportion of American Protestant clergy are generally sympathetic toward greater federal involvement in addressing a variety of perceived problems related to the socioeconomic welfare of the American people. For example, nearly three-fifths of Protestant clergy in 2009

Table 5.1 **The Positions of Clergy on Social Welfare Issues over Time**

Agree	1989 (%)	2001 (%)	2009 (%)
The federal government should do more to solve social problems such an unemployment, poverty	72	55	58
More environmental protection is needed, even if it raises taxes or costs jobs*	75	43	43
We need government-sponsored national health insurance so that everyone can get adequate medical care	x	46	42
Current welfare reform laws are too harsh and hurt children	x	24	18

* This question was not asked of CRC and RCA clergy in 1989, so the comparisons across time are based on only clergy from the five denominations surveyed in 1989.

believed that the federal government should do more to solve social problems such as those related to unemployment and poverty.

However, American Protestant clergy do not indiscriminately call upon the federal government to solve problems related to the broader social welfare of the American people. For example, even though nearly three-fifths of clergy in 2009 expressed the desire that the federal government do more to address social problems, only about two-fifths of American Protestant clergy that same year agreed that the national government should provide universal health insurance so that "everyone (could) get adequate medical care." In fact, nearly one-third (31 percent) of those clergy who agreed that the federal government should do more to address social problems nevertheless stood in opposition to the national government providing universal health insurance (data not shown).

Finally, some rather substantial changes in the political attitudes of American Protestant clergy occurred during the twelve years between 1989 and 2001, while relatively little change transpired in the aggregate in the eight years following. Of course, our assessment here is limited by the fact that there are only two questions that assess the level of change occurring between 1989 and 2001, but both items reveal the same pattern—namely, substantial change over that relatively short interval of time. For example, nearly three-quarters of the Protestant clergy surveyed in 1989 (72 percent) agreed that "the federal government should do more to solve social problems, such as unemployment and poverty," but only a little more than half (55 percent) did so twelve years later. An even greater change occurred with regard to the issue of environmental protection—as support for greater environmental protection among the clergy dropped from 75 percent in 1989 to 42 percent in 2001. Clearly, dramatic changes occurred in clergy attitudes on these issues across the twelve-year interval of time. On the other hand, all four items reveal little substantial change in clergy attitudes on such matters between 2001 and 2009.

Social Issues

The salience of noneconomic domestic issues has risen dramatically since the 1960s (Scammon and Wattenberg 1970). This broad category of issues has been variously labeled—sometimes identified as social issues and at other times as cultural issues. But, regardless of the label used, these issues typically involve differences of opinion related to the extent to which government should regulate certain kinds of social behavior. In fact, some analysts (e.g., Hunter 1991, 1994) have contended that these "lifestyle issues" have supplanted economic divisions as the primary basis of political conflict in the United States.

Far more survey questions have been asked of clergy related to "social issues" than social welfare concerns. Although these questions have addressed a variety of social issues, they can be roughly categorized in terms of (1) public policies related to particular groups in society, (2) public policies related to public and private education, and (3) public policies related to crime, particularly the ownership and use of handguns and the practice of capital punishment.

First, with regard to policies related to particular groups in society, clergy distinguish among different groups in society in terms of their relative need for protection through the enactment of public policies—as well as in terms of the changing circumstances such groups encounter over time. Only one-third of American Protestant clergy in 2009 agreed that "affirmative action" was necessary to help blacks and other minorities "achieve an equal place in America" or that "more legislation" was needed "to protect women's rights." On the other hand, clergy were much more willing to express agreement that "homosexuals should have all the same rights and privileges as others Americans," as a majority (53 percent) expressed agreement with the statement in 2009, with approximately the same percentage (55 percent) contending that a constitutional amendment was needed to prohibit most abortions.

Second, Protestant pastors are rather united in their policy positions on some matters related to public schools and education policy and rather divided on other issues. In terms of the former, American Protestant clergy tend to stand together regarding the content and focus of sex education programs in public schools. In fact, the highest level of agreement found in table 5.2 relates to sex education classes in public schools, as 63 percent of the clergy surveyed in

Table 5.2 **The Positions of Clergy on Social Issues over Time**

Agree	1989 (%)	2001 (%)	2009 (%)
Blacks and other minorities may need special governmental help to achieve an equal place in America	63	42	33
We need a constitutional amendment to prohibit all abortions unless necessary to save a mother's life or in case of rape or incest	55	55	55
Homosexuals should have all the same rights and privileges as other Americans	52	55	53
I oppose capital punishment	32	37	33
We need a constitutional amendment to permit prayer as a regular exercise in public schools*	39	35	35
We still need more legislation to protect women's rights*	41	31	34
Public policy should discourage ownership and use of handguns	x	46	32
Education policy should focus on improving public schools rather than encouraging alternatives such as religious schools	x	42	41
The government should provide vouchers to parents to help pay for their children to attend private or religious schools	x	43	46
Sex education programs included in the curricular of public high schools should be abstinence-based	x	77	63

*These questions were not asked of CRC and RCA clergy in 1989, so the comparisons across time are based only on clergy from the five denominations surveyed in 1989.

2009 expressed agreement that, when sex education programs are included in the curriculum of public schools, such programs should be abstinence-based. At the same time, however, Protestant clergy appear divided on whether educational policy should focus more on improving public schools or on enabling larger number of students to attend private or religious schools. Relatively identical, and stable, percentages of clergy agreed, on the one hand, that the focus of educational policy should be "on improving public schools rather than encouraging alternatives such as religious schools," and, on the other, that "the government should provide vouchers to parents to help pay for their children to attend private or religious schools."

With regard to issues related to crime, only about one-third of the clergy in 2009 stood opposed to capital punishment, with approximately the same proportion stating the belief that "public policy should discourage the ownership and use of handguns." Not surprisingly, those opposed to capital punishment were far more likely than those who favored to support a policy that discourages the ownership and use of handguns (73 percent versus 30 percent, respectively in 2009) (data not shown).

Finally, in relation to change over time, a variety of different patterns are evident in table 5.2. Some of these patterns are similar to those found in relationship to clergy views on social welfare issues; other patterns are distinctively different. First, in terms of matters related to what might be labeled "affirmative action," American Protestant clergy exhibited a major decline in their level of agreement that "blacks and other minorities may need special government help to achieve an equal place in America." Nearly two-thirds of clergy agreed with the statement in 1989, but only about two-fifths did so in 2001. Moreover, in contrast to the patterns found in table 5.1, support for "affirmative action" declined further between 2001 and 2009, as only one-third of Protestant clergy expressed agreement with the statement in 2009.

On the other hand, for the two statements related to constitutional amendments, a different pattern emerges. In each of the three surveys, a greater percentage of clergy expressed a need for a constitutional amendment related to restricting abortions than for an amendment permitting prayer in public schools. Nevertheless, for both issues, the percentage of clergy who expressed a desire for the enactment of such amendments was basically the same in 2009 as in 1989. Similar patterns of relative stability are found in clergy positions related to homosexual rights and capital punishment, with patterns of relative stability also evident between 2001 and 2009 about whether educational policy should focus on improving public schools and whether vouchers should be provided for children to attend private or religious schools.

Thus, in terms of change over time, we see that over the past twenty years, there has been a monotonic, and substantial, decline in clergy support for governmental action to help minorities achieve "an equal place" in American society. Likewise, we also see a decline between 1989 and 2001 in the extent to which Protestant clergy favored additional legislation to protect women's rights and a decline between 2001 and 2009 in the percentage of clergy who favor sex education programs in public schools being abstinence-based and that public policy should discourage the ownership and use of handguns. Other than these particular shifts, the stances adopted by American Protestant clergy over the past twenty years related to most social issues have remained generally stable over time.

Foreign Policy

In the aftermath of World War II, survey research typically revealed that most Americans were relatively uninterested in, and generally ill-informed about, international events, and that their foreign policy attitudes generally lacked both coherence and stability (Guth 2009, 243).[1] Although some scholars (e.g., Hero 1973) contended that religion shaped foreign policy attitudes, most others scholars largely ignored religion as a factor shaping such attitudes. In fact, Kohut and Stokes (2006, 94) have argued that "with the exception of policy toward Israel, religion has little bearing on how (Americans) think about international affairs."

Nevertheless, despite the apparent lack of coherence and stability in foreign policy attitudes, various analysts have contended that attitudes on foreign policy are organized in particular ways. For example, Wittkopf (1990) has argued that Americans tend to organize their thinking on foreign policy issues in terms of two different dimensions: militant internationalism and cooperative internationalism. And, more recently, Page (2006) has contended that Americans have "purposive beliefs systems" about foreign policy, entailing general orientations related to the degree to which America should engage in isolationism, multilateral cooperation, and unilateral interventionism.

Furthermore, it appears that a growing number of American religious leaders are playing an increasingly vocal role in addressing matters of foreign policy. Not only have some mainline Protestant clergy and councils chosen to engage in "a long tradition of 'prophetic witness' on international issues" (Guth 2009, 249), typically in a cooperative internationalist or at times pacifist vein (Kurtz and Fulton 2002; Tipton 2007), but they have now been joined by some evangelical Protestant leaders and clergy, who seemingly advance a more "militaristic" perspective on foreign policy (March 2007; Barker at al. 2008).

Though our surveys over the past twenty years have included a number of foreign policy questions asked over different points in time, only two foreign policy questions were asked of clergy across all three surveys: (1) whether the United States should spend more on the military and defense, and (2) whether Israel needed to make greater concessions to the Palestinians in order for a lasting peace to be achieved in the Middle East.

As can be seen from table 5.3, most American Protestant clergy in the months immediately following the 1988 presidential election[2] (and prior to the collapse of the Soviet Union) expressed stands on American foreign

Table 5.3 **The Positions of Clergy on Foreign Policy Issues over Time**

Agree	1989 (%)	2001 (%)	2009 (%)
The United States should spend more on the military and defense	17	36	26
A lasting peace in the Middle East will require Israel to make greater concessions to the Palestinians	62	43	45
China should not be given most favored nation trading status until it stops religious persecution	x	64	69
One of our top priorities should be a nuclear arms treaty with the USSR[a]	73	x	x
We should not support dictators, even those friendly to the United States[b]	53	x	x
The United States should impose economic sanctions on South Africa to pressure that country to change its racial policies	52	x	x
The United States should increase military aid to the "contras" in Nicaragua[a]	24	x	x
The United States should push development and deployment of the Strategic Defense Initiative (SDI)[c]	28	x	x
Despite the fall of communism, the United States should still be very cautious in dealing with Russia	x	54	x
The current war in Iraq is fully justified	x	x	32
Given the threat of terrorism, the United States must be able to take preemptive military action against other countries	x	x	45
The United States should coordinate its foreign policy more with the United Nations	x	x	33

[a]Does not include the CRC or RCA clergy, as they were not asked the question.

[b]Does not include the AOG and UMC clergy, as they were not asked the question.

[c]SBC, PC USA, and DOC clergy only, as clergy from other denominations were not asked the question.

policy that typically reflected positions that, while hardly isolationist in perspective, stood more in line with promoting multilateral cooperation than unilateral interventionism. Relatively few clergy (less than one-fifth) responded in agreement that "the United States should spend more on the military and defense," while clergy were overwhelmingly supportive of trying to negotiate a nuclear arms treaty with the Soviet Union, with 73 percent agreeing that it should be "one of our top priorities." Nor were clergy overwhelmingly sympathetic toward Israel in their efforts to achieve peace in the Middle East, as nearly two-thirds of clergy (66 percent) held that Israel would need to make greater concessions to the Palestinians if a lasting peace were to be achieved. Furthermore, a bare majority of clergy also favored the United States joining others in imposing economic sanctions on South Africa as a means of pressuring its government to abolish apartheid, while a similar percentage also responded that American foreign policy should not support dictators, even if such dictators were friendly to the United States. Finally, relatively few clergy (about one-quarter) advocated increasing military aid to the "contras" in Nicaragua or pushing the development and deployment of the Strategic Defense Initiative.

However, twelve years later, American Protestant clergy perceived the world somewhat differently. Whether, given the collapse of the Soviet Union, it was because of the dominant role the United States was now playing in the international order or because of the emergence of new threats to American foreign policy interests, the percentage of clergy who agreed that the United States should spend more on the military and defense more than doubled (moving from 17 percent to 36 percent) between 1989 and 2001—even before the events of 9/11. Moreover, over the course of the same period of time, Protestant clergy had also become much more sympathetic to the plight of Israel, with the percentage of clergy contending that Israel needed to make greater concessions to the Palestinians declining by a third (from 66 percent in 1989 to 43 percent in 2001). Nor were clergy overly sympathetic toward Russia or China. Despite the fall of the Berlin Wall and the collapse of the Soviet Union a decade earlier, American Protestant clergy remained rather suspicious of Russia, as a majority of clergy in 2001 (54 percent) agreed that "the United States should still be very cautious in dealing with Russia." And, an even greater percentage of clergy in 2001 (64 percent) indicated that they did not want China to be granted most favored-nation trading status until such time as religious persecution had ended within its borders.

Nevertheless, American Protestant clergy appeared, some years after the Iraqi invasion by American troops, to be rather divided in their foreign policy perspectives. Certainly, the clergy were relatively unified in terms of believing that the war in Iraq was not fully justified, as only about one-third of clergy in 2009 willingly expressed the opinion that, despite the controversies surrounding the incursion, the war in Iraq was fully justified. Likewise, following the economic collapse in the fall of 2008, clergy were generally opposed to greater military and defense spending, as only one-quarter advocated such increased spending. But, beyond these general points of agreement, clergy tended to part ways in what direction American foreign policy should pursue. On the one hand, about one-third of the clergy surveyed held that the United States should try to coordinate in foreign policy objectives more with the United Nations, whereas almost half advocated a much more unilateral approach contending that the United States "must be able to take preemptive military action against other countries." Similarly, about half of Protestant clergy continued to hold that Israel needed to make greater concessions to the Palestinians in order for a lasting peace to occur in the Middle East.

Interrelationship across Issues

Though the first three tables provide a snapshot of some of the important changes that have occurred in the issue positions of clergy, the data fail to reveal two other important changes that have transpired with regard to the political attitudes of clergy. First, with the passage of time, issue stands have become more highly intercorrelated. The issue positions adopted by clergy are far more interrelated today than in 1989. Thus, compared to two decades ago, one can now more easily predict where clergy stand on various issues of the day based simply on the knowledge of where they may stand on some other political issue.

This growth in the intercorrelations between the issue positions adopted by clergy can be seen in table 5.4. Since the analysis focuses on the changes in the strength of the relationships, and not on the particular direction of such relationships, all coefficients are presented as if the relationships are positive in nature.

The correlations presented for 1989 represent the starting point of the analysis, with twenty-eight different correlations presented between and among the eight items analyzed. When examining the correlations between the same two items in 2001 with those found in 1989, one finds that most of the relationships exhibit higher correlations in 2001. This is true for twenty of the twenty-eight correlations presented for 2001. Moreover, the remaining eight relationships that exhibit a weaker correlation over this span in time involve just three particular variables—namely, gay rights, abortion, and capital punishment—with only some of the relationships involving these three variables exhibiting a decline in the strength of their relationships with other issues.

However, when one compares the correlation coefficients found in 2009 with those found in 2001, the uniformity of stronger relationships is clearly present. Of the twenty-eight correlations presented in 2009, only one exhibits a weaker

Table 5.4 **Correlation Coefficients between Clergy Issues Positions over Time**

	Social problems	Affirmative Action	Abortion amendment	Gay rights	Capital punishment	Defense spending	Middle East	Ideology
1989								
Social problems	x	.46	.34	.35	.40	.32	.37	.47
Affirmative Action	x	x	.35	.38	.42	.27	.32	.47
Abortion amendment	x	x	x	.57	.55	.44	.40	.67
Gay rights	x	x	x	x	.54	.38	.42	.62
Capital punishment	x	x	x	x	x	.43	.41	.61
Defense spending	x	x	x	x	x	x	.43	.47
Middle East	x	x	x	x	x	x	x	.45
2001								
Social problems	x	.47	.37	.31	.42	.42	.34	.53
Affirmative Action	x	x	.39	.40	.45	.43	.43	.54
Abortion amendment	x	x	x	.53	.52	.47	.38	.68
Gay rights	x	x	x	x	.49	.43	.41	.57
Capital punishment	x	x	x	x	x	.55	.48	.65
Defense spending	x	x	x	x	x	x	.47	.61
Middle East	x	x	x	x	x	x	x	.52

(continued)

Table 5.4 (Continued)

	Social problems	Affirmative Action	Abortion amendment	Gay rights	Capital punishment	Defense spending	Middle East	Ideology
2009								
Social problems	x	.55	.42	.34	.48	.42	.46	.56
Affirmative Action	x	x	.48	.50	.56	.52	.55	.65
Abortion amendment	x	x	x	.59	.56	.50	.46	.70
Gay rights	x	x	x	x	.55	.50	.50	.66
Capital punishment	x	x	x	x	x	.52	.55	.69
Defense spending	x	x	x	x	x	x	.55	.62
Middle East	x	x	x	x	x	x	x	.60

relationship in 2009 than in 2001 (the relationship between one's position on capital punishment with one's position on defense spending). The same is true when one compares the coefficients in 2009 with those in 1989; of the twenty-eight different interrelationships examined, only one relationship exhibits a weaker relationship in 2009 than in 1989 (the relationship between one's position on gay rights and whether the government should solve social problems). Thus, the issue positions adopted by clergy are far more highly correlated today than they were two decades ago.

The second important change that has occurred in the issue positions adopted by clergy is that they are now much more closely aligned with their ideological self-classifications than was true previously. The last column in table 5.4 presents the correlation between the reported ideological self-classifications of clergy and the positions they adopt on the seven different issues examined over time. As seen in the table, the comparable correlation coefficients increase in magnitude as one moves from 1989 to 2001 (the only exception is the relationship between gay rights and ideological orientation) and then increases again between 2001 and 2009. Thus, all correlation coefficients between one's ideological self-classification and the particular positions one adopts on each of the seven political issues examined in the table are greater in 2009 than in 1989—and typically substantially greater as well.

This growing alignment of one's issue positions with one's ideological self-classification has occurred among Protestant clergy despite the occasional appearance of aggregate stability in some of the political attitudes of Protestant clergy across time. Nevertheless, even with such periodic appearances of stability, clergy were still sorting their positions on issues in a manner that made their positions on such issues more highly interrelated and more in line with their ideological self-classifications.

The Ideological Orientations of American Protestant Clergy

There are various reasons to anticipate that clergy would approach politics in a relatively systematic fashion and that their political attitudes would be more interrelated than those of the average voter.[3] First of all, those with more advanced levels of education, as is true with most clergy, typically exhibit more ideological thinking than those with lower levels of education. Second, ministers frequently think that, because of their particular place in society, they have "a special obligation to stay politically informed" (Quinley 1974, 64). This attentiveness, coupled with their typical possession of strong analytical skills, enable clergy not only to understand and comprehend the meaning of various ideological labels but to process and frame that political information in particular ways as well.

Scholars have frequently differentiated between what might be labeled *symbolic* ideology and *operational* ideology (e.g., Free and Cantril 1967; Stimson 2004). Whereas symbolic ideology denotes the particular placement one chooses in terms of classifying oneself along a "liberal-moderate-conservative" continuum, operational ideology designates one's average "left-to-right" position across a number of issues. Social scientists have long known that the ideological self-classifications citizens report do not always coincide with the types of positions they adopt on particular issues (e.g., Campbell et al. 1960; Converse 1964). But, scholars have also long recognized that ideological thinking, or "high attitudinal constraint," is much more prevalent among political activists and institutional elites than within the mass public (e.g., McClosky, Hoffman, and O'Hara 1960). Not surprisingly, therefore, there has been a high correlation between the ideological self-classifications that clergy report and their positions on particular issues (Guth et al. 1997)—and, as shown earlier, these correlations have only grown stronger over the past two decades.

Nevertheless, despite this greater issue constraint among clergy than among the mass public, it is less clear whether this greater constraint is along a single, liberal-to-conservative, dimension (that incorporates positions on social welfare, social issues, and foreign policy issues), or whether such constraint operates in terms of two or more dimensions that are somewhat unrelated to each other (in which, for example, the positions that one adopts on social welfare issues may be largely unrelated to the positions that one adopts on social issues or foreign policy issues). The bulk of the evidence suggests that, for the mass public, two dimensions of ideology are present; these two dimensions are not totally independent from each other, but, among the politically engaged, they may be very highly aligned (Federico 2012, 82).

The degree to which clergy structure their stands on individual issues has important consequences. If ministerial opinion is largely one-dimensional, political differences among clergy become highly polarized, whereas if pastoral opinions exhibit two or more cross-cutting dimensions, alliances may shift from issue to issue, as clergy who are opponents on one issue may find themselves allied on others.

Analysis of the 1989 clergy data, however, suggested that a powerful, single ideological dimension characterized the political worldview of the Protestant clergy, with data from surveys of Southern Baptist clergy conducted over time revealing that clergy attitudes on social justice and moral issues were becoming increasingly assimilated into a single dimension (Guth et al. 1997, 106–7).

And, given that the analysis here has further confirmed this growing correlation between issue positions and ideological orientation, regardless of whether they entail social welfare issues, social issues, or foreign policy issues (see table 5.4), the subsequent analysis of this chapter will focus on the reported ideological orientations of clergy rather than on the specific issue positions clergy may have adopted.

The Changing Ideological Orientations of Protestant Clergy

Ministers were asked across all three surveys to place themselves on a seven-point ideological scale, ranging from "extremely liberal" at one end to "extremely conservative" on the other. Table 5.5 reports the results of the distribution of these ideological self-classifications over time, in which the two most conservative and liberal options are collapsed together for ease of presentation.

Although several distinct patterns are evident from the data presented in table 5.5,[4] the most important pattern evident is the growing ideological polarization of Protestant clergy. The percentage of clergy classifying themselves as either extremely or very liberal rose from 9 percent in 1989 to 17 percent in 2009, while the percentage labeling themselves as either extremely or very conservative rose from 22 percent in 1989 to 44 percent in 2009. In other words, the political "middle" has been collapsing among Protestant clergy, as the percentage of clergy falling within the three middle categories has dropped from 69 percent in 1989 to 42 percent in 2009.

Moreover, this pattern of increasing polarization among Protestant clergy is not a function of changes occurring within just one or two particular denominations; it is present among clergy within each of the denominations surveyed.[5]

Table 5.5 **The Ideological Orientations of Protestant Clergy over Time**

Ideological self-classification	1989 (%)	2001 (%)	2009 (%)
Extremely/very liberal	9	11	17
Somewhat liberal	21	16	13
Moderate	21	16	14
Somewhat conservative	27	25	15
Extremely/very conservative	22	31	42
Total	100	99	101

Only among clergy in the Christian Reformed Church (CRC), the Reformed Church in America (RCA), and the United Methodist Church (UMC) does one find in 2009 a majority of clergy classifying themselves ideologically outside the "extremely or very liberal" or the "extremely or very conservative" designations—and even within these latter two denominations only 50 or 51 percent chose to do so (data not shown).[6]

Thus, despite the appearance of only modest change in the issue positions of clergy between 2001 and 2009, the ideological orientations of clergy clearly continued to shift over that same period of time. And, though a clear ideological divide that was present among clergy two decades ago (Guth et al. 1997), that divide has only since then increased substantially.

The Changing Bases of Clergy Ideological Orientations

What factors, then, are associated with this growing ideological polarization that is evident among Protestant clergy? This question is addressed in table 5.6, which presents a Multiple Classification Analysis based on seven variables tapping the demographic, contextual, and theological characteristics of the clergy, and which are available across each of the three clergy surveys.

Several particular patterns are noteworthy from the data presented. First, it is clear that the primary factors shaping the ideological orientations of Protestant clergy have remained relatively stable across time. Of the seven variables examined, theological orthodoxy ranks first and the social theology of individualism ranks second in terms of the magnitude of their beta coefficients across each of the three-time periods examined. However, while religious tradition ranked third in relative importance as an explanatory variable in 1989, gender replaced religious tradition as the third most important explanatory variable in 2001 and continued to retain that ranking in 2009. In other words, once the theological orthodoxy and social theology of individualism of clergy are taken into account, the gender of the clergyperson is now more important than religious tradition in shaping the ideological orientations of clergy.

Second, though the rankings of relative importance remains stable, the social theology of individualism has grown in general importance relative to theological orthodoxy in accounting for the particular ideological orientations of clergy. While the magnitude of the beta coefficient for theological orthodoxy has remained relatively stable across time, the magnitude of the beta coefficient for individualism as a social theology has monotonically increased from one time period to the next. In 1989, the magnitude of the beta coefficient for theological orthodoxy was nearly twice that of individualism as a social theology

Table 5.6 **Explaining Ideological Orientations of Protestant Clergy over Time**

	1989	*2001*	*2009*
Gender	.08	.15	.03
Age	.05	.07	.06
Seminary education	.02	.06	.00
Congregational size	.05	.06	.10
Religious tradition	.22	.34	.29
Theological orthodoxy	.34	.23	.36
Individualism	.17	.14	.22
R^2	.39	.37	.48

(.45 versus .23, respectively), but, by 2009, that ratio had declined to approximately 1.5 to 1 (.49 versus .30, respectively).

Third, despite the growing polarization of ideological orientations among Protestant clergy over the past twenty years, the relative capacity of our seven-variable model to explain variation in the ideological orientations of clergy has remained relatively constant over that period of time. The values of R^2 for the seven-variable model were .62 in 1989, .60 in 2001, and .64 in 2009, indicating that the seven-variables not only account for a substantial amount of the variation in clerical ideological orientations, but that their ability to do so has remained relatively constant over the past two decades.

The Issue Gap between Clergy and Parishioners

How then do the ideological views of pastors compare with those of their congregants? Any ideological differences are potentially significant for a number of reasons. First, in terms of more immediate considerations, ideological proximity would likely affect a clergyperson's ability to mobilize the congregation for political action. But, over the course of a longer period of time, there may well be other effects. When differences are evident, clergy might be able to modify the political attitudes of their congregants in either a more conservative or a more liberal direction. On the other hand, it is also possible that parishioners could have a moderating influence on their pastors, though this is more likely in terms of clergy behavior than in terms of clergy attitudes (Hadden 1969, 86–89). In addition, parishioners who disagree with the social and political ideologies expressed by their minister might well become less active in church life, reduce their financial support, or even leave and find another congregation to attend (Hadden 1969, 30–33; Guth et al. 1997, 110).

There are a number of reasons to anticipate that there will be differences between clergy and laity in their political attitudes and ideological orientations. Certainly, the classic studies of clergy conducted in the 1960s and 1970s revealed that Protestant ministers often expressed far more liberal attitudes than did their parishioners (Hadden 1969; Quinley 1974). In fact, it was this clergy-laity gap that prompted Hadden to warn of the "gathering storm in the churches."[7] But, much has changed religiously since then. The general vitality of denominations as organizational structures has waned, memberships in many historic denominations have diminished, and denominational loyalty on the part of many parishioners has weakened (Stetzer 2010; Weems 2010; Merritt 2013). Mainline Protestant clergy have become more theologically orthodox (see ch. 3), and during the 1980s and 1990s many evangelical leaders became more engaged politically as they sought to mobilize evangelical voters to get to the polls (Wuthnow 1983; Wilcox 1992). It is far from clear, therefore, whether the clergy-laity gaps evident several decades ago continue to be present in the same fashion today. Might not the growing theological orthodoxy among mainline Protestant clergy have, in turn, served to diminish the clergy-laity gap within mainline Protestant churches? And might not the increased political activism of evangelical clergy have also contributed to a greater clergy-laity gap within evangelical churches today than previously?

Clergy Perceptions of the Clergy-Congregational Gap

Table 5.7 examines clergy perceptions of the differences between their own views and those of the congregation they served first on economic issues and then on social issues, with the data drawn from the 2001 and 2009 surveys. When asked in 2001 how they would compare their own views on economic matters to those of their congregants, a majority of Protestant clergy (54 percent) reported that they were largely the same. To the extent that they differed, a larger percentage of clergy reported their views on economic matters tended to be more conservative (29 percent) than more liberal (18 percent) than those of their congregants. A similar pattern is evident with regard to positions on social issues. A majority of Protestant clery (51 percent) reported that they were largely the same as their parishioners. To the extent that they differed, a larger percentage reported that their views tended to be more conservative (29 percent) than more liberal (19 percent) than those of their congregants.

However, by 2009, fewer clergy stated that they held similar positions to those of their congregants, as less that a majority of clergy reported holding positions

Table 5.7 **Clergy Perceptions of "Clergy-Congregant Gap" on Economic and Social Issues**

	2001 (%)	*2009 (%)*
How would you compare your own views of **economic issues** with most members of your church?		
Mine much more conservative	3	3
Mine somewhat more conservative	26	16
About the same	54	49
Mine somewhat more liberal	14	26
Mine much more liberal	4	7
Total	101	101
How would you compare your own views of **social issues** with most members of your church?		
Mine much more conservative	3	2
Mine somewhat more conservative	26	17
About the same	51	43
Mine somewhat more liberal	14	29
Mine much more liberal	5	9
Total	99	100

similar to their parishioners on both economic and social issues. Moreover, in 2009, clergy were far more likely to report that, to the extent their perspectives differed, their positions now tended to be more liberal, than more conservative, than those of their congregants—regardless of whether such issues were economic or social in nature.

Still, even given these data, we do not know the extent to which the political views of clergy and their congregants are relatively similar in nature. What is needed is to see how the responses given to these two survey items relate to each other.

The data presented in table 5.8 do this by combining the responses given by clergy to the two separate survey items. This allows us to get a clearer picture of the extent to which clergy and congregants may differ in their economic and social political perspectives. Given three ideological positions (i.e., more conservative, the same, and more liberal)[8] and two issue dimensions (i.e., social and economic), nine different combinations are possible. And, the responses given by clergy fall within each of the nine possible combinations, though some possible combinations are relatively rare (e.g., clergy being more conservative on economic issues and more liberal on social issues, or vice versa).

The most common response in both 2001 and 2009 was for the pastor to report that they held similar positions to those of their congregants, with approximately one-third to two-fifths of the ministers surveyed so responding. However, if pastors did not report holding similar political views to their parishioners, then the next most typical responses were for clergy to report that they are either more conservative or more liberal than their congregants on both issue dimensions, as another one-third to approximately two-fifths of clergy responded accordingly.

Nevertheless, despite these commonalities across time, major changes were clearly evident across the first decade of the twentieth century in the ways in

Table 5.8 **Clergy Perceptions of "Clergy-Congregant Gap" on Current Issues**

Views of clergy in comparison with most members of congregation	2001 (%)	2009 (%)
Clergy more conservative on both social and economic issues	**20**	**11**
Clergy more conservative on social, same on economic, issues	8	7
Clergy same on social, and more conservative on economic, issues	7	6
Clergy more conservative on social, more liberal on economic, issues	1	1
Clergy and congregation about same on social and economic issues	**41**	**33**
Clergy more liberal on social, more conservative on economic, issues	1	1
Clergy same on social, and more liberal on economic, issues	3	4
Clergy more liberal on social, same on economic, issues	5	9
Clergy more liberal on both social and economic issues	**14**	**28**
Total	100	100

which clergy perceived their political proximity to their congregants. First of all, there was a major decline in the percentage of pastors reporting that they held similar political positions to their congregants. Second, there was a clear reversal in whether clergy saw themselves as more being more liberal or more conservative than their congregants. In contrast to 2001, clergy in 2009 were far more likely to perceive themselves as being more politically liberal than more politically conservative in relationship to their parishioners, with nearly as a many pastors now claiming to be more liberal than their congregants on both social and economic issues than as holding similar views to them (28 percent versus 33 percent, respectively).

What contributed to these changes in perceptions? Was it a function of clergy changing congregations, clergy themselves changing, or those in the pews becoming more conservative? Or, was it more a change in the political environment itself, with a change in the salience of particular political issues or perhaps a change in the political candidates[9] running for public office that served to shift these perceptions? Our data do not allow us to address these questions directly, but it is possible to try to assess what kind of change has occurred among those pastors who reported relatively similar political positions as their congregants in 2001 and then in 2009.

Table 5.9 presents the percentage of clergy across time who reported similar political stands as their parishioners—but now broken down according to various social, religious, and political characteristics of the clergy. The data clearly reveal that, regardless of the year analyzed, certain types of pastors are far more likely to report that they share the same political views as their congregation. For example, male clergy are far more likely than female clergy to do so, as do those with no seminary training in comparison to those who are seminary graduates. Similarly, those serving smaller (100 members of less), rather than relatively large, congregations are more likely to do so, as do those ministering in small town and rural areas than in more urban areas (data not shown). Religiously, evangelical Protestant clergy are more likely than mainline Protestant clergy to report that they hold similar political positions to their congregants, as do the highly theologically orthodox in comparison to those lower in orthodoxy. And, clergy who report that they are conservative politically are far more likely to report congruence than those who are more liberal politically.

However, when one seeks to discern the types of pastors who were the most likely to exhibit this decline in perceived political congruence over the course of the first decade of the twenty-first century, one is struck by the rather consistent level of decline evident across each and every category examined, as this decline transpired regardless of the particular social, religious, or political characteristics of the clergy. For example, as shown in table 5.9, the percentage of female pastors reporting similar political perspectives as their parishioners dropped

Table 5.9 **The Characteristics of Clergy Holding Positions on Issues Similar to Their Congregants**

	2001 (%)	*2009 (%)*
All	41	33
Gender		
Female	25	18
Male	42	35
Seminary education		
None, Bible college	61	51
Some seminary	51	39
Seminary graduate	36	29
Religious tradition		
Evangelical Protestant	53	42
Mainline Protestant	32	27
Theological orthodoxy		
Low	16	10
Medium	35	23
High	52	43
Political ideology		
Very Liberal	14	8
Liberal	16	12
Moderate	33	24
Conservative	50	43
Very Conservative	59	50

7 percentage points between 2001 and 2009 (25 percent to 18 percent), but it also dropped 7 percentage points among male clergy (from 42 percent to 35 percent). Likewise, the magnitude of the drop in percentage was relatively similar for evangelical as for mainline Protestant clergy, for the highly orthodox theologically as for the lowly orthodox theologically, and for pastors who were political conservatives as for ministers who were political liberals.

Given these similarities in the level of decline across the various categories examined, perhaps a clearer picture might emerge if one examines where growth has primarily occurred in the percentage of clergy who report that they are more politically liberal than their congregants. To do so, we combine together all clergy responses that fall within the last three rows of table 5.8 and then seek to ascertain among what types of clergy this increase in percentage has particularly occurred, using the same social, religious, and political characteristics analyzed in table 5.9. These data are presented in table 5.10.

Classified in this manner, the percentage of clergy who reported that they held more politically liberal positions than their congregants nearly doubled between 2001 and 2009—from 21 percent to 41 percent. Moreover, the data reveal two relatively distinct patterns. The first is that almost every category of pastor analyzed exhibited an increase in the percentage who reported that they held more liberal political perspectives than their congregants (the only

Table 5.10 **The Characteristics of Clergy Holding More Liberal Positions on Political Issues than their Congregation**

	2001 (%)	*2009 (%)*
All	21	41
Gender		
Female	33	72
Male	20	37
Seminary education		
None, Bible college	8	8
Some seminary	13	29
Seminary graduate	25	49
Religious tradition		
Evangelical Protestant	14	23
Mainline Protestant	27	55
Theological orthodoxy		
Low	40	87
Medium	25	66
High	14	21
Political ideology		
Very Liberal	43	91
Liberal	39	85
Moderate	24	62
Conservative	15	32
Very Conservative	9	5

exceptions occurred among those with no seminary training and among those who reported that their ideological self-classification was "very conservative"). Thus, even among evangelical Protestant clergy, the highly theologically orthodox, as well as clergy who labeled themselves as political conservatives, one finds a larger percentage reporting in 2009 than in 2001 that they are more liberal politically than their parishioners. Still, despite this relatively uniform pattern, some clergy were far more likely than others to report rather substantial increases, as major jumps in such disparities (i.e., increases of 25 percent or more) occurred among female clergy; seminary graduates, mainline Protestant clergy, those who exhibited low and medium levels of theological orthodoxy, and those who classified themselves as either political moderates or political liberals.

The most likely explanation for the change in clergy-laity gap is the growing perception that those who fill the pews of their churches are more conservative today politically than ten years ago. Just why congregations are more likely to be perceived in this fashion in 2009 than in 2001 is unclear. Perhaps some of this difference stems from the growth in aging congregations or from the fact that those who attend church are increasingly more politically conservative that those who do not attend church.[10] Certainly, as shown earlier in this chapter, there has been a growing ideological polarization of the clergy, but this polarization can hardly be the major explanation in accounting for the clergy-laity gap—as even among pastors who classified themselves as political conservatives one finds nearly one-third who perceive themselves to be more politically liberal in orientation than the congregants they serve.

Conclusions

The issue positions of American Protestant clergy have exhibited both stability and change over the past several decades, with patterns of aggregate change or stability being dependent upon the particular issue under investigation. On some matters, hardly any change has been evident in the issue positions adopted by clergy over the past two decades, whereas on other issues substantial changes have been evident in their adopted positions. Overall, these particular patterns of change and stability do not seem to be confined to particular domains of public policy, as patterns of change and stability are evident within each of the three domains of economic, social, and foreign policy.

Generally speaking, however, far more substantial changes in the issue positions of clergy transpired between 1989 and 2001 than between 2001 and 2009. Although this greater level of change for the former time period may be, at least in part, a function of the longer interval of time analyzed, it may also be due in part to the greatly diminished proportion of the "new breed" of clergy (who were ordained in the 1960s) in 2001 when compared to 1989, as 28 percent of the clergy surveyed in 1989 were ordained in the 1960s but only 4 percent of the clergy surveyed in 2001 had been ordained in the 1960s.

Moreover, for those issues in which there have been changes in the policy positions of clergy, the positions adopted by clergy generally have moved in a more conservative, than a more liberal, direction politically. Yet, despite the appearance of a certain level of relative stability in the issue positions of clergy on other matters of public policy, there were nevertheless other important changes that have occurred. Not only are the issue positions adopted by clergy far more highly related to each other now than several decades ago, but the policy positions adopted by clergy have also become much more closely related to the ideological self-classifications that they report.

Moreover, the ideological orientations of clergy have also shifted consistently over the past two decades. First, the percentage of clergy who choose to classify themselves as politically conservative in some fashion has increased over time— though the percentage who classify themselves as politically liberal has increased slightly over the period of time. Today, nearly twice as many Protestant clergy classify themselves as political conservatives than as political liberals. And, there has also been a substantial growth in the ideological polarization found among Protestant clergy. Not only has the percentage of clergy claiming to be political moderates declined over time, but the percentage of clergy adopting ideological self-classifications falling at the extreme ends of the ideological continuum has increased substantially.

Finally, clergy are less likely today than at the beginning of the millennium to report that they hold similar political positions to those of their congregants. Surprisingly, despite the increase over time in the percentage of clergy adopting more conservative positions on matters of public policy and choosing to classify themselves as political conservatives, clergy are nevertheless far more likely today to perceive themselves as more liberal politically than their congregants.

The Political Norms and Psychological Resources of Clergy

The willingness of clergy to express their positions on matters of public policy in the anonymity of social surveys does not necessarily mean that they would choose to express their positions publicly, endeavor to mobilize their congregations to secure the realization of such policies, or even publicly support political candidates. Clearly, though some clergy may choose to do so, not all do. What then accounts for such differences?

Several factors likely shape the probability of clergy publicly voicing their political opinions or choosing to engage in the political process. Certainly one factor is the extent to which clergy believe it may be it appropriate for pastors to engage in such endeavors, as studies of both the mass public and political elites have revealed a strong relationship between approving an action and undertaking that activity (Barnes and Kaase 1979; Guth et al. 1997, 146–50; Djupe and Gilbert 2003, 58–59). Likewise, personal orientations such as one's level of political interest or the desire for greater political involvement can serve to enhance or inhibit pastoral political engagement (Rosenstone and Hansen 1993; Verba, Schlozman, and Brady 1995; Guth et al. 1997), and clergy actions can also be shaped by the extent to which one's congregation may approve of such activities, as "clergy more often move in synchronicity with their churches rather than in opposition to them" (Djupe and Gilbert 2003, 57). And, finally, a large body of research has demonstrated that actions are shaped by perceptions of the extent to which they are perceived to be effective or efficacious (e.g., Rosenstone and Hansen 1993, 15–16; Verba, Schlozman, and Brady 1995), and so clergy may not choose to engage in certain congregationally based endeavors should they believe such actions to be relatively ineffective.

This chapter examines changes related to factors that may constrain or enhance clergy political activities and whether clergy today feel more constrained or more motivated than clergy several decades ago to be engaged politically. Clergy are, after all, persons whose stock and trade consists of norms and values, and it is highly likely that professional, as well as personal, norms might well shape their behavior. Consequently, the first portion of the chapter examines the extent to which clergy approve of pastors engaging in various activities related to public life (e.g., should clergy address matters of public policy from the pulpit, work publicly on a candidate's political campaign, or engage in civil disobedience?), the extent to which these norms may have changed over time, as well as those factors that serve to shape the expression of these norms.

The second portion of the chapter then analyzes several personal attitudes that might encourage or discourage political engagement, some of which relate to attitudes that clergy may share with other citizens and others of which are more specifically related to their role as clergy. The former includes the level of political interest clergy exhibit, while the latter relates to clergy perceptions of their potential to shape the political views of their congregants. Obviously, even if clergy believe that certain political endeavors are appropriate for them to do, they would be less likely inclined to engage in such endeavors if they are relatively uninterested in politics or believe their actions would have little, if any, effect on those whom one seeks to persuade or influence. The second part of the chapter therefore examines the changing nature of these potential motivating factors that can shape clergy involvement in public life.

The Changing Political Norms of Protestant Clergy

Members of different professions typically hold certain norms about what types of behavior may, or may not, be appropriate for members of their particular profession to exhibit, as norms constitute "shared expectations about appropriate behavior held by a community of actors" (Finnemore 1996, 22). Sometimes, these shared expectations may be formally expressed in a written code of conduct that one publicly takes an oath to follow (e.g., when medical doctors affirm the Hippocratic oath or nurses the Nightingale pledge), or they may be more informal in nature, typically held by most, but not necessarily all, of those within the profession.

But, regardless of whether such professional norms are formal or informal in nature, they are likely to vary according to the particular circumstances under consideration—with the behavior being inappropriate under certain, yet acceptable under other, circumstances. For example, given the Protestant emphasis on preaching from the Word of God, distinctions are frequently made between activities appropriately taken "from the pulpit" from those undertaken "off the pulpit"—as certain activities may be deemed appropriate for clergy, but not when conducted from the pulpit.

Likewise, norms about what may be appropriate can change over time. Although it is highly unlikely that clergy norms would change substantially over the course of a year or two, norms could well change over a period of several decades. For example, several decades ago, no pastor would likely have thought it appropriate to wear shorts during a worship service, but such informal attire may now be deemed appropriate for clergy when conducting "contemporary, seeker services."

Political Cue-Giving

In each of the three clergy surveys, pastors were asked whether they approved of various politically related activities in which clergy might engage. Given the particular questions asked, scholars have typically divided these activities into two categories: cue-giving activities and direct action activities (e.g., Guth et al. 1997, 147). Political cue-giving entails revealing to others one's position on some matter related to issues or candidates (e.g., which particular issues may be viewed as important, how such issues should be interpreted, where one stands on an issue, or whom one supports as a political candidate). Such revelations can occur in different ways and in different places. But, regardless of its content, form, or setting, political cue-giving constitutes some public disclosure of where one stands politically.

Across the three surveys, pastors have been asked their level of approval for eight specific ways in which they might disclose their political preferences: (1) urging your congregation to register and vote,[1] (2) publicly taking a stand on some moral issue while preaching, (3) publicly taking a stand on some political issue while preaching, (4) delivering a whole sermon on some controversial social or political issue, (5) endorsing a candidate from the pulpit, (6) publicly taking a stand on some moral issue while not preaching, (7) publicly taking a stand on some political issue while not preaching, and (8) publicly supporting a candidate while not preaching. Table 6.1 presents the percentage of clergy across time who expressed approval for each of these distinct forms of political cue-giving.

Certainly, as evident from the data presented, clergy vary considerably in their expressed level of approval for such actions. Some actions are viewed as appropriate by virtually all the pastors surveyed; other actions are overwhelmingly deemed inappropriate. For example, nearly all the ministers surveyed in 2009 reported that they approved of clergy urging their congregation to register and vote (96 percent of clergy did so), while nearly all clergy failed to express

Table 6.1 **The Political Norms of Clergy over Time**

	Approving (%)		
	1989	*2001*	*2009*
Approval of Cue-Giving			
From the Pulpit			
Urge your congregation to register and vote	99	x	96
Take a stand on some moral issue while preaching	x	92	93
Deliver sermon on controversial social/political topic[a]	80	72	78
Take a stand while preaching on some political issue	56	52	54
Endorse a candidate from the pulpit	7	x	7
Off the Pulpit			
Publicly (not preaching) take a stand on a moral issue	x	95	97
Publicly (not preaching) take a stand on a political issue[a]	92	79	82
Publicly (not preaching) support a political candidate[a]	69	48	51
Approval of Direct Action			
Congregationally Based			
Organize a study group in church to discuss public affairs	80	72	78
Organize an action group in church to accomplish a social or political goal	65	53	55
Protest-Related			
Participate in a protest march	60	61	66
Commit civil disobedience to protest some issue	42	41	46
Campaign-Related			
Join a national political organization to work for your political beliefs	59	50	54
Contribute money to a candidate, party, or political action committee	75	68	75
Work actively in a candidate's political campaign	x	35	40

x = not asked.

[a]Because AOG and UMC clergy were not asked this question in 1989, the responses of clergy from these two denominations are not included in the 2001 and 2009 percentages, so as to insure comparability across time.

approval of clergy endorsing candidates from the pulpit (only 7 percent of clergy expressed approval).

Second, as previously noted (Guth et al. 1997, 150–51), clergy differentiate between moral and political matters, with almost all clergy viewing their profession as being more directly related to moral than political matters. There is, for example, a relatively high level of approval for taking a stand while preaching on moral issues, with 93 percent of clergy in 2009 expressing their approval for such activities, but clergy are far more divided in their approval for doing so with regard to political issues, as only about one-half of clergy (54 percent) indicated that they approved of taking a stand on some political issue from the pulpit. Clearly, clergy express little hesitation in addressing moral issues from the pulpit, but they are far more reluctant to approve of doing so for political issues.

Third, in addressing public matters, clergy clearly distinguish between activities conducted on and off the pulpit, as clergy generally see the need to act more cautiously when speaking politically from the pulpit. As can be seen from table 6.1, more than four-fifths of pastors in 2009 approved of clergy publicly taking a stand on some issue when done off the pulpit, whereas only half did so when expressed from the pulpit. And, though pastors in 2009 overwhelmingly approved of clergy addressing moral issues from the pulpit (93 percent did so), and even higher percentage (97 percent) approved of doing so when not preaching.

And, fourth, even when off the pulpit or outside a house of worship, clergy express different levels of approval for different forms of public disclosure. Whereas pastors generally approve of clergy taking positions on political issues when off the pulpit (more than four-fifths did so in 2009), they are far more hesitant to express approval of clergy publicly supporting candidates outside the worship context (as only about half of the clergy expressed approval in 2009).

Nevertheless, table 6.1 reveals one apparent anomaly related to clergy political cue-giving norms. Only a little more than half of the pastors surveyed in 2009 reported that they approved of clergy taking a stance on a political issue from the pulpit, yet nearly three-quarters expressed approval of pastors preaching a whole sermon that addressed some controversial social or political issue. It is unclear why clergy are far more willing to approve of delivering a sermon on some public issue than taking a stand from the pulpit on a political issue. The drop-off of approval may stem from the fact that preaching a whole sermon on a political matter need not entail disclosing one's own position on the matter. Furthermore, delivering a sermon on a particular issue may provide pastors with an opportunity to examine various biblical passages that may suggest somewhat different perspectives on the matter, thereby allowing clergy to work through some of the moral complexity related to that particular issue. The fact that choosing to devote a whole sermon to the topic need not entail taking a position in relationship to such an issue is evident from the fact that, in 2009, one-fifth of those clergy (20 percent) who approved of delivering a sermon on a controversial social or political or political topic nevertheless disapproved of clergy publicly taking a stand from the pulpit on some political issue (data not shown).[2]

Finally, in terms of change over time, it appears that clergy approval for engaging in political cue-giving has not increased over the past twenty years; in fact, if anything, approval for engaging in such activities has diminished somewhat over that period of time. Certainly, approval for certain forms of cue-giving has remained rather steady over the past two decades. Relatively few pastors (7 percent) approved of endorsing candidates from the pulpit in 1989, and relatively few continued to do so in 2009 (7 percent).[3] Similarly, most pastors in 2001 (92 percent) approved of clergy taking a stand on some moral issue while preaching, and basically the same percentage continued to do so in 2009. And, some of the percentage declines found in table 6.1 are so small that one can hardly claim that such shifts necessarily constitute any real decline in approval.

Nevertheless, in terms of other cue-giving activities, there has been a pattern of decline in approval. The percentage of pastors who expressed approval for clergy delivering a sermon on some controversial social or political topic, for example, actually decreased between 1989 and 2009 (from 80 percent to 73 percent)—with the largest drop in approval occurring between 1989 and 2001. The same pattern is evident with regard to approval of clergy cue-giving endeavors off the pulpit—as the percentages of approval for clergy taking a stand on some political issue and publicly supporting a political candidate while not preaching both dropped considerably between 1989 and 2001, only to recover slightly in 2009.

Overall, therefore, these data do not reveal any growth over the past several decades in clergy approval for engaging in various political cue-giving activities. In fact, if anything, clergy are less accepting of such activities today than previously. So to the extent that norms serve to constrain behavior, Protestant clergy today continue to express a similar, if not greater, level of constraint related to political cue-giving than what clergy reported in the late 1980s.

Direct Political Action

The clergy surveys also inquired about clergy approval for a number of direct political actions (see table 6.1). When asked in 2009 about the two congregationally based activities, clergy were far more likely to approve of the formation of study groups (78 percent) than action groups (55 percent), with this greater approval for the former than the latter mirroring previous findings (e.g., Guth et al. 1997; Penning 2009).

In terms of protest-related activities, clergy are, not surprisingly, far more likely to express approval for legal than illegal means to express one's protests.

Interestingly, however, clergy were far more willingly to express approval for participating in protest marches than forming congregationally based action groups to address some social or political problem (66 percent versus 55 percent, respectively). Why this may be the case is not clear, though it perhaps relates to the historic roll that clergy played in the protest marches of the Civil Rights Movement of the 1960s. But, whatever its basis, two-thirds of the Protestant clergy surveyed in 2009 expressed approval for clergy participating in protest marches, whereas slightly more than half that year expressed approval for forming congregationally based action groups.

Somewhat more surprisingly, perhaps, is the fact that clergy are sometimes far more willing to express approval for clergy engaging in civil disobedience than they are for clergy engaging in more conventional forms of election activity. In fact, a rather substantial portion of the ministers surveyed in 2009 withheld approval of clergy being too actively involved in the political process—even if done as a private citizen. For example, a higher percentage of clergy expressed approval for clergy engaging in civil disobedience to protest an issue (46 percent) than for clergy working actively in some candidate's political campaign (40 percent).

Moreover, when considering campaign-related activities, it is also clear that clergy clearly take into account the relative public visibility of such campaign activities—with clergy expressing greater levels of approval for those activities less visible to others. Hence, a larger percentage of pastors approved of clergy contributing money to a party, candidate, or political action committee (75 percent) than approved of their actively working in some candidate's campaign (40 percent).

In the end, clergy may choose to engage in politics based on one of several roles: as a pastor, as a professional, or even as a private citizen. And, certainly as individuals, clergy are citizens who have the right to speak out on issues, display campaign signs, contribute money to political campaigns, and work for political candidates. But, regardless of the particular role in which they may choose to engage in such activity (e.g., in the role of an individual citizen rather than a pastor), it remains hard for others to discern just what role they may have adopted when engaging in that activity. As a result, the less publicly visible the campaign-related activity, the greater the likelihood of clergy approval, as such less publicly visible activities are likely to create fewer problems for clergy among their parishioners (and possibly less likely to tarnish the image of the church culturally).

Thus, overall, those actions that clergy are typically most likely to approve are those that tend to carry the least amount of risk, while the activities garnering the lowest levels of approval generally exhibit the greatest levels of risk—whether in terms of creating divisions within the congregation or violating existing laws. And, despite what might be appearances of growing clergy involvement in politics, clergy were no more likely in 2009 than in 1989 to express approval for clergy engaging in direct political action. This is true both with regard to congregationally based endeavors as well as to campaign-related activities. Approval for such endeavors typically declined between 1989 and 2001, only to be followed by a modest increase in approval between 2001 and 2009. But, even with the increase in approval between 2001 and 2009, levels of approval generally remained at far lower levels in 2009 than in 1989.

Interestingly, the one exception to this general pattern of stability, if not decline, in clergy approval for direct political action relates to political protest and civil disobedience activities. In contrast to campaign-related activities, pastoral approval for these endeavors did not decline between 1989 and 2001, but similar to the other activities examined in table 6.1, there was an upswing in approval between 2001 and 2009. As a result, these two protest-related activities were the only political actions for which greater clergy approval was expressed in 2009 than in 1989.

The Changing Frequency of Approval

In order to assess the overall changes in the political norms of clergy, two composite measures of clergy norms were created—one related to cue-giving and one related to direct political action,[4] with only those items asked over each of the three time periods being retained for use in constructing these measures.[5] The changing frequency distributions of these two measures are presented in table 6.2.

These distributions reveal there has been a decline in the level of clergy approval for both political cue-giving[6] and direct political action. For both norms, there were major declines in approval between 1989 and 2001, followed by a slight recovery in high levels of approval between 2001 and 2009. Nevertheless, for each measure examined, the percentage of pastors expressing high levels of approval for clergy engaging in the specified forms of political engagement was actually lower in 2009 than in 1989.[7]

These data suggest therefore that clergy are somewhat more cautious today than several decades ago in terms of expressing approval for members of their ranks entering into political life—whether through political cue-giving or direct political action. Certainly, there are some clergy who continue to exhibit high levels of approval for these particular endeavors, but, overall, clergy as a whole are less likely now than several decades ago to express high levels of approval for clergy engaging in either kind of political action.

Sources of Approval for Cue-Giving and Direct Action

Who then among Protestant clergy are the most likely to express high levels of approval for these political endeavors? Early analysts of ministerial politics

Table 6.2 **Frequency Distributions of Approval of Political Cue-Giving and Direct Political Engagement**

	1989 (%)	2001 (%)	2009 (%)
Cue-Giving[a]			
Low	16	31	29
Medium	44	43	43
High	40	26	29
Total	100	100	101
Direct Political Action			
Low	26	28	24
Medium	38	43	44
High	36	29	32
Total	100	100	100

[a]Since not all of the component items were not included in the 1989 survey of AOG and UMC clergy, the analysis for cue-giving over time is based on responses from the other five denominations only.

generally contended that theologically orthodox clergy were largely "other-worldly" in orientation, and, as a result, were less interested in politics, expressed less desire to be politically involved, noted greater difficulty in shaping political outcomes, and anticipated that less would be accomplished through politics than their modernist "this-worldly" clergy counterparts (e.g., Stark et al. 1970). But, given the political changes that transpired during the 1970s and 1980s, later research revealed that "positive attitudes about political involvement were on the rise among more theologically orthodox ministers" (Guth et al. 1997, 160). Still, this apparent narrowing of the gap between "orthodox" and "modernist" clergy was based on data collected in the late 1980s, and it is far from clear whether that gap has totally closed or whether it has changed in some fundamental fashion.

Moreover, though the classic studies of ministerial politics sought to determine the nature of clergy attitudes toward a variety of political activities, very little research has been subsequently conducted related to what particular factors might shape these norms and attitudes.[8] The research that has been conducted related to political norms suggests that the bivariate relationships tend to be stronger with norms related to direct action than with cue-giving (Guth et al. 1997, 153). Whereas gender, education, age, theological orthodoxy, individualist social theology, and political ideology were found, using the 1989 clergy data, to be significantly related to approval for direct political action, none of these variables proved to be significantly related to approval for political cue-giving (Guth et al. 1997, 155).

Do these patterns then continue to hold over time? Analysis reveals that it is those clergy who are male, older, non-seminary graduates, serving smaller congregations and churches in smaller communities, and who see themselves as more conservative than their congregants who are more likely to exhibit higher levels of approval for political cue-giving than their counterparts. And, in contrast, it is those clergy who are female, younger, seminary graduates, serving larger congregations and churches in larger communities, and who see themselves as more liberal than their congregants who are most prone to exhibit higher levels of approval for direct political action, with these relationships generally holding across time (data not shown).

Moreover, the percentage differences found across the various independent variables examined are typically much larger when examining approval for direct political action than when examining approval for political cue-giving, and this is true regardless of the year of the survey (data not shown). Put another way, the size of the correlation coefficients between the independent variables examined and political cue-giving are typically much smaller than coefficients between those same independent variables and direct political action. Thus, despite the passage of twenty years, bivariate relationships continue to be stronger with regard to norms related to direct action than with cue-giving (Guth et al. 1997, 153).

However, despite this continuity over time, there is at least one pattern which did not conform to some of the projections anticipated by the authors of The Bully Pulpit. Early studies of clerical politics (e.g., Quinley 1974) had revealed that the more theologically orthodox were far less likely than those less orthodox to approve of direct political action, but clergy data collected in the late 1980s suggested that this gap was narrowing, as there appeared to be "a considerable increase in approval (for direct political action) among orthodox clergy" (Guth et al. 1997, 148). Given that some theologically conservative clergy had begun to protest and engage in civil disobedience related to abortion and other social issues, and given the widely publicized efforts of various Christian Right organizations to mobilize Christians to the polls during the 1980s, it was speculated that such actions may have bolstered approval ratings for protest-related behavior and conventional political engagement among more theologically orthodox clergy. Indeed, further analysis revealed that, among theologically orthodox clergy,[9] it was the younger pastors who were leading the way—suggesting that the approval gap related to direct political action between those clergy high and low in theological orthodoxy would likely narrow, if not disappear, with the passage of time.

Consequently, table 6.3 examines how religious tradition and theological orthodoxy relate over time to norms about political cue-giving and direct political action. Clearly, as is evident from the data, clergy from evangelical denominations and theologically orthodox clergy continue to be far more likely to exhibit higher levels of approval for political cue-giving and far less likely to exhibit lower levels of approval for direct political action than their mainline and theologically less orthodox brethren. Thus, clergy continue to be divided in terms of the particular form of political endeavor they generally approve, with those who are most likely to approve of political cue-giving differing from those who are most likely to approve of direct political action. In fact, those clergy low in theological orthodoxy in 1989 were nearly three times more likely than those high in orthodoxy to express high levels of approval for direct political action (63 percent to 23 percent, respectively), and, twenty years later, the percentages continue to be basically identical to those found in 1989.[10] Thus, the anticipated narrowing of differences in levels of approval for direct political action has not occurred.

Table 6.3 **The Religious Location of Clergy Political Norms over Time**

	Religious tradition			*Theological orthodoxy*			
	Evangelical (%)	*Mainline (%)*	*r*	*Low (%)*	*Medium (%)*	*High (%)*	*r*
1989							
Political cues[a]	39	40	.00	51	38	36	.11
Direct action	25	45	.25	62	43	23	−.35
2001							
Political cues[a]	32	22	−.10	26	18	30	.05
Direct action	19	38	.21	61	33	18	−.32
2009							
Political cues[a]	37	23	−.15	24	19	34	.08
Direct action	25	38	.16	62	39	23	−.32

[a]Not all the component items were asked of AOG and UMC clergy in 1989. Consequently, in order to insure comparability across time, the responses of clergy from these two denominations are not included in the 2001 and 2009 cue-giving percentages.

The Changing Attitudinal Resources for Clergy Political Engagement

If the overall approval for political cue-giving and direct political action has diminished somewhat among clergy over the past twenty years, can the same be said about those psychological factors that may serve to encourage their political engagement? Four psychological factors that could shape the political engagement of clergy—namely, political interest, desire for greater political involvement, sense of efficacy related to shaping the political opinions of congregants, and strength of partisan identification—are examined here, with table 6.4 presenting the distributions of these variables over time.

The link between political interest and political activism has long been established, as those with higher levels of political interest are far more likely than those less interested to engage in political acts of various kinds. And the data clearly reveal that clergy have been, and continue to be, very interested in politics; in fact, the percentage of clergy who report that they are very interested in politics far exceeds the combined percentages of those who indicated that they are only mildly interested, somewhat interested, or not very interested in politics. In 1989, more than half of the clergy (54 percent) reported that they were very interested in politics, with one-quarter indicating that they were somewhat interested and less than a quarter noting that they were mildly, or even less, interested in politics.[11] Over time, however, the percentage of clergy who report that they are only mildly or somewhat interested in politics has declined, while the percentage who report they are very interested in politics has grown from 54 percent in 1989 to 64 percent in 2009. Thus, even though clergy reported very high levels of interest in politics in 1989, they expressed even greater levels of interest twenty years later.

Reporting a high level of interest in politics, however, does not necessarily indicate the desire to be more politically engaged. Hence, a more relevant question might be whether clergy want to become more politically involved. And, clergy typically report, regardless of the year surveyed, a desire to be more involved politically than their current level of involvement. In fact, about one-third of clergy report that they wished they could be "much more involved," while about a quarter indicate that they would like to be "somewhat more involved" with the distribution in the desire for greater involvement remaining rather stable over time. Nevertheless, despite this relative stability, the fact remains that many clergy express a strong desire to become even more involved politically than that evident by their current level of political involvement.

A third factor that might facilitate clergy engagement in politics is the extent to which they perceive themselves as being able to shape the political views

Table 6.4 **The Changing Psychological Resources for Political Engagement over Time**

	1989 (%)	2001 (%)	2009 (%)
Level of political interest			
Very interested	54	57	64
Somewhat interested	25	23	20
Mildly interested	17	14	8
Somewhat disinterested	4	5	6
Not very interested	*	2	2
Total	100	101	100
Desire for political involvement			
Much more involved	30	30	33
Somewhat more involved	25	25	23
Same involvement as now	41	41	39
Somewhat less involved	3	3	2
Much less involved	2	2	3
Total	101	101	100
Ministers have great potential to influence the political beliefs of their congregations[a]			
Strongly agree	13	16	15
Agree	54	46	56
Uncertain	19	23	16
Disagree	14	14	11
Strongly disagree	1	2	2
Total	101	101	100
Party identification			
Strong Democrat	13	15	17
Weak/Leaning Democrat	23	18	17
Independent	10	9	9
Weak/Leaning Republican	36	31	31
Strong Republican	17	27	26
Total	99	100	100

* = less than 1 percent.
[a] CRC and RCA pastors were not asked this question in 1989, and so the percentages across time are for the remaining five denominations only.

of their congregants. Even if clergy believe that certain political endeavors are appropriate for them to do, they are less likely to engage in such endeavors if they believe their actions will have little, if any, effect on those they seek to persuade or influence. Over the three clergy surveys, clergy have been asked whether they agree that "pastors have a great potential to influence the political beliefs of their congregations." And, as shown in table 6.4, overwhelming majorities of clergy have expressed agreement with the statement over the past two decades, with the percentage doing so growing from 66 percent in 1989 to 71 percent in 2009.

Finally, strength of partisan identification has been shown to be related to political activism, as those who identify strongly with a political party are far more likely to be engaged politically than those who identify more weakly. And, once again, there has been an increase in this resource as well, as the percentage of strong partisan identifiers has also grown among clergy over time from 30 percent in 1989 to 43 percent in 2009.

Overall, then, the psychological resources for political engagement among Protestant clergy have not diminished over the past two decades—but have actually grown. A majority of clergy continue to desire, as was true several decades ago, to be more politically involved than they currently are. But, in terms of their political interest, their perceived efficacy in shaping the political opinions or their congregants, and the strength of their partisan identifications, the psychological resources for political involvement were even greater among clergy in 2009 than they were in 1989.

Psychological Resources and Political Norms

How, then, do these relatively growing psychological resources relate to clergy norms? Are those with greater resources more likely to approve of clerical activism? And, do such relationships vary by whether such norms relate to cue-giving or to direct action?

Table 6.5 addresses these questions in part by examining the relationships between two of the psychological factors (specifically, the desire for greater involvement and perceptions of efficacy) and norms related to cue-giving and direct action. Several important patterns emerge from this analysis. First, the desire to be more involved politically is clearly related to high levels of approval for both political cue-giving and direct political action. Although the absolute level of approval for each form of engagement has diminished somewhat across time among those clergy desiring to be more involved politically (see table 6.5), the same is true among clergy who do not wish to be more politically involved (data not shown). As a result, the strength of these relationships has remained

Table 6.5 **Clergy Political Norms by Clergy Psychological Resources over Time**

	Desire for involvement				*Ministers have potential*[b]			
	Less	Same	More	r	Disagree	Not sure	Agree	R
% High cue-giving norms[a]								
1989	18	33	47	.21	30	36	44	.13
2001	15	21	31	.20	16	30	38	.23
2009	21	21	34	.22	21	30	38	.13
% High direct action norms								
1989	11	23	48	.33	33	30	30	−.01
2001	16	20	38	.27	28	30	29	.02
2009	10	22	42	.29	26	34	31	.02

[a]Not all the component items were asked of AOG and UMC clergy in 1989. Consequently, in order to insure comparability across time, the responses of clergy from these two denominations are not included in the 2001 and 2009 cue-giving percentages.

[b]CRC and RCA pastors were not asked this question in 1989, and so the percentages across time are for the remaining five denominations only.

rather equivalent across time (though at somewhat higher levels for direct action than for cue-giving).

Second, though perceptions of clergy efficacy are related to cue-giving norms, they are not related to norms concerning direct political action. Moreover, the relationships between ministerial potential and cue-giving norms are typically weaker than those between desire for greater political involvement and cue-giving norms. Perhaps, one might have anticipated that the relationship between ministerial potential and cue-giving might have been stronger had one restricted the cue-giving measures to only those two actions done within a worship service (namely, delivering a sermon that addresses a political issue and taking a political stand while preaching)—given that the wording of the ministerial potential item relates specifically to shaping congregants' political beliefs. But, such is not the case. Even when the cue-giving measure is divided into two separate measures (i.e., one related to the worship context and the other to a broader public context), the strength of relationships between ministerial potential and each of these two separated measures of cue-giving continue to be weaker than that exhibited by a pastor's desire for greater political involvement and political cue-giving (data not shown). Hence, these perceptions of ministerial potential (1) exhibit virtually no relationship whatsoever with regard to norms related to direct action, and (2) are more weakly related to cue-giving and direct action norms than is the desire to be more involved politically.

Patterns by Partisanship

Of course, the fact that some clergy are more likely than others to approve of cue-giving and direct action norms is not necessarily politically neutral in their effects. If approval were equally distributed across the partisan spectrum, then such differences might not be significant politically. But, if clergy from one political party were more likely to approve of these norms than clergy of the other party, then the resultant differences could have important political ramifications because, as noted earlier, there is a strong relationship between approving an action and undertaking that activity (Barnes and Kaase 1979; Guth et al. 1997, 146–50; Djupe and Gilbert 2003, 58–59).

Consequently, table 6.6 examines the relationship between partisan identification[12] and norms related to cue-giving and direct political action as well as the relationship between partisan identification and the other attitudinal resources that encourage political engagement. Overall, the data reveal that Republican clergy are more likely than Democratic clergy to exhibit high levels of approval for political cue-giving and to believe that ministers have a great potential to influence the political views of their congregants. However, patterns related to approval of political cue-giving have changed over time. Clergy who were strong Democrats were far more likely than those who were strong Republicans to express approval of political cue-giving in 1989, but by 2001 this relationship had reversed and then became even stronger by 2009—with the percentage difference found between strong Democratic clergy and strong Republican clergy being basically the same in 2009 as it was in 1989, only reversed.

On the other hand, Democratic clergy tend to exhibit higher levels of approval for direct political action than Republican clergy. In fact, the strongest relationships evident in table 6.6 are found between partisan identification and high levels of approval for direct political action, with the percentage of clergy exhibiting high levels of approval for direct action generally declining monotonically as one moves from strong Democrats to strong Republicans. These strong relationships and patterns have been consistently evident across each of the three clergy surveys.

Democratic clergy are also far more likely than Republican clergy to express the desire to be more involved politically. A curvilinear, and consistent, relationship exists between partisan identification and the desire to be more involved politically, as the percentages reporting a desire to be more involved politically are larger among the strong identifiers of each party than among those who reported weak identifications with that party.[13] However, across all three clergy

Table 6.6 **Clergy Political Norms and Psychological Resources by Partisan Identifications over Time**

	Strong Democratic	Weak/Leaning Democratic	Independent	Weak/Leaning Republican	Strong Republican	r
% High approval cue-giving						
1989	56	44	29	34	37	-.14
2001	28	20	17	25	36	.06
2009	25	21	20	26	46	.11
% High approval direct action						
1989	64	53	33	24	20	-.31
2001	60	42	23	21	17	-.28
2009	58	40	28	19	22	-.30
% High political interest						
1989	74	53	49	45	63	-.07
2001	75	50	43	47	67	-.00
2009	76	61	55	53	72	-.02

(continued)

Table 6.6 (Continued)

	Strong Democratic	Weak/Leaning Democratic	Independent	Weak/Leaning Republican	Strong Republican	r
% Desire greater involvement						
1989	70	59	47	50	50	–.12
2001	73	57	45	45	56	–.09
2009	73	63	49	44	56	–.12
% Minister has potential[a]						
1989	59	60	65	69	75	.13
2001	56	52	57	69	73	.16
2009	62	64	65	74	82	.18

[a]CRC and RCA pastors were not asked this question in 1989, and so the percentages across time are for the remaining five denominations only.

surveys, weak Democrats far exceeded weak Republicans in their expressed desire to be more politically involved—with the percentages found among weak Democrats even exceeding those found among strong Republicans.

Finally, the weakest relationships are evident in terms of political interest. Both strong Democrats and strong Republicans generally report high levels of politic interest, but the percentage of strong Democrats doing so exceeds the percentage found among strong Republicans across each of the three cross-sections in time, as does the percentage among weak/leaning Democrats in relationship to weak/leaning Republicans.

Thus, in the final analysis, the partisan ramifications associated with these political norms and psychological resources basically "even out," as clergy identifying with each major party tend to approve of different means of political engagement and draw upon somewhat different psychological resources for engagement. Democratic clergy are more likely than Republican clergy to approve of clergy engaging in direct political action, while the reverse is true with regard to political cue-giving. And, though Republican pastors are more likely than Democratic ones to contend that ministers have the potential to shape the political views of their congregants, the reverse is true in relationship to the expression of the desire to be more involved politically.

Explaining the Clergy Norms of Protestant Clergy

What then best explains differences in the political norms held by Protestant clergy from the seven denominations surveyed, and how might their capacity to explain variation in holding such norms have changed over time? To answer this question, a Multiple Classification Analysis was conducted as a means to assess the relative importance of seven independent variables in shaping responses to each of the dependent variables: gender, age, level of seminary education, religious tradition, level of theological orthodoxy, partisan identification, and the desire to be more involved politically.[14] The results of the analysis are presented in table 6.7.

First, given what was reported earlier, namely, that the bivariate relationships of independent variables tended to be stronger in relationship to direct political action than for political cue-giving, it is not surprising that the variables used to explain variation in clergy norms account for far more variation in the former than the latter. Across the three different cross-sections in time, the R^2 for norms related to direct political action never fell below a value of .22, whereas it never exceeded a value of .11 for norms related to cue-giving.

Moreover, over time, several important developments have occurred with regard to explaining the political norms of clergy. First, despite changes in the political environment over the two-decade period of time, it is the desire to be

Table 6.7 **Explaining Clergy Political Norms**

| | Clergy norms | | | | | |
| | Cue-giving[a] | | | Direct action | | |
	1989	2001	2009	1989	2001	2009
Gender	.02	.04	.02	.02	.03	.02
Age	.06	.01	.08	.14	.12	.07
Seminary education	.05	.03	.06	.26	.19	.13
Religious tradition	.05	.05	.11	.05	.03	.01
Theological orthodoxy	.10	.10	.10	.14	.18	.14
Partisan identification	.09	.08	.11	.12	.12	.16
Desire for more involvement	.21	.24	.27	.22	.29	.21
R^2	.08	.07	.11	.33	23	.22

[a]Not all the component items were asked of AOG and UMC clergy in 1989. Consequently, in order to insure comparability across time, the responses of clergy from these two denominations are not included in the 2001 and 2009 cue-giving percentages.

more involved politically that most strongly shapes approval of political actions related to both cue-giving and direct political action, as its beta coefficient is the largest regardless of the year analyzed.

Second, the importance of religious tradition has grown in relationship to cue-giving norms—with evangelical clergy being far more likely to approve of such actions than mainline clergy. However, over time, religious tradition has declined in its relative importance in explaining clergy norms related to direct political action.

Third, despite the passage of time, the level of theological orthodoxy exhibited by clergy has remained a rather steady contributor to shaping clergy norms for both political endeavors. But, it has done so in different ways. Across each of the three clergy surveys spanning twenty years, higher theological orthodoxy contributes to greater approval for political cue-giving, whereas lower theological orthodoxy contributes to greater approval for direct political action.

Finally, for both cue-giving and direct action norms, a rather similar, and perhaps noteworthy, development has occurred. In 1989 and 2001, the beta values associated with theological orthodoxy marginally exceeded those associated with the partisan identifications of clergy, indicating that one's level of theological orthodoxy was slightly more important than one's partisan identification in shaping norms related to clergy cue-giving and direct political actions. However, in 2009, partisan identifications became relatively more important than theological orthodoxy in coloring expressions of approval for both endeavors. In other words, the partisan identifications of clergy have now become more important than the theological beliefs of clergy, a core component of their profession, in shaping the political norms of clergy.

Conclusions

This chapter has examined several potential factors that may serve to shape clergy involvement in politics. Norms related to political cue-giving and direct political involvement clergy involvement were first examined, as any lack of clergy approval for these particular forms of political engagement are likely to constrain clergy from engaging in them. Clergy express different levels of approval for different forms of political cue-giving and direct political action. With regard to the former, the nature (e.g., moral vs. political issues), the context (e.g., whether on or off the pulpit), and the relative visibility of the action shape the level of approval expressed by clergy. With regard to the latter, the nature (e.g., forming study versus action groups), legality (e.g., participating in protest march versus engaging in civil disobedience), and the relative visibility of the action (e.g., contributing money versus actively working in a political campaign) shape expressions of approval by clergy.

Clergy differ in terms of their approval for political cue-giving and approval for direct political action. Both religious tradition and theological orthodoxy continue to shape expressions of clergy norms, as clergy from evangelical denominations and those who are more theologically orthodox tend to exhibit higher levels of approval for political cue-giving, while the converse is true with regard to approval for direct political action.

However, despite what might be appearances to the contrary, the level of approval that clergy express for pastors engaging in political cue-giving as well as for engaging in direct political action has actually declined over the two decades examined. As a result, Protestant clergy today are actually less likely to express approval for clergy engaging in political endeavors than several decades ago. This is particularly true with regard to clergy engaging in political cue-giving.

In addition to an examination of clergy norms that may constrain political activity, this chapter has also analyzed various psychological factors that can serve to encourage political engagement. Four psychological factors were examined: level of political interest, desire for greater political involvement, sense of efficacy related to the potential of clergy shaping the political opinions of their congregants, and strength of partisan identifications. In contrast to patterns related to political norms, there has been an increase in the psychological dispositions that motivate such involvement, as clergy today report higher levels of political interest, greater efficacy in relationship to their congregants, and stronger partisan identifications than twenty years previously. Only the expressed desire to be more politically involved has remained relatively stable over the past several decades, but even here it is noteworthy that a majority of pastors continue to express the desire to be more involved politically than what is evident by their current level of involvement. And, the distributions of these psychological resources for political engagement are not politically neutral, as these resources are far more prevalent among Democratic, than Republican, clergy.

Finally, when engaging in multivariate analysis to account for variation in clergy norms related to political cue-giving and direct political action, it is the desire to be more involved politically that most shapes these clergy norms. But, after taking into account the desire to be more politically involved, it is the theological orthodoxy and the partisan identifications of clergy that most serve to shape clergy norms. However, over time, the relative importance of each has shifted: whereas theological orthodoxy initially outranked partisan identifications in their relative effects, the partisan identifications of clergy now outweigh theological orthodoxy in structuring clergy expressions of approval related to political cue-giving and direct political action.

The Political Activities of Clergy within Congregational Life

Although knowing what political endeavors clergy approve and disapprove may be related to the likelihood of engaging in those activities, such approval in no way insures that clergy will actually engage in those particular endeavors. And, ultimately, what really matters is the extent to which clergy choose to engage in these various forms of political action.

When studying clergy as public leaders, it is important to recognize that there are different roles, contexts, and means by which clergy may choose to exert their influence. Sometimes clergy may seek to exert their influence outside their congregation and in roles not directly related to being a pastor. A pastor, for example, may seek politically to persuade family members or influence others through contributing financially to a political campaign. But, in each of these endeavors, the fact that one is a pastor has little bearing on whether such efforts may succeed or fail. For the most part, these endeavors are conducted by pastors primarily in their role as "private" citizens.

At other times, clergy may seek to influence the public and foster public engagement in their role as clergy, but outside the context of their particular congregation. Clergy who engage in such activities may, or may not, be pastors of a local congregation. For example, clergy who head denominational agencies may seek denominational adoption of particular positions related to matters of public policy. And, even clergy who serve local churches may choose to publicly engage important public issues or participate in public matters outside the context of the local church, when, for example, clergy serve as members of civic boards, participate in public ceremonies, or seek to influence the public position of denominational agencies with which they may be affiliated (Djupe and Gilbert 2003, 93).

However, it is the conjunction of their role as pastor within the context of serving specific congregations that clergy are likely to have their greatest opportunity to influence members of the American electorate. As discussed in chapter 1, relatively few members of the American electorate occupy the same strategic position, possess the particular kind of authority, or enjoy the unique opportunities that are available to clergy when they minister to members of the congregations they serve.

This chapter therefore focuses its attention on two major ways in which clergy may seek to shape the political thinking and actions of their congregants. First, the chapter examines the reported political cue-giving behavior of clergy within congregational life, particularly the worship context. Second, the chapter analyzes congregational life as a site for the development of political learning among parishioners and the role that clergy may play in endeavors such as fostering the study of political issues, forming political action groups, and organizing candidate forums within the congregations they serve.

In part, this focus on political endeavors within congregational life is due to the fact that religious houses of worship have been, and continue to be, important sites of public life within American society.[1] Corporate worship is a public occasion, and participation in these public events and spaces provides a wide variety of opportunities for worshippers both to develop an interest in, and a concern for, public life, as well as to learn important civic values and skills (e.g., Verba, Schlozman, and Brady 1995; Putnam 2000; Djupe and Grant 2001; Smidt et al. 2008). Those who gather to worship may be reminded in sermons, prayers, and other proclamations of the ethical imperatives of their religious faith in ministering to those in need; they may learn of opportunities to volunteer and serve others in their community through announcements, classes, or informal conversation with fellow worshippers; and, through the organizational life of the church, they have additional opportunities to organize activities, make collective decisions, express their views, acknowledge the contrasting view of others, and compromise on positions. In fact, as Lichterman and Potts (2005, 2) point out: "Religious congregations may be the most widespread and egalitarian sites of civic engagement in the United States."

The Political Cue-Giving of Clergy

Research has suggested that one of the primary mechanisms that clergy employ to influence political opinion, set political agendas, or politically mobilize parishioners is public speech (Djupe and Gilbert 2002, 596). Although the political voice of clergy can play an important role within the broader political community, particularly when the congregation constitutes a minority locally (Djupe and Gilbert 2003, 65), the primary arena within which most clergy are likely to exercise their political voice is within the life of the congregation they serve.

This is not to suggest that this is the only setting in which pastors have the potential to wield political influence over their parishioners, but the worship context is a particularly important one. Corporate worship is the central act in the church's life, as it is the one public activity in which members of the congregation most commonly gather together. Moreover, since the Reformation, the primary role of the Protestant clergy has been to exposit the Word of God to the people gathered for worship. Given the relative centrality of the preaching of the Word within the Protestant tradition compared to the sacraments in the Roman Catholic tradition, the words and actions of Protestant clergy during worship services are likely to carry more weight within the worship service than outside that context.

As a result, the three clergy surveys have largely focused on the political cue-giving of clergy done within the context of congregational life.[2] Cue-giving here refers to any communication, however brief, that directs the receiver's attention to civic or political phenomena during the worship service.[3] Although clergy may only occasionally address political matters directly in the worship service (Brewer, Kersh, and Petersen 2003; Woolfalk 2012), many sermons nevertheless contain implicit political messages (Woolfalk 2012). These implicit cues, however, should not be dismissed as being unimportant, as implicit political cues within religious communications can actually prove to be more effective than explicit cues in achieving their intended end (Woolfalk 2014). Given that many parishioners value the principle of separation of church and state, any explicit messages can heighten the resistance of parishioners to the messages delivered, but implicit cues may circumvent such resistance, thereby contributing to the greater efficacy of implicit political messages in religious communications.

Cue-Giving within the Worship Context

Clergy can use a variety of means by which to transmit politically relevant messages during a worship service. Table 7.1 examines seven possible forms of cue-giving from the pulpit[4] and the percentage of clergy reporting that they had engaged in these particular activities during the course of the 2000 and 2008 presidential election years.

The means by which pastors choose to address public life within the context of worship service are quite diverse, and clergy report that they frequently engage in many cue-giving activities. In fact, as can be seen from table 7.1, clergy report having done most, though not necessarily all, such cue-giving activities during the course of the 2008 presidential campaign.[5] Noteworthy, however, is the fact that, based on their own reports, relatively few clergy endorse candidates while preaching, as only 2 percent of clergy reported in 2009 having done so in the past year.[6]

Table 7.1 **Percentage of Clergy Providing Civic and Political Cues over Time**

	1989 (%)	2001 (%)	2009 (%)
Cue-giving from the pulpit			
Urged your congregation to register and vote	x	55	83
Prayed publicly about an issue	x	56	81
Touched on controversial issue while preaching	x	49	76
Prayed publicly for political candidates	x	40	62
Took a stand from pulpit on some political issue	x	28	43
Preached a sermon on controversial issue	x	15	23
Endorsed candidate while preaching	x	4	2
Cue-giving off the pulpit			
Publicly (not preaching) took stand on public issue[a]	64	43	63
Publicly (not preaching) supported candidate[a]	41	30	45
Index of cue-giving from the pulpit			
0	x	28	4
1	x	9	7
2	x	13	12
3	x	16	20
4	x	14	25
5	x	12	20
6	x	7	13
7	x	1	1
Total		100	100
Index of cue-giving off the pulpit[a]			
0	21	54	32
1	54	19	28
2	26	27	40
Total	101	100	100

[a]CRC and RCA pastors were not asked this question in 1989. Over time figures therefore are for the remaining five denominations only.

x = only asked of clergy from three denominations or less.

Clergy are far more likely to address political matters through prayer than through the sermon itself, with clergy being more likely to pray about an issue than pray for political candidates. Still, political issues are also discussed within sermons as well. Three-fourths of clergy reported having touched on some political issue in a sermon over the course of the presidential election year, while slightly less than a quarter of the clergy reported that they had over the same period of time preached a whole sermon on some civic or political issue.

Touching on some issue from the pulpit does not necessarily mean that one actually takes a political stand from the pulpit; the two are analytically distinct phenomena. Whereas more than three-quarters of the clergy reported in 2009 that they had touched on some political issue in a sermon, only about two-fifths of all clergy reported that they had, in the past year, actually taken a stand from the pulpit on some political issue. But among those who had preached a whole sermon on some controversial issue, 85 percent reported having taken a pulpit stand on some issue (data not shown).[7]

Overall, therefore, clergy willingly report that they engage in cue-giving endeavors and that they engage in a variety of such cue-giving endeavors from the pulpit. Nevertheless, while clergy may adopt a number of different means by which to provide political cues, clergy typically choose to engage in those cue-giving actions that require less, rather than more, pulpit time. However, time is not the only factor shaping such cue-giving actions, as it does not entail more time to take a position on an issue than pray about an issue; yet, substantial differences exist between the reported level of praying about an issue and issue-taking activities. Thus, considerations related to appropriateness and potential divisiveness within the congregation are also likely to shape such cue-giving activities.

Clearly, certain cue-giving actions from the pulpit are widely reported as being performed by clergy, while others are rarely done at all. What percentage then report that they engage in a variety of cue-giving activities or indicate that they rarely, if ever, do so? In order to answer this question, an index of cue-giving from the pulpit was created consisting of all seven cue-giving activities. As shown at the bottom of table 7.1, almost all pastors reported that they had engaged in some sort of political cue-giving activity during the course of the 2008 election year, as only 4 percent of the clergy in 2009 reported that they had not done any of these seven acts over the past year.[8] Thus, the number of clergy who engage in political cue-giving appears to be quite extensive, as nearly all reported that they were at least minimally involved in addressing political matters from the pulpit in 2008, and more than one-third of the clergy surveyed were substantially engaged in doing so (reporting that they had engaged in five or more such actions over the past year).

Cue-Giving outside the Worship Context

Of course, clergy are not limited to cue-giving within the worship context. Though there may be a number of different means by which clergy could provide cues outside that setting, only two items addressing cue-giving outside the worship context were included in the clergy surveys: (1) publicly taking a stand on some political issue, and (2) publicly supporting some particular political candidate. Neither action specifies to whom such cues are given, though they could well be offered to congregational members in personal discussions, adult education classes, or through various other means (e.g., campaign signs in the front lawn of one's home). But, regardless, one can likely assume that these cues occurred outside the worship context.[9]

Given these two particular items, one can see that most clergy do not limit their cue-giving to the worship context. A substantial number (63 percent) of the clergy surveyed in 2009 reported they had taken a public stand on some political issue over the past year, though far fewer clergy (45 percent) indicated that they had publicly supported some political candidate over the same course of time. Still, using only these two items in creating an index of cue-giving off the pulpit, more than two-thirds of the clergy in 2009 reported having done at least one of these activities, with two-fifths indicating that they had done both cue-giving actions in the past year.

Change over Time

A final consideration is the extent to which clergy cue-giving activity has changed over time. It may be that in some election years, for example, clergy feel the need to provide cues more readily than in other election campaigns. Likewise, given certain national and international events (e.g., 9/11 or the war in Iraq), clergy may choose to provide more cues in some years than in other years. Hence, some assessment of whether there may be a waxing and waning of the provisions of such cues helps to place these activities within a broader historical context.

Clearly, as evident from table 7.1, the most common practices of political cue-giving from the pulpit reported in 2001 were generally the most common practices reported in 2009, with the rank ordering of the percentages being virtually similar across the divide of time. But, probably the most noteworthy pattern, regardless of its particular form, is that clergy cue-giving from the pulpit jumped substantially between 2001 and 2009, with a similar jump in political cue-giving off the pulpit occurring over the same course of time. The only exception to this pattern is the decline in reports by clergy that they had endorsed some candidate while preaching (from 4 percent in 2001 to 2 percent in 2009). Clearly, based on these data, it would appear that clergy were far more politically engaged during the course of the 2008 election cycle than the 2000 one.

This increased cue-giving by clergy between 2001 and 2009, however, was not the result of clergy from certain denominations "ramping up" their political cue-giving in 2009, as this dramatic increase in political cue-giving occurred across each of the seven denominations surveyed. As shown in table 7.2, the percentage of clergy who reported in 2001 that they had not done any of the seven pulpit cue-giving activities over the past year ranged from 22 to 38 percent across the seven denominations, but in 2009 those percentages ranged between 2 and 6 percent.

Nor was the increase in cue-giving activity limited to the pulpit, as reports of off-the-pulpit political cue-giving also increased between 2001 and 2009. These increases in cue-giving off the pulpit, however, were not nearly as dramatic. Still, clergy were far more involved in political cue-giving both on and off the pulpit during the course of the 2008 election cycle than the 2000 cycle, and this greater level of political cue-giving was evident among clergy across all seven denominations surveyed.

What is less clear, however, is whether the increase in political cue-giving activity between 2001 and 2009 is a reflection of the growing issue polarization found among clergy (see chapter 5). The limited evidence presented in table 7.1 would suggest that this may not be the case, as neither of the two forms of political cue-giving off the pulpit reveals a higher level of cue-giving among clergy in 2009 than in 1989.

Nevertheless, it would be helpful to have data related to political cue-giving from the pulpit that span three or more elections in order to ascertain whether it has vacillated from one election cycle to the next or has generally increased over time. Fortunately, some assessment can be made, though the data are limited to a smaller number of denominations. These data are presented in table 7.3.

Based then on data drawn from varying numbers of denominations, it would appear that, just like the case with regard to political cue-giving off the pulpit, there has not been any major growth in political cue-giving from the pulpit either. Rather, it appears that patterns are more related to the particular forms of political cue-giving that clergy may employ and to the particular election cycle examined. Some cue-giving patterns exhibit a steady increase over time: the percentage of clergy who reported that they used prayer over the past year as a means for conveying political cues, for example, increased steadily over the two-decade period of time. Some cue-giving activity, such as touching on an issue while preaching, declined between 1989 and 2001, only to increase again between 2001 and 2009, with the net result being that reported levels in 2009 of this activity are identical to those evident in 1989. Other cue-giving activity (namely, delivering a whole sermon on some public issue over the past year) declined

Table 7.2 Percentage of Clergy Providing Civic and Political Cues by Denominational Affiliation over Time

	AOG (%)	CRC (%)	DOC (%)	PCUSA (%)	RCA (%)	SBC (%)	UMC (%)
Cue-giving from the pulpit							
2001							
None	22	23	27	38	22	34	32
Some[a]	44	58	62	54	57	39	53
Most/All[b]	34	19	11	8	22	27	15
Total	100	100	100	100	101	100	100
Mean Number Acts	3.06	2.70	2.17	1.76	2.80	2.58	2.17
2009							
None	5	4	4	6	4	2	4
Some[a]	45	63	76	70	67	46	69
Most/All[b]	50	33	20	24	30	52	27
Total	100	100	100	100	101	100	100
Mean Number Acts	4.15	3.78	3.27	3.31	3.70	4.31	3.40
Cue-giving off the pulpit							
2001							
None	42	52	56	66	52	51	56
One	17	22	22	17	21	16	22
Two	41	25	22	16	28	33	23
Total	100	99	100	99	101	100	101
Mean Number Acts	0.98	0.73	0.66	0.50	0.76	0.82	0.67

(continued)

Table 7.2 (Continued)

	AOG (%)	CRC (%)	DOC (%)	PCUSA (%)	RCA (%)	SBC (%)	UMC (%)
2009							
None	26	41	35	33	41	26	41
One	24	31	25	32	26	31	30
Two	50	28	40	36	32	43	29
Total	100	100	100	101	99	100	100
Mean Number Acts	1.25	088	1.06	1.03	0.91	1.17	0.87

[a]One to four acts.
[b]Five to seven acts.

Table 7.3 **Percentage of Clergy Providing Civic and Political Cues from the Pulpit, 1989–2009**

	1989(%)	1997 (%)	2001 (%)	2005 (%)	2009 (%)
Multiple denominations					
Urged your congregation to register and vote[a]	74	y	57	y	87
Prayed publicly about an issue[a]	45	y	54	y	80
Touched on controversial issue while preaching[b]	79	y	42	y	79
Prayed publicly for political candidates[a]	18	y	42	y	64
Took a stand from pulpit on some political issue[c]	x	y	28	y	43
Preached a sermon on controversial issue[d]	40	y	10	y	18
Endorsed candidate while preaching[e]	3	y	4	y	3
Christian Reformed and Reformed Church					
Urged congregation to register and vote	x	x	56	82	79
Prayed publicly about an issue	x	x	67	91	87
Touched on a controversial issue while preaching	x	77	55	66	75
Prayed publicly for political candidates	x	46	52	64	74
Took stand from pulpit	x	48	26	41	36
Preached a sermon on controversial issue	x	26	17	25	23
Endorsed candidate while preaching	x	*	2	*	*

* = less than 1 percent.

x = not asked.

y = no survey conducted.

[a]AOG and UMC clergy only.

[b]DOC, PC USA, and SBC clergy only.

[c]Clergy from all seven denominations.

[d]DOC and PC USA clergy only.

[e]AOG, DOC, PC USA, SBC, and UMC clergy only.

between 1989 and 2001, only to increase again between 2001 and 2009, but the level of increase failed to match the previous level of decline, and, as a result, the percentage reporting that they had delivered a whole sermon addressing some public issue was far less in 2009 than in 1989. Finally, only a small percentage of clergy reported that they had endorsed some candidate from the pulpit over the past year, with the percentage remaining rather constant over time.

The bottom portion of table 7.3 provides additional data for the 1996 and 2004 election cycles so as to cover all four election years between 1996 and 2008, but this time confined to Christian Reformed and Reformed Church in America clergy. Once again, it appears that the cue-giving patterns differ depending on the particular form of political cue-giving examined and particular election cycle under consideration. Generally speaking, the overall pattern suggests no major increase in political cue-giving from the pulpit over the four election cycles, as the percentages found in the 1997 clergy survey either generally mirror the percentages found in the 2009 clergy survey or were substantially more than that found in 2009. The exception to this pattern relates to praying publicly for political candidates, which exhibits a steady increase over the sixteen-year period. Moreover, it appears that the 2000 election cycle was somewhat distinctive in terms of its relative absence of clergy cue-giving from the pulpit, as the lowest percentages found for many cue-giving activities are those in the 2001 survey.

Overall, therefore, the data presented in table 7.3 suggest that there has not been a substantial increase in clergy political cue-giving from the pulpit over the past twenty years. Rather, patterns in political cue-giving appear to be related to the particular form of political cue-giving examined and to the particular election cycle under consideration. The frequency with which clergy have employed some forms of political cue-giving from the pulpit has declined over the past twenty years, while other means by which they have done so have become more frequently utilized. As a result, the overall percentage of clergy offering political cues from the pulpit is not necessarily greater today than it was two decades ago.

Explaining Political Cue-Giving among Clergy

What variables then best account for differences in clergy patterns of political cue-giving, and how might their capacity to explain variation in political cue-giving have changed over time? These questions were addressed in a Multiple Classification Analysis that assessed the relative importance of seven independent variables in shaping political cue-giving both on and off the pulpit. These variables were: gender, age, level of seminary education, religious tradition, level of theological orthodoxy, partisan identification, and the desire to be more involved politically. The analysis of political cue-giving from the pulpit was limited to the 2001 and 2009 surveys, given the desire to compare results from all seven denominations for each form of cue-giving across each cross-section in time.

Overall, these seven variables accounted for only a modest amount of the variation evident in cue-giving—whether done from the pulpit or off the pulpit. The maximum value of R^2 reached only .10 for the former and only .13 for the latter. However, the values for R^2 increased over time, indicating that their explanatory capacity had grown with the passage of time. Moreover, the variables that best accounted for differences in cue-giving among clergy shifted with the passage of time, as some variables became more important, and others less important, in accounting for differences in political cue-giving among clergy.

Clearly, it was the desire for greater political involvement that most consistently ranked as the primary variable shaping political cue-giving—regardless of whether it occurs on or off the pulpit. Moreover, over time, the relative importance of theological orthodoxy diminished in its capacity to explain such differences, while the capacity of partisan identifications to account for differences grew. Thus, as was true with regard to expressions of clergy norms related to cue-giving and direct political action, partisan identifications have eclipsed theological orthodoxy in their capacity to explain differences among clergy related to cue-giving both on and off the pulpit.

Political Deliberation and Action within Congregational Life

Few, if any, congregations exhibit uniformity in their political thinking, as a broad range of opinions can be present along with considerable disagreement on many key issues (Djupe and Gilbert 2009). Moreover, most members of a congregation do not see their church as pursuing some specific political goal or desire that it do so (Wald, Owen, and Hill 1988; Coffin 2005).

Still, congregational life serves as an important arena for political learning and for the development of civic skills (Peterson 1992; Verba, Schlozman, and Brady 1995; Smidt et al. 2008). Participation in congregational life, like involvement in other voluntary associations, offers its members opportunities by which to generate civic skills, whether it be in terms of writing articles for the church's newsletters, chairing church committees, serving on a church council, or discussing issues during congregational meetings.

Moreover, given the presence of these differences in political opinions among congregational members, churches can be "a potentially significant (yet largely unexamined) milieu in which (political) deliberation can occur" (Djupe and Neiheisel 2008, 413). Clergy, in turn, can play a potentially "important role in promoting deliberative processes" through various means at their disposal, for example, by initiating discussions, by providing information to be used in such deliberations, and by modeling how such deliberation can be conducted (Djupe and Neiheisel 2008, 419). Thus, political cue-giving need not constitute the only means by which clergy may seek to shape the political thinking and actions of their congregants.

One means by which such deliberation might occur is through the formation of church study groups in which the dissemination of information related to an issue would be coupled with mutual discussion about that issue. If such study groups are organized and led by the pastor, then the clergyperson could well model the process of political deliberation within a pluralistic, democratic system.

Drawing upon some of the early studies of clergy, the clergy surveys have asked pastors whether they have "organized a study group in church to discuss public affairs" or have "organized an action group in church to accomplish directly some social or political goal," though these two items were not asked in the CRC and RCA clergy surveys of 1989. Certainly the wording of the item related to the formation of church action groups does not include either the word "study" or "discussion." Nevertheless, it would seem that, prior to engaging in any action to accomplish some social or political goal, members of such groups would need to engage in some background analysis and discussion of the situation to be addressed. As a result, it is likely that some level of mutual discussion transpires as well within these action groups.

The top portion of table 7.4 examines the frequency distribution of clergy-organized study and action groups across the last two surveys based on the responses of clergy from all seven denominations, whereas the bottom portion of the table presents the resultant frequency distributions when limited to the responses of clergy from the five denominations for which the questions have been asked across all three surveys. Several important points can be drawn from the table. First, like patterns related to political cue-giving, there was an increase in clergy use of both study and action groups between 2001 and 2009, but the levels to which clergy report their formation in 2009 still lags behind the levels reported in 1989. Thus, once again, the data suggest that clergy political activism is no greater today than what was evident several decades ago.

Second, clergy reports related to the use of study and action groups lag far behind their reports of engaging in other church-related political endeavors. Only 11 percent of clergy reported in 2009 that they had organized either a study or an action group in the past year, but more than twice as many clergy in 2009 reported having preached a whole sermon on some controversial issue over the same period of time (see table 7.1).

Table 7.4 **Percentage of Clergy Who Engaged in Congregational Organizing, 1989–2009**

	1989 (%)	2001 (%)	2009 (%)
Congregational organizing			
Organized study group in church	x	7	11
Organized an action group in church	x	8	11
Congregational organizing			
Organized study group in church[a]	17	7	11
Organized an action group in church[a]	14	8	11

[a]AOG, DOC, PC USA, SBC, and UMC pastors only.

In some ways, the reported levels that clergy give for organizing such groups may seem relatively low—particularly in relationship to the formation of study groups. Given the presence of adult education classes within congregational life, perhaps one might have anticipated a greater number of clergy reporting that they had formed a study group to discuss some public issue. Several factors may account for this apparently low level of church discussion groups. First, it may be a function of the time period analyzed (i.e., within the past year). Perhaps, some groups were formed at earlier points in time and continue over the course of a year or two, so that reports related to the past year simply underestimate the presence of such groups. However, when one examines whether clergy have *ever during the course of their ministry* formed such groups, one finds that only 44 percent of the clergy surveyed in 2009 reported that they had ever formed a study group, while only 35 percent reported that they had organized an action group at some time in their ministry (data not shown). Clearly, clergy are not prone to congregational organizing—even when cast simply in terms of organizing groups for the purpose of studying public issues.

However, there are several other possible explanations for these seemingly low levels of congregational organizing. Quinley (1974) regarded both forms of church organizing as types of political activity favored by the New Breed activist clergy of the 1960s. And, even in the late 1980s, major differences were evident in the formation of study and action groups between those low and those high in theological orthodoxy (Guth et al. 1997, 169)—suggesting perhaps that "group and committee formation is a characteristic liberal strategy, inculcated in Mainline seminaries (Carroll and Marler 1995, 12) and honed by experience in denominational bureaucracies" (Guth et al. 1997, 171). It is also likely that the formation and presence of such groups are a function of the size of the congregations served, with pastors serving smaller congregations being far less likely than clergy serving larger congregations to report their formation and presence.

And, in fact, both the religious tradition and size of the congregation shape the likelihood that clergy report organizing such groups, as evident in table 7.5. Regardless of religious tradition, pastors serving smaller congregations are less likely than those serving larger congregations to have organized some kind of study or action group. But, at the same time, mainline Protestant clergy are far more likely than evangelical Protestant clergy, regardless of the size of the congregation they serve, to report such organization efforts.

Moreover, these patterns hold across all three clergy surveys. Mainline Protestant clergy are generally more than twice as likely as evangelical Protestant pastors to report having organized some study or action group during the course of the past year. And, like many of the previous patterns reported, the level of clergy political activity related to organizing congregational study or action groups drops between 1989 and 2001, only to recover somewhat between 2001 and 2009—with the levels found in 2009 still falling below those reported in 1989.

Finally, most congregations offer some type of weekly adult education classes—whether on Sunday or some other day of the week. Hence, in terms of assessing the level of political deliberation that might transpire within congregations, the reported organizational endeavors by clergy to form study or action groups may well underestimate the extent to which political discussion actually occurs within the congregations they serve.

Fortunately, clergy were asked within the 2009 survey whether their adult education sessions had addressed any of nine different political issues over the course of the past year: hunger and poverty, environmental stewardship, Islam, the economy, race relations, gay rights and homosexuality, immigration, the war

Table 7.5 **Percentage of Clergy Having Organized a Study or Action Group in Past Year by Congregational Size, Controlling for Religious Tradition, 1989–2009**

Size of congregation	1989		2001		2009	
	Evangelical	*Mainline*	*Evangelical*	*Mainline*	*Evangelical*	*Mainline*
Under 50 members	7	18	5	10	7	17
50–100 members	7	25	9	13	9	22
101–250 members	9	28	6	15	6	19
251–500 members	12	37	10	15	12	31
501+ members	24	49	11	19	20	36
All sizes	12	32	8	15	10	23

in Iraq, and the 2008 presidential election. Of course, such a listing does not capture the full range of potential political issues that may have been addressed in adult education classes over the past year. But, the list does provide some insight into the relative frequency by which certain adult members of Protestant congregations may engage in political discussions in some organized fashion.

Table 7.6 presents the frequency with which clergy in 2009 reported that adult education classes in their church had addressed any one of these nine issues, and then breaks down these frequencies by the religious tradition of the pastor and their level of theological orthodoxy. First of all, it is clear that the questions related to the clergy's organizing of study and action groups do not fully capture the extent to which political matters are actually discussed within congregational life. A full 40 percent of the clergy surveyed across the seven denominations reported that their church had had during the past year an adult education class related to at least one of these nine topics. Based on this listing, the topics most frequently discussed in the churches these pastors served were those of hunger and poverty (27 percent), environmental stewardship (23 percent), and Islam (20 percent).[10]

Mainline Protestant churches were also somewhat more likely than evangelical Protestant churches to offer classes that addressed these particular political

Table 7.6 **Percentage of Congregations Addressing Selected Political Topics in Adult Education Classes during Past Year, 2009**

	ALL (%)	Religious tradition (%)		Orthodoxy (%)		
		Evangelical	Mainline	Low	Medium	High
Hunger and poverty	27	18	34	46	36	19
Environmental stewardship	23	13	30	42	31	15
Islam	20	19	22	27	24	17
Economy	17	16	18	22	16	16
Gay rights/ homosexuality	16	7	17	26	16	8
Race relations	15	13	16	20	18	12
Immigration	13	4	11	16	11	5
2008 election	8	10	7	9	7	8
War in Iraq	8	5	9	15	8	5
Any one of the above	40	32	46	59	49	32

topics. Overall, about half of the mainline clergy (46 percent) noted that their congregations had had an adult education class addressing one of these issues, whereas only one-third (32 percent) of the evangelical clergy did so.[11] However, the rank ordering of the relative frequency with which these class were offered are relatively similar for both traditions, with a larger frequency reported by mainline than evangelical Protestant clergy for each topic listed. The one exception to this pattern, however, relates to the 2008 presidential election, for which evangelical Protestant clergy were somewhat more likely than their mainline counterparts to report having had an adult education class on the matter (10 percent versus 7 percent, respectively).

Clergy who were lower in theological orthodoxy were also more likely than those higher in orthodoxy to report having had one of the classes listed. Nearly three-fifths of clergy low in orthodoxy reported such, while only one-third of clergy high in orthodoxy did so. Once again, the rank ordering of the relative frequency with which these different classes were offered is relatively similar across the different levels of theological orthodoxy exhibited by the clergyperson, though the relative frequency with which each topic was addressed monotonically declines as one moves from those clergy lower to those higher in orthodoxy. The one exception to this pattern is once again related to classes focusing on the 2008 election, as the frequencies cited by the clergy (between 7 and 9 percent) were relatively similar regardless of their level of theological orthodoxy. Interestingly, despite the fact that clergy low in theological orthodoxy were the most likely to report classes related to these particular political topics listed, they were the least likely to report having had some adult education class related to the 2008 election.

Of course, simply having a class on some topic related to public affairs does not necessarily imply that rules related to democratic deliberation were followed. Some scholars see voluntary organizations, such as churches, as unlikely places for quality deliberation to occur, as they express considerable skepticism that reasoned deliberation can transpire in religious settings (e.g., Scheufele et al. 2004; Mutz and Mondak 2006). These expectations likely stem from the fact that theorists of deliberative democracy typically caution against moral fanaticism and appeals to divine authority when engaging in public deliberation (e.g., Gutmann and Thompson 1996).

Consequently, clergy were also asked several questions in the 2009 clergy survey about the desired goals and processes in conducting these adult educational classes and forums. These particular questions addressed the relative importance of (1) having participants learn how their particular religious beliefs and values relate to the various social and political issues under discussion, (2) having a range of viewpoints being presented, (3) encouraging participants to think seriously about the opinions or others, and (4) having participants talk through their differences of opinions on the matter under discussion. The frequencies with which clergy expressed agreement with these matters are presented in table 7.7, along with how such expressions of agreement differed by the religious tradition and the theological orthodoxy of the pastors surveyed.

Almost all clergy expressed agreement with these particular goals and processes. Not surprisingly, perhaps, nearly all clergy (94 percent) expressed the desire that those participating in such classes and forums learn how their particular religious beliefs and values relate to the social and political issues under discussion. But, an equal percentage of clergy stated that is was essential for those engaging in such discussion "to talk through their differences of opinions on such matters." However, when considering the viewpoints of others, particularly those outside the congregation, there was a somewhat lower level of agreement expressed. Still nearly nine in ten clergy (87 percent) indicated that participants were encouraged "to think seriously about the opinions of others," with the lowest level of support expressed for the goal of having a range of viewpoints presented—though even here well over three out of every four pastors expressed agreement with the idea that it was "essential that a range of viewpoints be presented."

Table 7.7 **The Goals of Adult Forums within Congregational Life, 2009**

Goals of adult forums	All (%)	Religious tradition (%)		Orthodoxy (%)		
		Evangelical	Mainline	Low	Medium	High
It is essential that participants learn how their values and religious beliefs relate to social and political issues	94	92	95	98	95	93
It is essential that a range of viewpoints be presented	78	64	89	95	93	69
We explicitly encourage participants to think seriously about the opinions of others	87	79	94	97	95	82
It is essential for participants to talk through their differences of opinions on such matters	94	91	96	98	97	91

Moreover, relatively few major differences between pastors emerge when controlling for either their religious tradition or their level of theological orthodoxy. Where such differences do occur relate to the necessity of having a range of viewpoints be presented and the need for thinking seriously about the opinions of others. Evangelical clergy and those clergy high in theological orthodoxy are somewhat less likely than mainline clergy and those lower in orthodoxy to agree with these processes, but even at their lowest levels, approximately two-thirds of evangelical and highly orthodox clergy still stand in agreement that these processes be evident. In part, though not fully, these differences between evangelical and mainline clergy and between clergy high in theological orthodoxy and those lower in orthodoxy are a function of differences in levels of seminary education of the pastors surveyed (data not shown). But, regardless of these differences, it is clear that clergy overwhelming support these particular goals and processes when public issues are discussed within the life of the congregations they serve.

Conclusions

The primary mechanism by which clergy seek to influence others is that of public speech, with congregational life being the primary arena within which their political voice is exercised. This chapter therefore focused initially on the reported political cue-giving activities of clergy within congregation life, examining different means by which clergy may offer political cues during services in which congregant members gather to worship together in a public fashion.

Clergy willingly report that they engage in various forms of political cue-giving from the pulpit as a means to address social and political issues. The level of cue-giving varies by the form which such cue-giving can take. Some forms are widely employed; others are rarely employed. Clergy are more likely to report engaging in cue-giving activities that require less, rather than more, time. But, the amount of time required for such cue-giving is not the sole determinative factor shaping cue-giving, as clergy report different frequencies in cue-giving activities that require relatively similar amounts of time. Most clergy, however, report that they engage in multiple forms of political cue-giving, though a few pastors hardly engage in any political cue-giving activities at all.

Pastors also report that they engage in cue-giving behavior outside the worship context, though clergy less frequently engage in political cue-giving outside the worship context. This lower level of "off-the-pulpit" political cue-giving may be a function of ministers either having fewer opportunities to engage in these forms of public cue-giving or simply reflect a greater reluctance to engage in such behavior. But, it may also be due to the fact that far fewer questions were asked about such cue-giving behaviors outside the context of worship. Still, regardless of its basis, it appears that clergy engage in political cue-giving more frequently within, rather than outside, the congregations they serve.

Overall, the frequency with which clergy report cue-giving behavior, whether from or off the pulpit, varies with the passage of time. Although there were substantial jumps in the level to which clergy reported having engaged in political cue-giving between the 2001 and 2009 clergy surveys, the reported levels to which such cue-giving was evident during the 2008 election campaign did not match the levels evident during the 1988 election campaign. Hence, despite what may be appearances to the contrary, clergy are no more likely today to engage in political cue-giving activity than what was evident among clergy several decades ago.

Nevertheless, certain changes have occurred with regard to political cue-giving among clergy. Over time, the relative importance of partisan identifications has grown, while the relative importance of theological orthodoxy has diminished in their capacities to explain differences in the frequencies with which clergy engage in such cue-giving activity. Thus, as was evident earlier with regard to the expression of political norms, partisan identifications have overtaken theological orthodoxy in their relative contribution for explaining differences in political cue-giving among clergy.

But, the political activity of clergy within congregational life need not be limited to political cue-giving; clergy can also play an important role in encouraging the study and deliberation of public issues among congregational members. To a certain extent, these activities may be fostered by clergy organizing study and action groups within congregational life. However, the frequencies with which clergy report that they have organized such groups lag far behind the frequencies reported for engaging in various cue-giving endeavors. In part, such differences may be due to the differential amount of time and energy expended in engaging in these various endeavors, but such differences are also due to the fact that cue-giving behavior can occur regardless of the size of the congregation served, whereas congregational size has a more decided effect in shaping the likelihood of organizing study and action groups.

Regardless, clergy reports related to the formation of study and action groups fail to capture the full range of opportunities available to congregational members to engage in discussion and deliberation of public matters. Most churches provide weekly adult educational opportunities for its members, and many of these opportunities do relate to the study and discussion of current political issues of various types. In fact, given the relative presence of these various weekly classes examining public issues across the host of churches dotting the political landscape, one would likely be hard pressed to find anything similar occurring within American life that captures as many Americans engaging in such regular and frequent discussion of various public issues confronting American social and political life than that found within American congregational life.

Despite the restricted listing of only nine particular topics provided in the 2009 clergy survey, a full two-fifths of the clergy reported that an adult education class of some sort had, during the past year, addressed one of the topics listed. These classes were somewhat more likely to be offered in mainline, as opposed to evangelical, denominations, and were somewhat more likely to be found within congregations pastored by clergy lower, than higher, in theological orthodoxy. Nevertheless, both one-third of evangelical clergy and one-third of those clergy high in theological orthodoxy indicated that their congregations had had within its adult education offerings some class within the past year that addressed one of these particular matters.

Finally, Protestant clergy are highly united, regardless of religious tradition or level of theological orthodoxy, that congregational discussion of social and political issues exhibit certain qualities. These include the need for congregational members to talk through their differences of opinions related to these political matters as well as the need to take seriously about the opinions of others outside the church itself.

8

The Political Activism of Clergy

Neither denominational life nor politics is static in nature. Old patterns of clergy involvement in politics may dissipate, and new patterns may emerge over time. Changing environmental conditions (whether in terms of changing economic conditions, deteriorating social structures, increasing global interdependence, changing leadership within political parties, etc.) may affect both religious and political life, altering the way in which the two spheres interrelate. Moreover, the nature of the clergy ordained by each denomination may also change over time (as can the nature of the parishioners they serve), thereby changing the ways in which clergy may choose to relate to those whom they both serve and lead. As a result, the ways in which clergy choose to engage in politics today may well diverge from patterns evident only a decade or two previously.

Of course, clergy do not just act politically within the congregations they serve, they also engage in various forms of political action outside that context. Some of their political activity may be done in relationship to their role as clergy (e.g., participating in protest marches or engaging in civil disobedience), though other political actions may be done more as an individual citizen (e.g., voting in primary elections or contributing money to a political candidate or party). And, there are a variety of other activities for which it is unclear whether clergy are engaging in some political action in their role as clergy or as an individual citizen (e.g., contacting governmental officials, boycotting products, or becoming involved in partisan politics).

This chapter examines the political activism of clergy. Although scholars may elect to organize their analysis of clergy political activism in different ways (e.g., Guth et al. 1997; Djupe and Gilbert 2003), they are united in the recognition that clergy may choose to be engaged politically through various means. Hence, in order to fully capture the political activism of clergy, it is necessary to examine a spectrum of activities by which clergy may choose to participate.

This chapter therefore first analyzes the particular political topics clergy report they publicly address. Speech is a political action, and clergy report that they have made their views known publicly across a host of different political issues. Hence, the chapter begins with an analysis of the content of the political voice of clergy (i.e., the particular kinds of issues that clergy choose to address publicly). An examination of the issues that clergy choose to address most often is then used to reveal the particular political agendas advanced by clergy, how these agendas are advanced by different types of clergy, and how the relative emphasis given to such agendas has changed over time.

The second portion of the chapter then examines the reported political activities of clergy done outside the physical context of the congregation they serve. Here, three forms of political engagement are analyzed—namely, activities related to political campaigns, political contacting, and political protesting— along with changes in the levels to which clergy report engaging in these forms of activism to ascertain whether clergy are more politically active today than several decades ago.

The last portion of the chapter examines the partisan nature of clergy engagement in politics. It has been argued that the political actions of clergy done more directly in relationship to members of their congregations are the behaviors that collectively are most likely to have the greatest significance politically. However, not all clergy efforts in relationship to their congregants need be directed toward the same political ends, as clergy hold different theological perspectives and partisan preferences that move them in different directions politically. Consequently, even though casting a vote is a solitary act done outside the congregational context, the political preferences undergirding those clergy votes nevertheless have relevance to congregational life, as the partisan preferences of clergy likely shape and color the nature of their thoughts, speech, and actions. Consequently, the last section of the chapter examines the partisan identifications of clergy, how their identifications have changed both individually and collectively, and the partisan nature of their votes cast in presidential elections over the past two decades.

The Changing Political Speech of Clergy

Of course, knowing that clergy offer political cues, both on and off the pulpit, does not reveal anything about the content of such cues. Whether cues are offered to influence opinions on public issues, set political agendas, to mobilize parishioners to action, the primary mechanism by which such cues are delivered is through public speech (Djupe and Gilbert 2002, 596). Not surprisingly, therefore, scholars have long examined both the frequency and content of the public speech of clergy and have sought to discern just what factors may serve to shape and affect the content of such cues (Hadden 1969; Stark, Foster, Glock, and Quinley 1971; Quinley 1974; Guth et al. 1997; Olson 2000; Crawford and Olson 2001; Djupe and Gilbert 2003).

The Topics Clergy Address

Researchers have typically attempted to ascertain the content of what clergy discuss politically by providing them with a list of issues and inquiring how frequently (e.g., "never," "seldom," "often," or "very often") they have made their views publicly known related to the list of issues provided. The listing of issues tends to be topical in nature, without necessarily inquiring where the clergyperson stands politically in relationship to the particular issues provided.

It is also important to note that these questions do not inquire about the particular context within which these views have been made known. Part of the apparent discrepancies in the findings between ethnographic research and survey research is that the former has typically focused on the sermons of clergy, whereas the latter usually poses its questions more broadly, asking clergy whether they have addressed particular issues and made their views "known publicly, whether inside or outside the church." Of course, clergy can choose to address an issue without taking a position on the issue, but clergy willingly reveal that they make their views publicly known, and with some regularity, about a wide variety of different issues (e.g., Guth et al. 1997, ch. 5; Djupe and Gilbert 2003, 32–35). Thus, even though clergy may report that they only occasionally touch on political issues within their sermons, they nevertheless indicate they address particular matters of public policy with far greater frequency.

Over the three clergy surveys, clergy have been provided with a listing of twenty-five different political topics, though not every topic has been included in each of the three surveys. Table 8.1 presents the particular topics asked, and the changing percentage of clergy who report that they have made their views known either "very often" or "often" on these matters (which may be noted, for stylistic purposes, in the text as "regularly" or "frequently").

Clearly, clergy consistently report that they make their views known publicly across a wide range of issues. When asked in 1989, four-fifths of the clergy surveyed indicated that they had often addressed the issues of family decline, hunger and poverty, as well as alcohol and drug abuse, while a majority had done so related to the issues of abortion, race relations and civil rights, and pornography. However, in 2009, only one issue was addressed regularly by at least four-fifths of the clergy: the issue of hunger and poverty. But, two-thirds or more reported that they had frequently discussed publicly the issues of alcohol and drug abuse, race relations and civil rights, and unemployment and the economy, while a majority noted that they had frequently addressed pornography, family decline, domestic violence, abortion, religious persecution abroad, and gender equity. Thus, given the particular issues listed, there were more instances in 2009 than in 1989 in which a majority of clergy reported having made their views publicly known

Table 8.1 **Percentage of Clergy Addressing Specific Public Policy Issues "Often" over Time**

Policy issue	1989 (%)	2001 (%)	2009 (%)
Family decline	83	56	57
Alcohol and drug abuse	80	72	72
Hunger and poverty	80	78	82
Abortion	59	58	54
Pornography	54	56	58
Race/civil rights	53	71	68
Environmental problems	50	39	47
Unemployment, the economy	41	x	66
Defense	37	18	33
Gender Equity	34	55	51
Gay rights, homosexuality	32	49	49
Gambling	32	35	33
School prayer	31	37	34
Israel and the Middle East	28	39	43
Capital punishment	28	25	23
Domestic violence	x	54	54
Religious persecution abroad	x	48	53
Issues of aging	x	36	43
Scandals in government	x	35	x
Public education	x	33	35
Health care	x	33	38
Gun laws	x	21	15
Immigration	x	15	27
The war in Iraq, terrorism	x	x	46
Budget policy, taxes	x	x	27

Note: Cell entries report responses for "often" or "very often".

concerning these specified issues. In other words, more clergy today are talking more frequently about more political issues than was true two decades ago.

What particular kinds of issues, then, appear to be discussed with greater regularity by clergy today compared to several decades ago? In other words, what particular types of issues have waned, while others issue have gained, in terms of the frequency with which clergy report they have addressed them? Basically, it appears that the issues which clergy report they address far more regularly now compared to two decades ago (i.e. those issues for which there has been a 10 percent or more increase) are those that relate largely to what might be labeled matters of "justice" and "equality," in that they involve the issues of unemployment, race and civil rights, gender equity, gay rights, and Israel and the Middle East. Conversely, the only issue for which there has been a 10 percent or more drop is that of "family decline."

Still, to address some topic and make one's views publicly known about the matter does not necessarily indicate where one stands on the issue. For example, some of the clergy who report they have made their views known about capital punishment may oppose the practice, while others may favor it. And, this is the case. Among those clergy who reported in 2009 that they had frequently addressed the topic of capital punishment, 42 percent later[1] agreed with the statement "I oppose capital punishment," whereas 55 percent disagreed (data not shown).[2] The same is true in terms of the topic of gay rights/homosexuality: 49 percent of the clergy who indicated they had regularly discussed the matter later agreed with the statement "Homosexuals should have all the same rights and privileges as other Americans," while 44 percent expressed disagreement (data not shown).[3]

However, for many issues, those who usually address a topic with some regularity tend, generally speaking, to adopt a particular stance related to that issue when compared to those who rarely, if ever, address the topic. For example, 78 percent of those clergy who reported in 2009 that they had frequently addressed the topic of abortion later agreed with the statement that a constitutional amendment was needed "prohibiting all abortions unless necessary to save the mother's life or in case of rape or incest," whereas only 12 percent did so among those who reported that they never addressed the issue (data not shown). The same is true with regard to environmental stewardship; most clergy (69 percent) who regularly addressed the topic agreed that "more environmental protection is needed, even if it raises prices or costs jobs," whereas among those who never addressed the issue, relatively few (15 percent) did so (data not shown).

The Two-Agenda Thesis

Because those addressing a particular topic with regularity frequently adopt policy positions on that issue that differ from those who discuss the matter far less regularly, scholars have used clergy reports about the issues they regularly address as a means to discern the particular political agendas they advance. Typically, these agendas are divided into two broad categories: a "moral reform agenda" and a "social justice agenda" (e.g., Beatty and Walter 1989; Hofrenning 1995; Guth et al. 1997; Djupe and Gilbert 2003). The assignment of specific issue topics to each of these agendas is frequently done by statistical means,[4] though sometimes it is done simply by assigning issues to one agenda or the other.

The research literature on clerical politics conducted during the 1960s and 1970s generally revealed the presence of these two different agendas, with mainline clergy usually advancing the social justice agenda and evangelical clergy typically advancing the moral reform agenda (e.g., Stark et al. 1971; Quinley 1974). And, despite scholarly contentions that the political agendas of evangelicals had broadened during the 1980s (e.g., Buzzard 1989; Himmelstein 1990; Reed 1996), the different political agendas advanced by evangelical and mainline Protestant pastors continued to remain largely intact even by the end of the 1980s (Guth et al. 1997, 94).

Perhaps then, with the additional passage of time, the two-agenda thesis may now be less evident than it was several decades ago. In order to ascertain whether this is the case, measures of the two agendas were created, with each agenda based on four component items.[5] The moral reform agenda was tapped by the frequency with which pastors reported that they had regularly addressed the issues of abortion, pornography, the decline of the nuclear family, and school prayer, while the social justice agenda was tapped by regularity with which the issues of hunger and poverty, gender equity, race relations, and the environment were addressed. The extent to which clergy promoted a particular agenda was measured by an additive index based on the number of issues clergy reported they had addressed "often" related to that agenda.

Has, then, the frequency with which Protestant clergy addressed these different agendas changed over time? As table 8.2 reveals, slightly less than half of the clergy in 1989 (47 percent) reported that they had frequently expressed their views on most of the issues of the moral agenda, with the percentage holding rather steady, though decreasing slightly, between 1989 and 2009. More significantly, however, the percentage of clergy who report that they only infrequently, if ever, addressed any of these four issues, increased from 9 percent in 1989 to 22 percent in 2009.

Similarly, nearly half of the pastors surveyed in 1989 (44 percent) reported that they had regularly addressed most or all of the component issues of the social justice agenda. But, in contrast to the moral reform agenda, the percentage of clergy who expressed their views on most of the social justice issues grew over the next twenty years (from 44 percent to 55 percent), while the percentage of clergy reporting that they had not regularly addressed any of the component issues declined over the same period of time (from 15 to 11 percent).

Table 8.2 **The Changing Percentage of Clergy Addressing Moral Reform and Social Justice Agenda Issues over Time**

	1989 (%)	*2001 (%)*	*2009 (%)*
Moral reform agenda			
Addressed none	9	19	22
Addressed some[a]	44	36	33
Addressed most or all[b]	47	44	45
Total	100	99	100
Social justice agenda			
Addressed none	15	12	11
Addressed some[a]	41	33	34
Addressed most or all[b]	44	54	55
Total	100	99	100

Note: Moral Reform Agenda: abortion, school prayer, family decline, pornography; Social Justice Agenda: hunger, civil rights, gender equity, environment.

[a]Addressed one or two issues often.

[b]Addressed three or four issues often.

Of course, table 8.2 does not reveal anything about the nature of the relationship between the moral reform agenda and the social justice agenda. Do some clergy, for example, remain largely silent on both agendas? Or, do some clergy address the social justice agenda and largely ignore the moral reform agenda, while other clergy do the converse?

One means by which to assess the relationship between the two agendas is to examine some net level of emphasis given to one agenda over the other, simply by subtracting the total number of issues frequently addressed in relationship to one agenda from the total number of issues frequently addressed in the other. These results are presented in table 8.3.

Clearly, there is both change and stability evident in the political agendas addressed by Protestant clergy over time. In terms of stability, approximately the same proportions of clergy have exhibited a "balanced" pattern of emphasis, in which clergy report addressing an equal number of issues from both agendas (or not addressing any of the issues from either agenda). About one-fifth of clergy did so in 1989, and the same is true in 2001 and 2009. On the other hand, the percentage of clergy who have exhibited a predominantly social justice emphasis in their political agendas increased over time (from 23 percent in 1989 to 31 percent in 2009), while the percentage of clergy emphasizing a moral reform agenda declined (from 25 percent in 1989 to 18 percent in 2009)

Table 8.3 **The Relative Balance of Issue Agenda Emphasis over Time**

	1989 (%)	*2001 (%)*	*2009 (%)*
Predominantly social justice[a]	23	31	31
Marginally social justice[b]	15	15	15
Balanced[c]	21	21	20
Marginally moral reform[b]	17	15	16
Predominantly moral reform[a]	25	19	18
Total	101	101	100

[a]Given the four issues associated with each agenda, a marginal difference represents a net difference of addressing one additional topic within the agenda than within the other agenda.

[b]Given the four issues associated with each agenda, a predominant difference represents a net difference of addressing two or more additional topics within the agenda than within the other agenda.

[c]A balanced score represents addressing an equal number of topics within each agenda.

Explaining Differences in Clergy Agendas

Previous research has found that both the gender of clergy and their level of theological orthodoxy shape the likelihood of clergy addressing a particular political agenda (e.g., Guth et al. 1997, ch. 5; Djupe and Gilbert 2003, 35), and that personal motivations have greater direct effects on clergy public speech than either congregational or denominational influences (Neiheisel and Djupe 2008, 438).[6] Have these relationships, then, strengthened or weakened over time? Table 8.4 addresses this question.

Female clergy have been found to be far more prone than male clergy to focus on social justice issues (Olson, Crawford, and Guth 2000; Crawford, Deckman, and Braun 2001; Djupe and Gilbert 2003, 34–35), and this tendency has only grown over time, as the percentage of female clergy focusing predominantly on issues related to the social justice agenda jumped significantly between 1989 and 2009 (from 49 percent to 67 percent). Though the corresponding percentage among male clergy has also grown, it only grew from 22 percent to 26 percent over that same period of twenty years. Consequently, given these differential rates of growth, even though the "social justice" gap between male and female clergy was already sizable in 1989, it has now become even more pronounced.

Previous research has also shown that those clergy higher in theological orthodoxy are more likely to emphasize the moral reform agenda, while those lower in orthodoxy are more prone to emphasize the social justice agenda (Guth et al. 1997, ch. 5; Djupe and Gilbert 2003, 34; Deckman et al. 2003). And, as shown in table 8.4, a strong relationship between theological orthodoxy and

Table 8.4 **Issue Agendas by Gender and Theological Orthodoxy over Time**

	Gender (%)		Theological orthodoxy (%)		
	Female	Male	Low	Medium	High
1989					
Predominantly social justice[a]	49	22	58	33	4
Marginally social justice[b]	20	14	23	23	7
Balanced[c]	14	21	14	24	21
Marginally moral reform[b]	6	18	3	12	25
Predominantly moral reform	12	26	1	7	42
Total	101	101	99	99	99
	r = .13		r = .65		
2001					
Predominantly social justice[a]	58	27	76	45	10
Marginally social justice[b]	16	15	15	22	12
Balanced[c]	14	22	8	20	25
Marginally moral reform[b]	4	16	1	7	22
Predominantly moral reform[a]	8	20	1	5	30
Total	100	100	101	99	99
	r = .22		r = .61		
2009					
Predominantly social justice[a]	67	26	83	52	10
Marginally social justice[b]	16	16	11	21	15
Balanced[c]	10	21	5	17	25
Marginally moral reform[b]	5	17	1	6	23
Predominantly moral reform[a]	3	20	0	3	28
Total	101	100	100	99	101
	r = .28		r = .63		

[a]Given the four issues associated with each agenda, a marginal difference represents a net difference of addressing one additional topic within the agenda than within the other agenda.

[b]Given the four issues associated with each agenda, a predominant difference represents a net difference of addressing two or more additional topics within the agenda than within the other agenda.

[c]A balanced score represents addressing an equal number of topics within each agenda.

issue agenda was evident in 1989, as those scoring low in theological orthodoxy were far more likely than those scoring high to place a greater (either marginal or predominant) emphasis on the social justice agenda, with the converse being true in relationship to the moral reform agenda. And, though there has been a growth in an emphasis on the social justice agenda among clergy high in orthodoxy, the gap in emphasis previously evident between those low and those high in theological orthodoxy nevertheless continues to remain much the same today.

What variables then best account for differences in the political agendas advanced by clergy, and to what extent, if at all, have such relationships changed over time? Here, as in the previous chapters, a Multiple Classification Analysis (MCA) was conducted to track the relative importance of different variables in explaining the differences in addressing issues related to the moral reform and social justice agendas.

For this MCA, seven independent variables are examined: gender, age, seminary education, religious tradition, theological orthodoxy, partisan identification, and desire for greater political involvement (see table 8.5). In 1989, theological orthodoxy served as the primary factor shaping differences in the political agendas advanced by Protestant clergy (beta = .36), with partisan identification ranking second in importance (beta = .26) and seminary education ranking a distant third in relative importance (beta = .14). However, over time, the relative importance of both theological orthodoxy and seminary education has declined in importance, while partisan identifications have grown in importance. As a result, the partisan identifications of clergy (beta = .41) have now

Table 8.5 **Explaining the Issue Agendas of Clergy**

	Net agenda		
	1989	*2001*	*2009*
Gender	.03	.02	.05
Age	.03	.01	.06
Seminary education	14	.12	.05
Religious tradition	.13	.11	.12
Theological orthodoxy	.36	.30	.28
Partisan identification	.26	.35	.41
Desire for involvement	.09	.02	.02
R^2	.51	.50	.55

replaced their theological orientations (beta = .26) as the most important factor shaping differences in the political agendas advanced by clergy. Thus, once again, just as was true with regard to the norms that clergy express and the political cue-giving they report, the partisan identifications of clergy have now eclipsed theological orthodoxy in serving as the major factor shaping the political agendas advanced by clergy.

The Political Activism of Clergy

As is true with American citizens as a whole, there are a variety of ways by which one can choose to become engaged politically (e.g., writing letters to the editors of newspapers, voting, or boycotting products). Table 8.6 presents the reports of clergy concerning whether they had, over the past year, engaged in any of fifteen

Table 8.6 **Percentage of Clergy Who Engaged in Direct Political Actions, 2001 and 2009**

	1989 (%)	2001 (%)	2009 (%)
Political campaigning			
Voted in presidential election	x	96	98
Voted in presidential primary	x	70	79
Publicly supported a political candidate	x	30	42
Contributed money to candidate, party, or PAC	x	20	31
Tried to persuade a friend or colleague	x	x	23
Displayed a campaign button, yard sign	x	15	22
Attended a political rally	x	12	17
Joined a national political organization	x	11	16
Actively campaigned for a party or candidate	x	7	12
Political contacting			
Contacted a public official	x	35	50
Signed a petition	x	39	43
Wrote a letter to editor/op-ed piece	x	18	16
Political protesting			
Boycotted a product	x	22	24
Participated in a protest march	x	6	6
Practiced civil disobedience	x	2	1

different political actions organized under three different categories: political campaigning, political contacting, and political protesting. Although some questions concerning political activism were asked of clergy in 1989,[7] a more extensive battery of activism questions was inaugurated in 2001. Hence, table 8.6 presents data for 2001 and 2009 only, in order to examine this greater breadth of the possible political activities in which clergy might engage.

Two particular patterns are clearly evident in the data presented. First, outside the acts of casting votes in terms of presidential primaries or presidential elections, the most frequently reported activities that clergy report having done are those related to political contacting, particularly in terms of contacting public officials and signing petitions. Some other campaign activities are also widely reported (e.g., publicly supporting a political candidate), but for the most part, less than one-quarter of all clergy surveyed typically report having engaged in any of the fifteen activities examined over the course of the past year.[8] Depending on one's basis of comparisons, these levels of reported activity may seem relative high, or hardly distinctive, in nature. On the one hand, the levels to which clergy report engaging in these various activities is likely to be much higher than those reported by most Americans. But, when compared to the level of activism exhibited by other highly educated leaders and professionals within American civic life, these levels of activism are hardly likely to be particularly distinctive in nature.

Second, clergy were far more politically active in 2009 than in 2001. For eleven of the fifteen activities examined, a higher percentage of clergy in 2009 than in 2001 reported that they had engaged in the activity during the previous year. The only endeavors not exhibiting an increase between the two points in time are participation in a protest march, writing a letter to an editor, and having engaged in civil disobedience. Some increases in activism were rather dramatic (e.g., contacting a public official, publicly supporting a political candidate, and contributing money), while other increases were less so. Nevertheless, overall, clergy were far more likely to report that they had engaged in a variety of political endeavors in 2009 than in 2001.

Given the increased polarization evident in American politics, these data may seem to suggest that clergy are far more politically engaged today than clergy several decades ago. However, this does not appear to be the case. Table 8.7 presents data comparing responses of clergy from five denominations related to a more limited number of political activism questions asked across all three clergy surveys. Clearly, these data do not reveal any consistent increase in the political activism of clergy between 1989 and 2009. What appear to be rather dramatic surges in activism between 2001 and 2009 are not so dramatic when examined in the context of clergy activism reported in 1989. The only activity exhibiting a monotonic increase across the three points in time was voting in presidential

Table 8.7 **Percentage of Clergy Who Engaged in Direct Political Actions over Time**

	1989 (%)	2001 (%)	2009 (%)
Political campaigning			
Voted in presidential election	98	96	98
Voted in presidential primary	63	70	79
Publicly supported a presidential candidate[a]	41	30	45
Contributed money to candidate, party, or PAC[a]	28	20	34
Joined a national political organization[a]	17	10	17
Political contacting			
Contacted a public official[a]	47	34	53
Political protesting			
Participated in a protest march[a]	6	6	6
Practiced civil disobedience[a]	2	2	2

[a]AOG, DOC, PC USA, SBC, UMC pastors only.

primaries, as the percentage of pastors reporting they had cast a presidential primary vote jumped from 63 percent in 1989 to 78 percent in 2009. Part of this increase, however, can be attributed to the growth in the number of presidential primaries that transpired over this period of time, as fewer states held presidential primaries in 1988 than in 2008 (Hagen and Mayer 2000; Hershey 2013, 193).

Moreover, most of the activities examined in table 8.7 reveal a decline in clergy activism between 1989 and 2001, only to be followed by a jump in activism between 2001 and 2009. Not all forms of activism exhibit fluctuation over time. A small, but rather constant, percentage of clergy report engaging in political protesting activities, but other forms of clergy activism, particularly in terms of political campaigning behavior, tend to be much more election specific— waxing and waning depending on the issues or candidates associated with the particular election examined. And, though the percentages of clergy reporting some campaign endeavors are greater in 2009 than in 1989, they are only marginally greater, hardly suggesting any dramatic surge in clergy activism over time.

Thus, overall, the level of political activism over the past year reported in clergy in 2009 largely mirrors the levels of activism reported by clergy in 1989. Some increases in political activism (e.g., voting in presidential primaries) are more a function of opportunity structures than changes in clergy activism per se, whereas other increases between 1989 and 2009 are rather modest in scope

(6 percent or less), masking substantial declines in activity between 1989 and 2001 and substantial increases in activity between 2001 and 2009. And, still other forms of political action exhibit patterns of stability over each of the three surveys. Consequently, the data suggest that there has not been any major increase in clergy political activism over the past several decades; rather, activism tends to wax and wane depending more on the political environment at the time.

The Changing Partisanship of Protestant Clergy

To what partisan ends have these clergy activities likely been directed? Of course, not all political endeavors necessarily encompass specific partisan ends, as some goals may be more related toward the implementation of specific policy matters than to the particular fortunes of specific political parties. Nevertheless, in American politics, it is the two major political parties that dominate the organization of government and constitute the major actors in proposing, implementing, and administering public policies. Hence, knowing the partisan preferences and inclinations of clergy provides important insights related to the particular political ends for which clergy likely direct their political endeavors.

The Changing Partisan Identifications of Clergy

Collective-Level Change

Partisan identifications have been at the center of most scholarly analyses that examine the political attitudes and behavior of the American electorate. This is because they reveal "more about (an individual's) political attitudes and behavior than does any other single piece of information" (Hershey 2013, 109): partisan identifications structure political perceptions, forge positions on political issues, and shape evaluations of political candidates (Campbell, Gurin, and Miller 1954; Campbell et al. 1960). Nevertheless, over time, generational replacement can shift the collective partisan identifications of clergy, as newer clergy who have had different socialization experiences enter the ranks of ministry and replace older pastors who are retiring and exiting its ranks.

And, over the past two decades, important changes have occurred in the collective partisan identifications[9] of Protestant clergy. Earlier research using the 1989 clergy survey noted that "many clergy shun strong party ties and prefer an independent or, more often, an independent-leaning classification" (Guth et al. 1997, 118). And, as can be seen from table 8.8, once all independents are classified together, they constituted nearly a majority of the clergy surveyed in 1989 (49 percent). However, over the past several decades, the percentage of clergy

Table 8.8 **The Changing Partisan Identifications of Protestant Clergy over Time**

Partisan identification	1989 (%)	2001 (%)	2009 (%)
Strong Democrat	13	15	17
Weak Democrat	9	8	6
Independent, Leaning Democratic	15	11	12
Independent	10	9	9
Independent, Leaning Republican	24	15	16
Weak Republican	13	16	15
Strong Republican	17	27	26
Total	101	101	101

who claim to be political independents has dropped considerably—from nearly half of the pastors in 1989 to a little more than one-third of the clergy in 2009.

Second, the overall shift in partisan identifications among Protestant clergy has been in a more Republican, than Democratic, direction. Given the seven denominations from which clergy were surveyed, a somewhat higher percentage of clergy in 1989 claimed to be Republican than Democratic in their partisan identifications (30 percent versus 22 percent, respectively), but by 2009 that Republican advantage over Democratic identifiers was even greater (41 percent compared to 23 percent).

Finally, the percentage of pastors claiming strong partisan identifications has also grown, as there has been a monotonic increase in the percentage of clergy claiming to be strong Republicans as well as strong Democrats. In fact, the combined percentage of strong party identifiers has increased from 30 percent in 1989 to 42 percent in 2009, so that a plurality of clergy now express strong partisan preferences. Thus, just as was the case in relationship to ideological orientations, Protestant clergy are now far more polarized politically than was the case several decades ago.

Individual-Level Change

The status of partisan identifications being understood as "causally prior" to other political attitudes and behavior stems, in part, from seminal studies in the field which revealed that partisan identifications were typically acquired relatively early in life, and once formed, tended to be relatively stable in nature (Campbell et al. 1960; Greenstein 1965; Beck and Jennings 1991). And, this scholarly perspective continues to hold true even today (e.g., Green, Palmquist,

and Schickler 2002; Hershey 2013, 110). Nevertheless, even though party identifications are generally viewed as rather enduring orientations, they are subject to change—particularly during periods of time in which groups of voters
undergo either dealignment[10] or realignment[11] with the two major parties (e.g.,
Key 1955, 1959; Burnham 1970; Petrocik 1981; Shafer 1991; Lawrence 1997;
Rosenof 2003).

In order to ascertain the extent to which clergy have shifted their own partisan identifications over time, a party change score was calculated by tallying
just how far, and in which partisan direction, ministers have moved along the
seven-point partisan scale between their present partisan identification and
what identification they reportedly held at age 21 (see table 8.9). For purposes
of presentation, those shifting one or two points on the seven-point scale were
classified as "weak" movers in the table, while those who moved three or more
points along the scale were deemed to have changed substantially and were
labeled "strong" movers.

Clearly, as the data reveal, many clergy report that their own partisan identifications have shifted over time. In the 1989 clergy survey, only 18 percent of
the clergy reported that their current location on the seven-point partisan identification scale was the same as when they were 21 years of age. Of those who
moved, nearly half moved "weakly" in one partisan direction or the other—
with a larger percentage moving in a more Republican than Democratic direction (29 percent versus 19 percent, respectively). However, slightly more than
one-third moved rather substantially in a different partisan direction, with a
slightly higher percentage once again having moved on a more Republican than
Democratic direction (19 percent versus 15 percent, respectively).

No question related to partisan identification at age 21 was asked in the
2001 clergy survey, but the item was once again included in the 2009 clergy
survey. And, the patterns found in 2009 are far different from those evident
twenty years earlier. First, far fewer clergy in 2009 than in 1989 reported shifts
in their partisan identifications: only 18 percent of clergy reported no change
in 1989, but 44 percent did so in 2009. Second, far fewer substantial shifts in
partisan identifications were reported in 2009 when compared to 1989: more
than one-third of the clergy reported substantial shifts in their partisan identifications in 1989, but only 8 percent did so in 2009. Finally, to the extent
that these shifts moved more in one partisan direction than the other, the
data in 2009 reveal, in contrast to previous patterns, a slight net advantage
for the Democratic, rather than the Republican, Party. Clearly, far more partisan change was reported in the lives of clergy who ministered during the late
1980s than among clergy during the waning years of the first decade of the
twenty-first century.

Table 8.9 **The Shifting Direction of Partisan Identification Change by Selected Variables**

	Direction of Partisan Identification Change (%)					
	Strongly Democratic	*Weakly Democratic*	*No Change*	*Weakly Republican*	*Strongly Republican*	*Total*
1989						
All	15	19	18	29	19	100
Gender						
Female	31	28	20	9	12	100
Male	14	18	18	30	19	99
Age						
Young	16	19	18	29	19	101
Middle-Aged	17	19	19	29	16	100
Old	11	18	19	30	22	100
Religious tradition						
Evangelical	7	13	20	36	25	100
Mainline	21	23	18	24	14	100
Theological orthodoxy						
Low	36	31	16	12	5	100
Medium	18	26	21	24	11	100
High	6	11	18	39	27	101
2009						
All	4	25	44	23	4	100
Gender						
Female	7	30	44	17	1	99
Male	4	24	44	23	5	100
Age						
Young	4	38	39	19	1	101
Middle-Aged	3	26	45	23	4	101
Old	5	20	45	24	6	100

(*continued*)

Table 8.9 (Continued)

	Direction of Partisan Identification Change (%)					
	Strongly Democratic	*Weakly Democratic*	*No Change*	*Weakly Republican*	*Strongly Republican*	*Total*
Religious tradition						
Evangelical	2	21	45	27	6	101
Mainline	6	28	44	20	3	101
Theological orthodoxy						
Low	10	28	50	12	0	100
Medium	7	33	39	19	3	101
High	1	21	45	27	6	100

The extent to which partisan change has occurred among different categories of clergy is also examined in the same table. As the data reveal, most female clergy reported in 1989 that they had moved their partisan identifications in a more Democratic, than Republican, direction, as nearly three times as many female clergy reported shifting in a Democratic than a Republican direction. In fact, a far greater number of clergywomen reported that they had moved in a strongly Democratic direction (31 percent) than in any Republican direction combined (21 percent). The converse, however, was true among male clergy; a far higher percentage of male clergy in 1989 reported becoming more Republican than more Democratic in their identifications (49 versus 32 percent, respectively). And, though far less partisan change was evident among clergy in 2009, clergy-women continued to report that they had moved in a more Democratic than Republican direction (37 percent versus 18 percent, respectively), whereas smaller, but similar, percentages of male clergy reported having moved from one party to the other in their partisan identifications.

When one examines partisan change among clergy in terms of age, religious tradition, and level of theological orthodoxy, similar patterns occur. First, regardless of the clergyperson's social or religious characteristics, far more partisan change was evident among clergy in 1989 than in 2009. Second, in terms of age, clergy across all age groups reported in 1989 that, over their lifetime, they had moved in a more Republican than a Democratic direction, but in 2009 nearly twice as many young clergy reported that they had moved in a more Democratic than Republican direction. Third, regardless of the year of the survey, a higher

percentage of evangelical Protestant clergy reported that their partisan identifications had moved more in a Republican than a Democratic partisan direction,
while the converse is true among mainline Protestant clergy.

Finally, partisan change in relationship to theological orthodoxy has been
consistent over time, as those low in orthodoxy have tended to move in a
Democratic direction, while those higher in orthodoxy have generally moved
in a more Republic direction. What has changed, however, is the magnitude of
the consistency of differences—particularly among the theologically orthodox.
In 1989, nearly two-thirds of those clergy who scored high in theological orthodoxy reported movement toward the Republican Party, while less than one-fifth
reported movement toward the Democratic Party (with nearly identical percentages, but in a reversed partisan direction, for those who scored low in theological
orthodoxy). In 2009, the balance in partisan shifts among those high in theological orthodoxy continued to advantage the Republican over the Democratic
Party, but the ratio was far smaller (being only 3:2 in 2009 compared to nearly
4:1 in 1989).

What variables, then, best account for the partisan identifications held by
Protestant clergy and for the partisan changes they report? Earlier studies have
revealed that, at the bivariate level, these partisan identifications are associated
with a variety of attitudes and social characteristics, with the political ideology
of clergy having the strongest correlation with their party identifications (Guth
et al. 1997, 124). Consequently, a MCA was conducted on the partisan identifications as well as the level and nature of partisan change among Protestant
clergy over time. In this instance, however, political ideology was used in addition to gender, age, seminary education, religious tradition, and theological
orthodoxy as the independent variables in the analysis, with the results presented in table 8.10.

In terms of explaining the current partisan identifications of Protestant clergy,
the two ideational variables (i.e., ideology and theology) exhibit the strongest
beta coefficients in 1989, though ideology far surpasses theology in terms of
accounting for the expressed identifications of clergy. But, even when ideology
is taken into account, the level of theological orthodoxy expressed by clergy still
contributes to accounting for variation in the dependent variable. But, once ideology and theology are taken into account, the additional variation explained by
gender, age, and seminary education becomes fairly minimal in nature.

The relative importance of political ideology in accounting for the partisan
identifications of Protestant clergy has only grown over time, as the beta coefficient for political ideology has grown monotonically from .54 in 1989 to .69 in
2009. The relative importance of theological orthodoxy, on the other hand, has
diminished somewhat (from a beta of .19 in 1989 to .15 in 2009), but retains its
status as being the second most important variable in accounting for the partisan

Table 8.10 **Explaining Partisan Identification and Partisan Change of Protestant Clergy over Time**

	Partisan Identifications			Partisan Change		
	1989	2001	2009	1989	2001	2009
Gender	.00	.04	.03	.01	x	.02
Age	.03	.03	.03	.05	x	.10
Seminary education	.01	.02	.03	.04	x	.07
Religious tradition	.01	.06	.05	.01	x	.00
Theological orthodoxy	.19	.13	.15	.18	x	.04
Political ideology	.54	.65	.69	.44	x	.38
R^2	.47	.63	.70	.33	x	.16

identifications of clergy. Only marginal changes are evident with regard to the beta coefficients for the other variables contained in the analysis, though the relative importance of religious tradition has grown over the two-decade period of time despite trailing considerably behind theological orthodoxy in relative importance.[12] Overall, however, the six-variable model has grown considerably in its ability to account for the partisan identifications of Protestant clergy, as the values of R^2 have monotonically increased over the three surveys from accounting for 47 percent of the variance in 1989 to 70 percent in 2009.

When using these same six independent variables to account for the direction and magnitude of reported lifetime changes in clergy partisan identifications, several similar, but also several different, patterns emerge. Since contemporary party alignments among clergy are predominantly ideological in nature, changes in partisan identification likely reflect these influences—and such is the case. Clearly, in 1989, the ideological orientations of clergy best account for reported changes in partisan identifications; theological orthodoxy, while ranking second in relative importance, trails significantly behind ideology in accounting for these reported shifts. And, while the age of clergy ranked third in 1989 in relative importance, it trailed significantly behind theological orthodoxy in terms of the magnitude of its beta coefficient, with gender and religious tradition contributing little to the explained variation.

Not surprisingly, then, ideological orientations continued to rank as the most important variable in accounting for the more limited level of lifetime partisan changes reported by clergy in 2009. But, by 2009, neither of the two religious variables, theological orthodoxy or religious tradition, contributed much to such reported changes. Rather, it was now age (beta = .10) and seminary education (beta = .07) that ranked second and third, respectively, in relative importance, with younger clergy and higher educated clergy moving in a more Democratic direction in terms of their political party identifications.

The Changing Partisan Vote of Protestant Clergy

Although partisan identifications shape voting behavior, the two variables are analytically distinct. Hence, knowing the changing distribution of partisan identifications among clergy does not necessarily reveal how such clergy may choose to cast their votes over time. Every four years, each major political party puts forth a candidate for the general election campaign as their nominee to serve as the President of the United States, and though the issue positions advanced by the nominees of the two major parties are not likely to change substantially from one presidential election to the next, the social and religious characteristics of the nominees can. And, these social and religious characteristics of the presidential candidates can also affect one's voting decisions (e.g., Smidt et al. 2010). Thus, even though partisan identifications strongly shape presidential vote choice, they do not fully determine them. Hence, the presidential voting patterns of Protestant clergy may reflect, but not fully mirror, the partisan identifications they express.

Table 8.11 presents the reported presidential vote choices of clergy across five presidential elections between 1989 and 2009. Although a couple of the presidential reports are based on recall data approximately four years after having cast the vote, it is not likely, given the highly educated nature of clergy and the high level of political interest they exhibit, that these recollections are very problematic in terms of being incorrect.

Overall, given the seven denominations under study, Protestant clergy have consistently cast a greater percentage of their ballots for Republican, than Democratic, presidential candidates. In 1989, three-fifths of the clergy surveyed

Table 8.11 **Vote for President over Time**

	1989 (%)	1992 (%)	1996 (%)	2000 (%)	2004 (%)	2008 (%)
Presidential Vote						
Democrat	37	x	34[a]	30	30[b]	38
No vote, other	4	x	9	10	8	7
Republican	60	x	57	60	62	54
Total	101	100	100	100	99	

[a]Based on recall drawn from the 2001 survey.
[b]Based on recall drawn from the 2009 survey.
x = no survey data.

indicated that they had voted for George H. Bush, while slightly more than one-third reported having cast their ballots for Michael Dukakis. A decade later, the same proportion of clergy reported that they had voted George W. Bush in the 2000 presidential election, but the percentage of clergy casting ballots for Al Gore was far smaller than it had been for Dukakis. And, though Protestant clergy still voted overwhelmingly Republican in 2008, Barack Obama secured the highest percentage of Democratic votes across the five presidential elections, as John McCain fared the most poorly of all the Republican nominees examined.

In part, these somewhat shifting partisan percentages are colored by a growing percentage of clergy who report that they have cast their ballot for a third party candidate. Given the voting turnout reports found in table 8.7, one can discern from table 8.11 that 2 percent of the Protestant clergy surveyed in 1989 reported that they had voted for a third-party candidate in the 1988 election. But, a far higher percentage of clergy have cast their ballots for third-party candidates more recently. In 2001, 6 percent of the clergy surveyed reported voting for a third party candidate in the 2000 presidential election—most likely at the expense of Al Gore—whereas 5 percent did so in the 2008 presidential election.

In seeking to ascertain which clergy were most likely to have swung their votes between the 2004 and 2008 elections, almost all (97 percent) of those clergy who voted for Kerry in 2004 reported having voted for Obama in the 2008 (data not shown). On the other hand, there were far greater defections among 2004 Bush voters, as 14 percent of Bush voters reported that they had cast their ballot for Obama in the 2008 presidential election (data not shown). These swings to Obama were far more pronounced among female than male clergy, among younger than older clergy, among mainline than evangelical clergy, and among those lower than those high in theological orthodoxy.

The Changing Sources of Clergy Partisan Voting

Finally, in order to assess changes in the relative importance of variables shaping the presidential votes of Protestant clergy, an MCA analysis was conducted using the same independent variables used previously in table 8.10, but this time substituting the partisan identifications of clergy in place of their reported ideological orientations. This analysis is presented in table 8.12.

As one would have expected given previous research, the partisan identifications of clergy overwhelm all other factors in shaping the presidential vote choices of Protestant clergy. When partisan identifications are dropped from the model, the magnitude of the beta scores for theological orthodoxy (approximately .55) are more than five times greater than those for the other remaining variables (data not shown). But, when such identifications are included, the

Table 8.12 **Explaining the Presidential Vote of Protestant Clergy over Time**

	1989	*2001*	*2009*
Gender	.03	.01	.01
Age	.01	.02	.02
Seminary education	.05	.01	.05
Religious tradition	.04	.03	.03
Theological orthodoxy	.19	.15	.09
Partisan identification	.66	.75	.77
R^2	.68	.77	.74

magnitude of the beta coefficients for theological orthodoxy drops considerably. Thus, to the extent that theological perspectives, religious tradition, as well as social and demographic factors influence electoral choices, they primarily do so through party identification.

Moreover, table 8.12 reveals once again what previous MCAs have also shown—namely the growing importance of partisan identifications and ideological orientations of clergy relative to their theological orientations. Of the six variables included in the analysis, theological orthodoxy ranked second to partisan identifications in 1989 in shaping the presidential votes cast by clergy in the 1988 election; it also ranked second in importance to partisan identifications in the 2008 election. However, over that period of time, the magnitude of the beta coefficient for theological orthodoxy declined in magnitude, whereas it increased in magnitude for partisan identifications. Of course, much of this decline in the relative importance of theological orientations is likely due to the greater level of congruence now between the level of theological orthodoxy exhibited by clergy and their reported partisan identifications. As a result, it is far easier today than twenty years ago to know the ideological orientation, partisan identification, and presidential voting behavior of a clergyperson simply on the basis of the particular level of theological orthodoxy they may exhibit.

Conclusions

This chapter has examined the political activism of Protestant clergy and how it may have changed over time. Three distinct topics were addressed in relationship to possible changes that may have occurred in their political activity: their public pronouncements, their forms of political activism, and their partisanship.

In terms of public pronouncements, clergy have been, and continue to be, quite vocal in terms of publicly addressing various matters of public policy. However, more clergy now report talking about more issues with greater frequency than was true several decades ago. Moreover, the content of what they address has also changed, as clergy now more frequently address topics related to social justice than moral reform.

In terms of the means by which clergy may choose to be engaged politically, there was a fairly uniform increase between 2001 and 2009 in reported levels of activity across all different forms of political activity. However, the levels to which clergy exhibited political activism in 2009 were only marginally different from what was evident in 1989. Hence, it does not appear that clergy today are more politically active now than they were several decades ago.

The partisan preferences of clergy have also shifted over the last couple of decades. Given the seven denominations under study, Protestant clergy are now more Republican in their partisan identifications than in 1989, and far less likely to report some form of being an "independent" in their identification. In addition, there has been a growing polarization in these identifications, as there are more strong identifiers today compared to several decades ago. However, there has been relatively little fluctuation in voting Republican in each of the presidential election since 1988, though there was a considerable drop in Republican voting between the 2004 and 2008 elections. Moreover, over time, the theological orientations of clergy have become more closely aligned with their ideological orientations in shaping the partisan identifications of clergy, and the level of orthodoxy exhibited by clergy has become more closely aligned with their partisan identifications in shaping the presidential votes they cast. As a result, in multivariate analyses, the relative importance of theological orthodoxy in shaping partisan identifications and partisan votes has seemingly diminished, as its influences are now largely subsumed within the effects that their ideological and partisan identifications exhibit.

Conclusion

Reflections on the Past, Thinking about the Future

Scholars have long been interested in matters related to change within social, religious, and political life, and studies that focus on change over time frequently embody a theme of "continuity and change." Even when it is not chosen as the undergirding theme, the idea of "continuity and change" generally surfaces because certain aspects related to the subject matter under consideration typically exhibit qualities that reveal continuity, whereas other facets reflect change. Change is certainly an ordinary part of many facets of life, but so too are elements related to continuity. In fact, sometimes the two appear to be so intertwined that common parlance notes that "the more things change, the more they stay the same."

This study has assessed continuity and change among American Protestant clergy, based on data collected through surveys of Protestant clergy drawn from the same seven denominations gathered over three points in time across a period of twenty years. And, certainly, the theme of "continuity and change" has revealed itself in that, though there are important facets of continuity among American Protestant clergy, there are also important sociological, theological, and political changes that have occurred as well. And, these changes have important implications for those who enter the doors of the congregations that clergy serve—as well as for American society as a whole.

This concluding chapter, therefore, addresses several related topics. First, as a concluding matter, it offers some reflection on the significance of the present study, highlighting some of the important findings of, and what has been learned from, the study. In other words, what has this study revealed theoretically, methodologically, and empirically?

Second, this study has been predicated on the contention that clergy have played, and continue to play, a central role religiously and politically within American public life. But, a variety of cultural changes are occurring that present challenges to the important role that clergy have played historically within American culture. Hence, the second section of the chapter examines the

distinctive nature of clergy and some of the challenges confronting the continued religious authority they exercise and their continued importance as intermediaries within American political life.

Finally, given these challenges that confront clergy in relationship to their
authority within congregational life, denominational life, and American culture,
in which directions should the study of American clergy go? In what possible
new directions might future studies of clergy be directed?

The Significance of the Present Study

Though clergy have been studied through a variety of contextual lens, no previous
study has systematically examined clergy through the context of time. The current
volume therefore constitutes the first study to systematically assess the nature and
level of change evident sociologically, theologically, and politically within the ranks
of American Protestant clergy over the past twenty years. Not surprisingly, the analysis has revealed some important sociological, theological, and political changes, as
well as some continuity, with ranks of Protestant clergy since the late 1980s.

Clergy occupy a unique position in American public life that enables them, as
a group, to play a potentially important role in shaping the character of American
civic and political life. Their distinctive position in American life stems from the
strategic position they occupy, the particular nature of the organizations they
lead, the authority and resources they possess, and the opportunities they enjoy.

Substantial numbers of Americans attend church regularly, with ministers
serving as the primary interpreters of the Christian faith for members of their
congregations. These particular resources and opportunities that clergy possess
could be largely ignored if clergy were unlikely to convey political messages or
chose not to engage in public life. But, for most clergy, this is not the case. When
clergy do act politically, they may, at times, engage in the political process outside their roles as pastors of local congregations, but it is in their capacity as leaders of the congregations they serve that clergy collectively are likely to exhibit
their greatest influence in American public life.

Empirical Findings

Sociological Changes

Sociologically speaking, the ranks of Protestant clergy in America look largely
the same today as they did twenty years ago, as clergy continue to be predominantly white, male, married, and rather well educated. Nevertheless, three
important changes have occurred since the 1980s within their ranks: a growth in

both female and second-career clergy, and this growth has contributed, in part, to a corresponding "graying" of the profession.

The prospect of whether the growing feminization of American Protestant clergy could fundamentally change the church has been widely debated. One of the major assumptions undergirding the expectation of change has been that the leadership styles of men and women differ (Nesbitt 2007, 307), with the leadership style of women being less authoritarian and more relational and egalitarian in nature. The idea that leadership styles may differ by gender is generated, in part, by the argument (Gilligan 1982) that men and women are different in terms of their moral evaluations.[1] Men are supposedly more inclined to think in terms of rules, while women are supposedly more inclined to make assessments through the lens of personal relationships. Certainly, as revealed in this study, clergywomen are far less likely than clergymen to subscribe to the idea that there are clear and absolute standards of right and wrong, but the extent to which this difference in moral perspective leads to a different approach to ministry remains to be determined.[2]

Given the more limited levels of education within the American population a century ago, those who were recruited to serve as clergy at that time were among America's "best and the brightest." But, this no longer is necessarily the case. There is some evidence, for example, to suggest that in more recent years there has been a decline in the academic abilities of students entering Protestant seminaries (Chaves 2004, 39–41), though academic ability is not the only quality associated with being an excellent pastor nor the quality necessarily most predictive of excellent pastoral leadership (Carroll 2006, 191). Others (e.g., Wheeler 2001) have suggested that the declining numbers of young adults choosing to enter the ministry coupled with the growth of second-career clergy also reveal a decline in the quality of those choosing to become pastors of local congregations. Nevertheless, despite the fact that there may be some truth to the declining academic qualities of those entering the ministry, the evidence related to such claims is rather "sparse and mostly impressionistic, especially when it comes to the actual performance of clergy as leaders" (Carroll 2006, 191).

Coupled with these sociological changes in the composition of clergy are the changes related to the social context of ministry. Given that there are more congregations per capita in rural and small-town settings than in more urban areas, the majority of opportunities for clergy to serve as pastors of congregations are to be found in rural and small-town settings. However, these are the very same social settings that are losing population to the larger, more urban, ones— contributing to both a thinning and aging of congregations in these smaller communities. And, declines in church membership and average weekly attendance have occurred across all types of communities within both the evangelical and mainline traditions, with declines having been greater within mainline churches.

These particular changes are likely to pose greater future challenges for rural and small-town congregations. It is likely that these congregations have always experienced the greatest disadvantage in attracting clergy within the "clergy labor market," but their disadvantage has only grown over the past decade or two through two relatively recent developments: (1) the growth of two-career families that makes serving rural and small-town congregations less attractive to clergy when one has to consider meaningful employment for one's spouse, and (2) the growth in second-career clergy who "demand higher salaries and are less geographically mobile than younger people" (Chaves 2004, 42–43). The problem is not so much the lack of available clergy to fill such positions, as the lack of willing clergy to do so, as the total number of clergy, within most denominations, exceeds the total number of congregations.[3]

Theological Changes

Protestant clergy have also changed theologically over the course of the past several decades, as there has been a growth in the percentage of clergy who score high in theological orthodoxy. This growth has occurred primarily within mainline Protestant denominations, given that clergy in evangelical Protestant denominations have consistently exhibited relatively high levels of theological orthodoxy across time. And, this growth in theological orthodoxy within mainline Protestant denominations has transpired even with the growing feminization of the ranks of mainline clergy, as clergywomen are, generally speaking, far more likely to exhibit lower levels of theological orthodoxy than their male counterparts. Yet, despite this growing proportion of clergywomen within mainline denominations, the overall level of theological orthodoxy has increased within those same denominations over that same span of time. Hence, the increased growth in theological orthodoxy within mainline Protestant denominations is due, in large part, to the increased levels of theological orthodoxy found among male clergy within those denominations, with the growth in theological orthodoxy among mainline clergy contributing to a narrowing of theological differences among Protestant clergy.

When one shifts attention to the social theology expressed by Protestant clergy, the ability to assess change over time is more limited in nature. Still, several important, over time, assessments can be made. First of all, most clergy agree that the church needs to be involved in public affairs in order for it to remain faithful to its mission, with relatively few clergy contending that such involvement in politics detracts from the church's primary mission. Fewer clergy, though a growing majority, contend that social justice stands at the center of the gospel message. Nevertheless, a rather steady, and large proportion of clergy (roughly four-fifths) reject the notion that the church should place greater

emphasis on transforming the social order and less emphasis on individual sanctification, likely in part because a growing number of Protestant clergy, now
nearly a majority, believe that simply bringing enough people to faith in Christ
would solve contemporary social problems.

Clergy are, overall, highly supportive of religious involvement in political life,
though clergy clearly differentiate between and among the political involvement
of religious institutions, religious groups, religious leaders, and religious people
in their evaluations. Depending on which religious category is examined, clergy
are somewhat more, or less, supportive of that particular religious category being
engaged in politics, with the general level of approval holding rather steady over
the course of the first decade of the twenty-first century. Finally, over that same
span of time, most Protestant clergy (roughly three-fifths) continued to perceive
clear threats to religious freedom within American society and political life.

Political Changes

Politically, the issue positions of American Protestant clergy have exhibited both
stability and change over the past several decades, with patterns of change and
stability related more to the particular issue under investigation than being confined to some particular domain of public policy. Generally speaking, far more
substantial changes in the issue positions of clergy occurred between 1989 and
2001 than between 2001 and 2009, and for those issues in which changes were
evident in the policy positions of clergy, clergy positions on those issues generally moved in a more conservative, than liberal, direction politically.

Moreover, over time, the issue positions adopted by American Protestant
clergy have become more tightly bound together and have become much more
closely tied to the ideological self-classifications they report. There has also
been a substantial growth in the level of ideological polarization found among
Protestant clergy, as the percentage of clergy adopting self-classifications falling at the extreme ends of the ideological continuum has increased substantially
over the past several decades. And, with these ideological changes, clergy are less
likely today than previously to report that they hold similar political positions to
those of their congregants. Clergy today typically see their congregants as being
more politically conservative than where they are politically, and this is true even
among those clergy who classify themselves as political conservatives.

Change has also occurred with regard to clergy expressing approval for members of their ranks engaging in either political cue-giving and direct political
action. The level of approval that clergy express for pastors engaging in political
cue-giving during church services or for engaging in direct political action outside that context has declined since the late 1980s, particularly so with regard to
clergy engaging in political cue-giving.

On the other hand, motivations that tend to spur political involvement have only grown among clergy over that same period of time. Clergy today report higher levels of political interest, greater efficacy in relationship to their congregants, and stronger partisan identifications than twenty years previously. Only the expressed desire to be more politically involved has remained relatively stable over the past several decades, but even in this case a majority of pastors continued to express a desire to be more politically involved. Overall, these psychological resources for political engagement were, and continue to be, far more prevalent among Democratic, than Republican, clergy.

Clergy willingly report that they engage in various forms of political cue-giving from the pulpit as a means to address social and political issues, with the level of cue-giving varying by the form which such cue-giving can take. Most report engaging in multiple forms of political cue-giving. But, regardless of whether such reported cue-giving occurs on or off the pulpit, their reported frequency clearly varies with the passage of time. However, despite substantial jumps in reported political cue-giving among clergy between 2001 and 2009, it appears that clergy are no more likely to engage in political cue-giving activity today than what was evident among clergy several decades ago.

The political activities of clergy within congregational life are not necessarily confined to political cue-giving within the context of worship; clergy can also play an important role in encouraging the study and deliberation of public issues among congregational members. To a certain extent, these activities may be fostered by clergy organizing study and action groups within congregational life, though the formation of these types of groups does not capture fully the range of opportunities available to congregational members to engage in the discussion and deliberation of public matters. Overall, the percentage of clergy who report they have organized such groups lags far behind the percentage who report they have engaged in various cue-giving endeavors. Moreover, the formation of study groups does not capture the presence of other adult education classes, many of which may focus on public issues of the day. In fact, two-fifths of the clergy surveyed in 2009 reported that during the past year at least one of nine specified topics related to public affairs had been the subject of an adult education class, though no overtime measures related to church classes on public issues are available by which to assess change over time.

In terms of public pronouncements, clergy have been, and continue to be, quite willing to address various matters of public policy publicly, with more clergy now reporting that they address a larger number of issues with greater frequency than was true several decades ago. Moreover, the content of what they address has changed, as they now more frequently address topics related to social justice than moral reform. With regard to the means by which clergy may choose to be engaged politically, the levels to which clergy exhibited political activism in 2009 was only marginally different from what was evident in 1989. Thus, clergy as a whole are no more politically active today than several decades ago. However, their partisan preferences have shifted over that same period of time, with clergy now being more Republican and polarized in their partisan identifications than in 1989. Moreover, over this same span of time, the theological orientations of clergy have become more closely aligned with their ideological orientations and partisan identifications, and, as a result, the relative independent effects of theological orthodoxy have diminished in relationship to explaining the partisan identifications and presidential voting behavior of clergy.

Challenges to the Central Role of Clergy

One of the core arguments of this volume has been that clergy occupy a distinctive position in American public life that enable them, as a group, to play a potentially important role in shaping the character of American civic and political life. As discussed in chapter 1, their unique position stems from five factors: (1) the strategic position they occupy, (2) the particular nature of the organizations they lead, (3) the authority they hold, (4) the resources they possess, and, (5) the opportunities they enjoy.

Consequently, any social, cultural, or political changes transpiring within contemporary American life that serve to diminish any one of these five particular qualities would serve to weaken the potential of clergy to significantly shape the character of American civic and political life. And, there are several current trends present in American society that are likely to diminish, though far from eliminate, the relative importance of two of these five qualities currently enjoyed by clergy—namely, the strategic position they occupy and the authority they hold.[4] Hence, the primary challenges to the distinctive role played by clergy derive from social trends related to these two factors.[5]

The Strategic Position of Clergy

The strategic position clergy currently occupy stems from the relative number of people who gather weekly to hear what they have to say. Any social changes diminishing the relative number of people gathering together within their churches on a regular basis would serve to reduce relative importance publicly. And, there are a number of social trends that are weakening their strategic advantage clergy possess. The first trend is the growing religious diversity in American religious life (Hout, Greeley, and Wilde 2001; Smith and Kim 2005; Wuthnow 2005; Fisher and Hout 2006; Chaves and Anderson 2012). The growth of religious diversity stems from various sources. First, there are increasing numbers of Muslims, Hindus, Buddhists, and others who are not Christians within the United States. And, their ranks have more than tripled since the last quarter of the twentieth century,[6] with their percentage of the population jumping more than 1 percent between 2007 and 2014 alone (Pew Forum on Religion and Public Life 2015). Nevertheless, despite such growth, the overall proportion of these religious "others" still remains fairly small, as it currently stands at about 6 percent of the American people (Pew Religious Landscape Survey Report 2015).

Second, and more importantly, the proportion of Americans who report that they have no religious affiliation has increased dramatically. In 1957, only 3 percent of Americans claimed no religious affiliation (Chaves and Anderson 2012, 215), but now that percentage stands at 23 percent (Pew Research Center 2015). Moreover, though this shift toward religious non-affiliation is evident across all age groups (Pew Research Center 2015), it is particularly evident among the young. Over the past two decades, the proportion of young people who claim no religious affiliation has grown dramatically, as more than one-third of those between the ages of 18 and 24 now choose "unaffiliated" when asked about their religious affiliation (Pew Research Center 2015).[7] And, though there is a tendency for young adults to reconnect with church life as they marry and have children (Wuthnow 2007, 54–56), it is likely that many of these religiously unaffiliated young adults will continue to remain unaffiliated as they grow older, marry, and raise their families. As a result, the proportion of the religiously unaffiliated will likely continue to grow in size within American society over the next several decades.

The Authority of Clergy

Not only has the strategic position of clergy been weakening over the past several decades, but so too has the authority of clergy. This decline in authority can be seen in the cultural shift from textual to visual materials, the general confidence Americans express in organized religion generally, and the level of honesty and ethical behavior Americans attribute to clergy.

First of all, through the advent of various technological innovations, there has been a gradual shift away from textual materials to visual materials in American culture. This cultural shift spreads far beyond the religious sphere of American life, and it is something which religious authorities and clergy cannot control. Nevertheless, this cultural change has clear ramifications for religious life and the authority of clergy. The stock and trade of Protestant clergy is the "preaching of the Word," with the authoritative content of that message being derived from textual materials. Hence, to the extent that the visual supplants the textual as the "basis of knowledge," the broader contours of clergy authority are being undermined.

However, the decline in clergy authority is not limited to such cultural changes, as Americans today are much less likely than several decades ago to state that they possess a great deal of confidence in leaders of religious institutions. The percentage of Americans expressing a "great deal" of confidence in leaders of "organized religion" has dropped from 35 percent in 1975 to 25 percent in 2008 (Chaves and Anderson 2012, 222). Although those who attend church regularly are more likely to express higher levels of confidence than those who attend less regularly, even regular attenders have exhibited a decline in confidence in leaders of organized religion across time (Chaves and Anderson 2012, 222). Moreover, this decline in American confidence in public leaders is not confined to leaders of "organized religion," as Americans now report lower levels of confidence in leaders of a variety of different institutions when compared to the 1970s (Smith 2012).

Perhaps more importantly, Americans are far less likely today than several decades ago to rate the honesty and ethical standards of clergy highly. Of course, many clergy are still held in high moral regard by their parishioners, but, as a group, their collective standing has diminished. For example, over the years, the Gallup Poll has asked Americans to rate the "honesty and ethical standards" of members of different professions, including those of clergy. In 1977, when the question was first asked, 61 percent of Americans responded that they rated clergy either "very high" or "high," with the highest percentage reaching 67 percent in 1985 (Gallup Poll 2014). Even at the turn of the millennium, 60 percent of Americans continued to rank the honesty and ethical standards of clergy as very high or high. But, by 2010, the percentage who did so had declined to 53 percent, and that percentage has declined every year thereafter to a point where in 2014 less than a majority of Americans (46 percent) ranked the ethical standards of clergy as either very high or high (Gallup Poll 2014). Of course, these changes in the evaluation of the ethical standards of clergy are tied to the growth in the number of Americans who report that they are religiously unaffiliated, as the ratings of clergy honesty and ethics monotonically declines as one moves from those who report that they attend church regularly to those who report less frequent attendance.[8]

Thus, these changes suggest that, over the past several decades, the authority of clergy has also diminished. Although the decline in the moral authority of clergy has transpired primarily among those who rarely, if ever, attend worship services, there also appears to be some decline in clergy authority even among regular church attenders (Jones 2009).[9] Nevertheless, those who sit regularly in the pews, who hear the messages delivered each Sunday by their pastor, still continue to attribute relatively high levels of moral authority to the ranks of clergy, as the decline in the attributions of clergy authority are primarily related to the previously noted decline in religious affiliation among the American people. Overall, therefore, these social and religious changes are likely to diminish, but far from eliminate, the important role that clergy play in American public life.

The Future Study of Clergy

The use of survey research as a methodological approach to the study of clergy has been widely employed for over fifty years. Like all methodological approaches, it has its particular strengths and weaknesses. Not all important questions related to the public role of clergy are necessarily best addressed through the use of surveys, and some questions can be addressed through more than one particular approach. However, many important questions related to clergy are best addressed through survey research, and, hence, it is likely that it will continue to be a major means by which to study clergy in the future.

Consequently, in closing this study, it may be appropriate to discuss briefly some areas of future research on clergy either raised by this study or left largely unaddressed by this study. Four particular areas will be briefly discussed: (1) the political socialization of clergy, (2) clergy and political deliberation, (3) the influence of contextual effects on clergy political endeavors, and (4) assessing the political influence of clergy on parishioners.

The Political Socialization of Clergy

The motivations for pastors to join the ranks of clergy differ, which likely in turn shape their perspectives related to clergy and public life. For a variety of reasons, it is likely that clergy "respond to different incentives from those drawn to other professions" (Guth 2001, 31). Although ministry can be viewed as a profession, it is also viewed by many who serve as clergy as a calling from God (Carroll 2006, 16–25), an incentive not always associated with recruitment patterns to other professions. Not surprisingly, therefore, most clergy have historically been drawn from the ranks of those socialized as young children within the life of the church, with a majority of clergy today coming from homes in which parents, particularly mothers, were weekly church attenders (Carroll 2006, 76–77).

Far greater scholarly attention should be given to the socialization processes that clergy undergo and how those different processes of socialization may relate to the ways in which clergy choose to serve their congregations. What we do know about these different processes suggest that they are formative in shaping the theological orientations of clergy and their approach to public life; for example, both the type of college attended and undergraduate majors help to produce divergent political orientations in mainline and evangelical pastors, with their later theological training often reinforcing these tendencies (Guth et al. 1997; Guth 2001, 33; see, however, Djupe and Gilbert 2003, 80–82).

However, socialization does not end following graduation from educational institutions. Little is known about how divorce may shape one's moral evaluations and approach to ministry. Likewise, though their earlier occupational experiences may be diverse, the prior professional experiences of "second career" clergy may serve to shape their theological orientations and political activities in ways that diverge from those for whom the ministry was their initial career.

Questions related to recruitment to the ministry, educational experiences, and professional socialization are particularly relevant to the changing composition of Protestant clergy. One component of this changing composition is the growing feminization of the clergy. As Guth (2001, 35) noted years ago, a fair amount of attention has been given to the career experiences of women clergy, but relatively little attention has been given to the question of how "feminization" of the clergy may affect the church and its ministry.

Likewise, little is known about what effects the growing influx of "second-career" clergy will have on denominational life and its programs of ministry. Of course, to a certain extent, the growing entry of women into ministry contributes to this influx of "second-career" clergy, but the two are indeed analytically distinct phenomena. Part of the challenge posed by "second-career" clergy concerns how socialization processes related to entry into their new profession (e.g., the instilling of particular clergy norms or the acceptance of the existing denominational culture) may mesh with the insights, experiences, and perspectives garnered through their previous career. "Late" entrants into ministry could well "present a dilemma for resocialization in tight conformity with traditional clergy norms and their supporting ideology" (Nesbitt 1997, 98), as the insights, experiences, and perspectives garnered through careers outside the ranks of clergy hold the potential for conflict between second-career clergy and those clergy who may be "preoccupied" with the maintenance of traditions within the denomination (Nesbitt 1998, 99). And, this tension is only likely to increase as the influx of second-career clergy continues to grow and more traditionally trained clergy, ordained primarily in their twenties, exit in retirement.

Clergy and Political Deliberation

Very little attention has been given to the role of churches and clergy in processes of public deliberation. Nevertheless, the research that has been done thus far (Coffin 2005; Djupe and Neiheisel 2008; Neiheisel, Djupe, and Sokhey

2009) suggests that churches hold the potential to act in the service of build-
ing democratic capacity by fostering religious civility through means of public
deliberation, particularly within the adult education classes sponsored by the
congregation (Neiheisel, Djupe, and Sokhey 2009, 637). Although many adult
education classes may focus on biblical texts or study various religious authors,
a substantial number of such classes address a variety of topics related to public
issues. Furthermore, these classes are generally offered in congregations where
partisan diversity is evident, as adult education classes tend to be less common
in politically unified (and likely, thereby, smaller) churches (Neiheisel, Djupe,
and Sokhey 2009, 636).

Clergy do not always lead these adult education classes, so the extent to which
clergy actually nurture the democratic capacity of their congregants remains to
be determined. When leading such classes, it is possible that clergy may well
choose to insert themselves within the discussion to insure that the right values
are promoted, but the research done thus far suggests that many pastors serve
as "relatively neutral moderators" of discussion, "affording parishioners with
relatively frequent opportunities to speak their mind and engage one another"
(Neiheisel, Djupe, and Sokhey 2009, 618–19). Although these findings are sug-
gestive of the democratic possibilities provided by these educational opportunities, far more research is needed to firmly establish these particular findings.

Similarly, additional research is needed on the sources by which clergy obtain
their political information for their discussion of public issues. Although a host
of studies have sought to ascertain the bases by which clergy derive their political
attitudes and issue positions, relatively little attention has been given to the role
that media may play in shaping the political orientations of clergy. What research
has been done has been limited to a group of clergy from a narrow range of
denominations (Brown and Smidt 2003). However, the findings of this research
suggest clergy derive their political information from a variety of sources, but
that different types of clergy tend to mix the relative balance of secular and religious media in different ways. These different patterns of media use have been
found to shape the particular kinds of issues clergy choose to address, even after
controlling for a number of variables, including the ideological orientations of
clergy. Whether these particular findings hold for clergy across a broader range
of denominations remains to be determined.

The Influence of Contextual Effects

Congregations within a denomination can vary greatly in terms of the theological perspectives expressed from the pulpit, the liturgy they employ, and the
social values they promote. In fact, the decline in denominationalism occurring

within American religious life has led to congregations experiencing greater freedom within the denominational structures of which they are a part—creating thereby a de facto form of congregationalism (Warner 1994, 74). This variation across congregations of the same denomination, coupled with the greater ease of travel, has led to local congregations now being constituted more by the characteristics of its members than by geography itself. Consequently, many parishioners may now travel past other churches of their denominational affiliation in order to worship with a congregation that is not located in the particular neighborhood where they reside. In fact, between 2006 and 2012, nearly one-third of Americans reported that they had switched the congregation they attended, with most (nearly 60 percent) doing so because they had moved to a different community (Briggs 2014). However, among those who had not moved but still switched congregations, the most frequently reason for the change (cited by 58 percent of those who had not moved to a new community) related to dissatisfaction with spiritual leaders, with an almost similar percentage citing dissatisfaction with the social and political views of congregational members (Briggs 2014). Consequently, given that people switch congregations more readily today, and frequently do so because of issues related to the pastor and spiritual leadership more generally, clergy are likely to be far more important to the strength of particular congregations today than was true previously.

Nevertheless, despite years of research related to clergy, we still know little about how the particular nature of the congregation serves to shape the political strategies of pastors. Are clergy more likely to conceal their political preferences and inclinations when they diverge significantly from those of their congregants, or are clergy more likely to provide political cues, form study groups, or develop action groups when their viewpoints stand apart from those typically expressed by their congregants. Moreover, it is possible that such patterns vary depending on the salience of the particular issue or the nature of the specific action under consideration. Finally, when clergy choose to engage in political cue-giving within the context of congregational worship, what factors serve to shape whether such cues are rather subtle or more direct in nature?

Finally, a number of research studies (e.g., Calfano 2009; Calfano, Oldmixon, and Gray 2014) have revealed that the congregation is not the only reference group which is taken into consideration when clergy choose to engage in various political endeavors. A variety of other reference groups (e.g., other clergy in the denominations, denominational leaders, etc.) can also come into play that shape the way(s) in which clergy act, or fail to act, politically. Thus, clergy must engage in a "delicate balancing act among their own personal commitments, the perceived and vocalized wishes of the congregations, and their professional networks of fellow clergy," and it remains to be determined under what condition "these contending pressures push clergy into activism" (Williams 1998, 724).

It is here, in particular, where scholars who study congregational life and those who study clergy could fruitfully join forces. Over the past several decades, there has been a revival in scholarly studies of congregational life (e.g., Ammerman 1997, 2005; Chaves 2004; Marti 2005, Emerson 2006). Answers to research questions about how the congregational context serves to move clergy both into, and perhaps out of, political activism could well benefit from ethnographic research done in relationship to congregational life.

Assessing the Political Influence of Clergy

As Guth (2001, 41) noted more than a decade ago, the "most recalcitrant research problem is whether and how clergy influence parishioners' social and political orientations." Not only do churchgoers frequently switch from one congregation to another, but clergy too move with some frequency (though this is somewhat dependent on the particular denomination in which the clergy is ordained to serve). Consequently, part of the difficulty in assessing clergy influence on the parishioners they serve results from differentiating between the short-term and long-term effects of clergy.

Certainly, clergy within a particular denomination can vary considerably in terms of their basic understanding about social theology and politics. Nevertheless, clergy within the same denomination typically hold relatively similar views related to social theology and politics, and, as a result, denominational clergy are likely, regardless of the particular pastor, "to deliver a fairly consistent message over time that reinforces and even shapes parishioners' attitudes" (Guth 2001, 42). Furthermore, given the de facto congregationalism noted earlier (and, when evident in terms of church polity, the desires of bishops to maintain congregational vitality), congregations are increasingly likely to either "call" pastors that appear to (though do not always) reflect the theological and political preferences of the congregants or have such pastors appointed to serve their congregations. As a result, there may be a fairly consistent message given to congregants over time—a relatively consistent message that likely has certain long-term effects on the attitudes and orientations of the congregants served by these various pastors.

However, regardless of these likely long-term effects, it is far more difficult to discern just what might be the short-term impact of particular clergy speech and actions. Clergy may seek to alter the priority of political issues to be addressed through agenda setting or endeavor to alter the particular political positions typically expressed by their congregants. Ascertaining whether attitudinal changes have occurred among congregants is readily subject to empirical verification, but there are methodological challenges in demonstrating the links between clergy speech and their effects on congregants. First, it requires pairing the study of clergy with the study of the congregants they serve. Although efforts have been made to do this (Djupe and Gilbert 2009), more needs to be done. Yet, to do so on a fairly broad scale becomes fiscally prohibitive for most research budgets. Hence, engaging in a number of case studies may be the most likely way to move forward in this regard. Second, though attitudinal changes related to agenda setting, issue positions, or partisan preferences can easily be demonstrated empirically, it is harder to demonstrate whether clergy messages resulted in reinforcement (which can be a significant political effect) or were simply ineffectual and had "no effect" on parishioner's attitudes or preferences.

Conclusion

Each research methodology has its particular strengths and weaknesses. Survey research has been a frequent means by which clergy have been studied, but its particular methodology cannot answer a variety of questions related to the public influence and significance of clergy. Ethnographic research can provide valuable information and offer important insights into the relationships that may be evident between pastor and congregants. Experimental studies can help to provide clues related to the conditions under which clergy statements and cues may influence those exposed to such messages. Hopefully, future research on clergy will more frequently employ multi-method strategies of inquiry so that the different modes of inquiry will serve to complement the research endeavor and capture more fully the breadth and depth of clergy endeavors in relationship to the congregants they serve.

Appendix A

NUMBER OF RESPONDENTS AND RESPONSE RATE BY DENOMINATION OVER TIME

				PC			
	AOG	*CRC*	*DOC*	*USA*	*RCA*	*SBC*	*UMC*
1989							
N	406	368	1,289	917	378	653	723
Response rate (%)	52	66	64	64	66	47	54
2001							
N	336	379	557	473	372	455	453
Response rate (%)	45	59	52	41	55	36	50
2009							
N	208	370	335	290	312	248	282
Response rate (%)	21	53	35	29	51	25	29

Appendix B

VALIDATING THE REPRESENTATIVENESS OF THE 2009 COOPERATIVE CLERGY SURVEY

1. Demographic Variables

	Cooperative Clergy Study All	Clergy Voices Study All
Median age	55	56
White (%)	94	93
Male (%)	80	80
Seminary graduate (%)	91	94

Sources: 2008 Mainline Protestant Clergy Voices Survey, N = 2,658; 2009 Cooperative Clergy Study, Mainline Protestant component only, N = 1,456. See Robert P. Jones and Daniel Cox, "Clergy Voices: Findings from the 2008 Mainline Protestant Clergy Voices Survey, March 2009, http://www.publicreligion.org, p. 8.

2. Theological Variables

	Cooperative Clergy Study		Clergy Voices Study	
	All (%)	PC USA (%)	All (%)	PC USA (%)
Jesus only way to salvation				
Agree	62	52	61	59
Not sure	10	14	9	11
Disagree	28	34	30	31
Total	100	100	100	101
Bible is inerrant				
Agree	34	25	29	22
Uncertain	5	4	4	2
Disagree	61	71	67	76
Total	100	100	100	100
The Devil actually exists				
Agree	68	56	61	53
Not sure	8	11	12	12
Disagree	24	33	27	35
Total	100	100	100	100
If enough people brought to Christ, Social ills take care of themselves				
Agree	34	30	38	28
Not sure	17	16	21	20
Disagree	49	54	41	52
Total	100	100	100	100
Social justice the heart of the gospel				
Agree	69	71	73	75
Not sure	7	6	7	8
Disagree	25	23	20	17
Total	101	100	100	100

Sources: 2008 Mainline Protestant Clergy Voices Survey, N = 2,658; 2009 Cooperative Clergy Study, Mainline Protestant component only, N = 1,456. See Robert P. Jones and Daniel Cox, "Clergy Voices: Findings from the 2008 Mainline Protestant Clergy Voices Survey, March 2009, http://www.publicreligion.org, p. 11. Most of the data reported here for the Clergy Voices study were reported in a personal correspondence with the author.

3. Political Variables

	Cooperative Clergy Study		Clergy Voices Study	
	All (%)	PC USA (%)	All (%)	PC USA (%)
Ideology				
Liberal	46	55	48	52
Moderate	18	16	19	16
Conservative	36	29	33	32
Total	100	100	100	100
Partisan identification				
Strong Democrat	29	30	29	30
Weak Democrat	9	13	10	10
Independent, lean Democrat	16	17	17	22
Independent	10	9	10	6
Independent, lean Republican	11	10	13	12
Weak Republican	11	10	9	10
Strong Republican	13	10	12	10
Total	99	99	100	100

Sources: 2008 Mainline Protestant Clergy Voices Survey, $N = 2,658$; 2009 Cooperative Clergy Study, Mainline Protestant component only, $N = 1,456$. See Robert P. Jones and Daniel Cox, "Clergy Voices: Findings from the 2008 Mainline Protestant Clergy Voices Survey, March 2009, http://www.publicreligion.org, p. 12. PC USA statistics for the Clergy Voices study were reported in a personal correspondence with the author.

NOTES

Introduction

1. For example, the Civic Participation Survey of 1997 (http://www.thearda.com/Archive/Files/Descriptions/CIVIC.asp) reveals that 60 percent of all Americans report church membership; when asked about membership in a listing of twenty-two broad categories of voluntary associations (e.g., arts, profession, veterans, environmental, union, school, etc.) a little less than 69 percent of all American reported membership with some kind of voluntary association.
2. Although the percentage of Americans who report that they attend church weekly has remained stable over the past several decades, the percentage of those who report that they rarely or never attend has increased over that same period of time.
3. This statement is based more on inference than direct evidence. Several factors contribute to making this inference. The first is a broader cultural turn from an emphasis on truth to an emphasis on experience. The second is the increased individualism and subjectivism within American religious life, reflected in part in the greater willingness of Americans to shift denominational affiliations. The third is the widespread presence of Moralistic Therapeutic Deism within the lives of emerging young adults (Smith and Denton 2005), a perspective that may be (and likely will be in the future) reflective of a growing number of American adults as well.
4. In other words, clergy licensed by the Evangelical Lutheran Church may, because of such arrangements, be called to serve congregations of the Reformed Church of America, and vice versa.
5. The prohibition of clergy endorsing candidates relates to the "Johnson Amendment" which was added to the IRS Code in 1954 that prohibits churches from intervening in election campaigns on behalf of candidates; to do so risks the loss of the church's tax-exempt status. At its inception, the amendment was largely noncontroversial, but for various reasons it has become much contentious (Dart 2013; Smietana 2013; Bade 2014).
6. Much of the discussion found in the next several paragraphs is drawn from Olson (2009).
7. Although the Notre Dame Study of Catholic Parish Life did not include data on the content of clergy messages related to capital punishment, it is likely, given the official stance of the Catholic Church related to pro-life issues, that such clergy messages were directed largely toward opposition to the practice of capital punishment. The Catholic Church does recognize the right of the state to engage in capital punishment under certain circumstances, but its Catechism, quoting Pope John Paul II, states that the cases in which execution of the offender is an absolute necessity "are very rare, if practically nonexistent."
8. In addition to surveying clergy from the two denominations, the authors also surveyed some of the congregational members who were served by a portion of the clergy surveyed. Thus, they were able to more directly assess the extent to which clergy actually shaped the attitudes and opinions of their parishioners.

9. The note at the bottom of table 2.1 indicates that "clergy are judged to have spoken about the (specified) issue if they gave a response other than 'never'" (Djupe and Gilbert 2009, 61). As a result, response options of "rarely" and "seldom" (see p. 255) were included in assessing congregational misperceptions of clergy cues.

10. Moreover, many clergy surveys inquire about the extent to which clergy may have addressed particular matters of public policy but do not assess the particular location in which such policy matters were addressed. Hence, even if clergy report that they have only rarely addressed the issue of gambling laws, the analyst has no way of knowing just where, and with whom, this discussion occurred. Consequently, if the clergyperson did so in this rare instance outside the context of congregational life, it is not necessarily a misperception on the part of the congregant (as their methodology would suggest) for them to believe that their pastor has not addressed such a topic.

11. Although this would limit the number of congregational members analyzed, it should be recalled that about 40 percent of Americans report that they attend weekly.

12. Perhaps, then, when clergy meet these particular religious expectations related to congregational vitality, clergy gain "the freedom" to act politically as a simple "by-product" of fulfilling these expectations, in that once their religious expectations are met, congregants simply choose to tolerate or ignore the clergy's politics (Djupe and Gilbert 2008).

13. Compare, for example, the frequencies with which clergy report engaging in cue-giving with that of engaging in direct political action as found in tables 9.1 and 9.2 within *The Bully Pulpit* (Guth et al. 1997).

14. In *The Bully Pulpit*, survey data drawn from clergy affiliated with the Evangelical Covenant Church were included, with these data being collected somewhat later by Richard Dodson (Guth et al. 1997, x). However, given that clergy from this denomination have not been subsequently surveyed, data drawn from this denomination are not reported in the 1989 wave of surveys.

15. Twenty-five different scholars were engaged in this cooperative research effort, with twenty-two different religious bodies surveyed. For a description of the study, participants, and religious bodies analyzed, see http://www.calvin.edu/henry/research/clergy.htm. Denominational findings related to this study can be found in Smidt (2004).

16. Indeed, the whole clergy population of some smaller denominations was less than the sample size drawn in larger ones.

17. Although surveys were mailed in the 2009 survey, pastors were notified that they could complete their survey online as well, with a survey posted on the Calvin Center for Social Research website.

18. In the 2009 survey, a total of five evangelical Protestant denominations were surveyed (the Assemblies of God; the Christian Reformed Church; the Mennonite Church, USA; the Lutheran Church, Missouri Synod; and the Southern Baptist Convention), as well as a total of five mainline Protestant denominations (the Disciples of Church; the Evangelical Lutheran Church of America; the Presbyterian Church, U.S.A.; the Reformed Church in America; and, the United Methodist Church).

19. Details related to the number of clergy from each denomination who responded as well as the resulting response rate for each denomination can be found in appendix A, with details listed by the year each survey was conducted.

20. This assignment to the evangelical and mainline Protestant traditions is based on whether the denomination is affiliated with the National Association of Evangelicals or the National Council of Churches (the primary organizational association of mainline Protestant denominations). For a discussion of the history, size, and social makeup of these seven denominations, see Guth et al. (1997, ch. 2) or the appropriate chapters in Smidt (2004).

21. Of course, given that the Mainline Clergy Voices study did not include surveys of evangelical Protestant pastors, there is no direct way to assess the representativeness of clergy responses from the three evangelical denominations included in this study. Nevertheless, should the responses of mainline Protestant clergy mirror each other across the two clergy studies, it would lead to some greater confidence that the results obtained from evangelical Protestant clergy might also be fairly representative as well.

Chapter 1

1. See introduction, n. 1. Of course, how the question related to church membership is asked can shape the results obtained. Sometimes, the survey questions are posed in terms of whether one is affiliated with some kind of religious institution/denomination; in other surveys, respondents may be simply asked whether they are a member of some church; and, in still other surveys, respondents may be asked whether they are affiliated with some denomination and then later asked whether they are member of some church. The percentage of Americans who report religious affiliation is greater than the percentage who report church membership per se.

2. The percentage of Americans who report that they attend church weekly has not changed substantially over the past fifty years. See, for example, Smidt et al. (2008, 44–45). On the other hand, the percentage who report that they attend church only occasionally or rarely has also increased—as those who in the past reported that they attended church once or twice a month has declined over the same period of time. However, it should be noted that some scholars question this reported level of weekly church attendance, contending that such reports are inflated; see, for example, Hadaway, Marler, and Chaves (1993) and Marler and Hadaway (1999). On the other hand, it is highly likely that the "social desirability effects" of reporting weekly church attendance were far greater several decades ago than presently. Hence, even the apparent stability in reported weekly church attendance continues despite the decline in social pressure to report such weekly attendance.

3. For example, if the Right Rev. James Jansen chose to sign the letter simply as James Jansen, then he would be doing so as an individual citizen. But, were he to sign the letter as the Rev. James Jansen, Pastor of St. John's Lutheran Church, then he would be adopting a different role—in this case, as a pastor of a local congregation. But, as noted in the next two paragraphs, were the Rev. James Jansen also the chair of the local ministerial association and had he signed the letter as the Rev. James Jansen, Chair, Middletown Ministerial Association, he would be doing so in a different capacity or role—this time as a representative of a "professional association" and less as a pastor of the local church he serves.

4. However, it is also true that on some issues that clergy report addressing with less, though relatively substantial, frequency, only about 60 percent of congregants correctly perceive whether their pastor had addressed the topic in the past year (Djupe and Gilbert 2009, 61).

Chapter 2

1. The term "lay pastor" can mean somewhat different things in different denominations. However, generally speaking, "lay pastors" have not completed a formal Minister of Divinity degree at some seminary, yet serve as ministers of Word and Sacrament where ordained clergy are unavailable for the local congregation. For a description of some denominational differences related to "lay pastors," as well as a discussion of some of the issues related to their use, see Wood (2010) and Wheeler (2010).

2. There are some exceptions. The Unitarians, for example, did ordain women in the late 1880s.

3. The granting of ordination to female clergy transpired at different times in different denominations, though for most denominations this occurred following World War II (Chaves 1997). In terms of the denominations under study here, the Assemblies of God ordained women from the start of the denomination in 1914. The forerunner of the current Presbyterian Church, U.S.A., ordained its first female minister in 1956, and the United Methodist Church approved full clergy rights to women in the same year. The Reformed Church in American did not ordain its first female minister until 1979. By tradition and custom, only males were ordained in the Southern Baptist Convention. But the Convention modified its "Baptist Faith and Message" Statement in 2000 to prevent any future ordination of women.

4. In terms of a longer time perspective, Gaustad (1990, 28) contends that what changed during the twentieth century was "the image of the minister: his role, his function, his self-esteem, his social standing, his political and economic clout."

5. Of course, clergy still rank relatively high in terms of their social standing, ranking sixth out of twenty-one professions. See http://www.gallup.com/poll/166298/honesty-ethics-rating-clergy-slides-new-low.aspx.

6. The graying, however, seems to have ebbed by 2009. Although there is a larger percentage of clergy over the age of 55 in 2009 than in 2001, the mean age of the Protestant clergy within the "56 years or more" category actually declined somewhat between 2001 and 2009: from 62.6 to 62.0 mean years of age.

7. When those who are currently separated or who are presently "divorced but not remarried" are added together with the "divorced, but remarried" category, the percentage increases from 14 to 15 percent.

8. Technically, the delineation and practice of ordination vary across denominations (Zikmund, Lummis, and Chang 1998, 3). Consequently, our surveys did not specifically ask if, and when, one had been ordained, but rather how many years one has served in the ministry. Hence, the use of the word "ordained" here and elsewhere in the volume is done more for stylistic purposes.

9. Analysis of change over time is dependent on the nature of the data available. Unfortunately, our earliest clergy surveys did not include a great number of questions related to the social context of ministry. As a result, the analysis of this topic is more limited in nature.

10. The percentages presented in the table are "rounded" up or down to reflect "full" percentages. Hence, in order to demonstrate that it was more than half of all female clergy, the actual percentage reported here does not fully mirror the percentage reported in table 2.3.

Chapter 3

1. As noted in the previous chapter, not all clergy necessarily attend seminary; it varies by denominational requirements. However, most clergy have some form of theological training whether in terms of attending Bible college or seminary.

2. Several new theological belief items were added to the clergy surveys of 2001, and they were then included again in the 2009 clergy surveys.

3. Dispensationalism is a theological interpretation that contends that God has chosen to relate to human beings in different ways over time, in a series of different "dispensations" or covenants during different periods of time. Dispensationalists adhere to a clear distinction between God's promises to Israel and those to the Church, whereas non-dispensationalists view the Old Testament promises to Israel as applying to New Testament church.

4. Universalism is a theological position adopted by some Christians which holds that, because of God's divine love and mercy, all people, regardless of their particular faith or lack thereof, will ultimately be reconciled to God and enjoy salvation.

5. This potential item asked clergy their level of agreement with the statement: "The Bible is the inerrant Word of God, both in matters of faith and in historic, geographic, and other secular matters."

6. The reliability coefficients for the four-item index ranged from an alpha of .914 in 1989 to .928 in 2009, indicating a high level of reliability for the four-item index.

7. For example, the Apostles' Creed notes that Jesus "ascended into heaven and sits at the right hand of God, the Father" which is followed by the phrase "from thence he shall come to judge the living and the dead." This latter phrase then suggests that Jesus will return from heaven to earth to engage in this judgment.

8. A sizable portion (though less than half) of those clergy who fall in the middle category of theological orthodoxy do so on the basis of their disagreement with the contention that "Adam and Eve were real people." If the "second coming" item were used in place of the "Adam and Eve" item in the 2001 and 2009 surveys, about 40 percent of those currently classified as "medium" in terms of their level of theological orthodoxy would instead be classified as "high" in theological orthodoxy. As a basis for comparison, if the second coming item is used instead of the Adam and Eve item for the years 2001 and 2009, the percentage of clergy who would be classified as high in theological orthodoxy would be 66 percent in 2001 and 70 percent in 2009. Thus, even using this particular measure of theological orthodoxy over a shorter period of time suggests that there has been a growth in theological orthodoxy over the eight years.

9. This figure is obtained when one subtracts the lowest level of theological orthodoxy evident—in this case, 15 percent—from the highest level of theological orthodoxy evident in 1989—in this case 98 percent.

10. Here I am using, somewhat arbitrarily, a 10 percent-point difference as constituting a "substantial" difference.

11. The major exceptions relate to those clergy low in theological orthodoxy, where evangelical clergy in both 2001 and 2009 expressed greater approval of liberation and feminist theology than did mainline Protestant clergy. However, these "exceptions" may well be a function of the relatively small numbers of evangelical clergy who are low in orthodoxy, making the resultant percentages within their ranks rather "unstable."

12. Table 3.7 also revealed that clergy differed substantially in their expressed levels of theological orthodoxy based on their differences in seminary education. However, when one controls for theological orthodoxy and examines the relative effects of seminary education on their expression of agreement with other theological matters, differences in seminary education have very little, and somewhat inconsistent, impact on the positions adopted on such matters.

13. Multiple Classification Analysis (MCA) first provides the means score on the dependent variable for each category of the independent variable. This procedure yields a bivariate measure of association (*eta*) between the independent and the dependent variables. In addition, MCA provides deviations from the mean score on the independent variable for each category of the independent variables after controls for each of the other independent variables have been entered into the analysis, with the statistic *beta* being the multivariate equivalent of *eta*—revealing the relative strength of the relationship once the effects of the other variables in the analysis have been taken into account. For simplicity of presentation, only the *beta* scores are entered into the tables here.

14. In other words, MCA provides a single score for the categorical variable rather than a number of scores for each of the non-suppressed categories of that variable when used in regression analyses.

Chapter 4

1. The fact that an individual may be committing an immoral act is not in itself grounds for governmental action. Nor are all sins necessarily crimes. In fact, of the Ten Commandments given by God on Mount Sinai, only the sixth (murder) and the eighth (theft) are always considered wrong by the state and worthy of punishment. While engaging in an extramarital affair is immoral, it does not mean that the state should bring criminal charges against those who do so. It should also be noted that government may choose to address a problem even though nothing immoral has occurred. For example, driving through an intersection is not immoral. But, for purposes of safety and convenience, governments may choose to place a traffic light at an intersection after which people are morally, and legally, obligated to stop when the light turns red. Only after a law has been passed and a traffic light placed at the intersection do such actions become matters of morality (Marshall 2002, 141).

2. Moreover, even the prevention of such behavior does not necessarily entail any moral improvement of the individual in the sight of God, as anyone who hates his neighbor has already committed murder in his or her heart. See Matthew 5:21.

3. In other words, one (though not necessarily the sole) mission of the church is to deepen and strengthen the faith of those who have already committed their life to Christ as well as to preach the gospel to those outside the church in order to bring others into the faith. Here, the emphasis is more on the vertical relationship between the individual and God.

4. This is the more horizontal dimension of the Christian faith. There are, of course, many biblical injunctions related to helping and aiding the poor. Such help may be offered by the individual Christian, but it may also be offered communally through the church (e.g., providing a "soup kitchen"). Certainly, some poverty may be a function of individual failure, but other forms of poverty, particularly those found among minorities and the disadvantaged, may be related to institutional arrangements and the particular existing structures of society. Hence, the social ministry of the church may also seek to transform society and alter institutional structures as a means of addressing human needs and seeking to secure social justice.

5. Thus, at times, the two may appear to be rather contradictory in nature. Nevertheless, to adopt positions that are "in tension" with each other is not unusual for Americans. For example, Americans have long cherished both the values of freedom and equality, though these two values always stand in tension with each other. Likewise, Bellah et al. (2007) discuss the presence of, and tension between, the liberal and republican ideals that historically have been held simultaneously by most Americans.

6. Liberation theology is a distinct approach to theology that emphasizes social justice and the liberation of the poor from unjust economic, social, and political conditions. It has been described by proponents as an interpretation of the Christian faith through the eyes of the poor and by its detractors as little more than a Marxist analysis of economic conditions.

7. Feminist theology is a movement to reconsider Christian traditions, practices, scriptures, and theologies from a feminist perspective.

8. Clergy were given a five-point continuum with "involvement in politics detracts from the church's primary mission" at one end of the continuum and "involvement needed to remain faithful to the church's primary mission" at the other end. For table 4.1 and the discussion in the chapter, the two positions closest to the "detract from" side of the continuum were coded together to establish the 16 percent of the clergy who responded that political involvement detracts from the primary mission of the church, with the two positions closest to the "involvement needed" end of the continuum being coded together to form the 63 percent who responded that involvement was needed to remain faithful to the church's mission.

9. The remaining percentage of clergy (21 percent) indicated that they were uncertain about the matter.

10. For a discussion of some of the potentially beneficial as well as potentially detrimental effects of religion on public life, see chapter 1 in Smidt et al. (2008).

11. Nevertheless, a tension exists between these two religion clauses of the First Amendment. Religion is more than a set of beliefs, as religion finds its expression in action. However, not all religiously motivated actions can be permitted by the state. For example, some religious faiths may emphasize faith healing, and others (at least hypothetically) might emphasize child sacrifice. However, clearly, there is a compelling state interest to protect vulnerable children by preventing the latter, and there may be, under certain circumstances, a compelling state interest to prohibit parents from engaging in faith healing of their children (e.g., when the life of the child is endangered without proper medical care).

12. Indeed, some theorists object to any presence of religion in public life on the basis of its being divisive and disruptive, thereby reinforcing and strengthening political divisions rather than bridging or healing them.

13. One would anticipate that religion would be more meaningful, stronger, and more salient in an individual's life when that religion is freely chosen than when it is socially imposed upon a person.

14. It should be noted, however, that there is a certain level of ambiguity in what the designation "founded as a Christian nation" may suggest to those responding to the statement. Hence, it is unclear whether clergy choose to interpret this statement in terms of (1) noting the religious faith of the vast majority of those living in the country at the time of the founding, (2) indicating what they believe to be the desire of the framers of the constitution in terms of the religious nature of its citizens, or (3) expressing their own assessment as to what particular religious faith serves to undergird the structure and operation of the country's political institutions (e.g., the principle of separation of powers found in the American constitution being built upon Christian understandings related to the fallen nature of humankind).

15. And, subsequent research among senior pastors in Protestant churches conducted in the later months of 2013 revealed that seven out of ten held that "religious liberty is on the decline in America" (Smietana 2014).

16. Gilligan's analysis has been criticized on a number of grounds. For a discussion of some of these criticisms, see Robbins (1998, 75) and Sommers (2000).

17. Some other items were asked across all three points in time, but only among clergy from five of the seven denominations surveyed in 1989.

18. For ease of discussion, rather than constantly referring to an "individualism-communitarian" orientation, discussion will simply be cast in terms of an "individualistic" orientation, with

those who score low on this orientation being labeled at times as having scored high in terms of a communitarian orientation.

19. In 1989, the three items selected formed a single factor what explained 56 percent of the variance; in 2001, they formed a single factor that accounted for 58 percent of the variance; and, in 2009, the same items again formed a single factor that explained 57 percent of the variance. The alpha coefficients for the individualism measure were .61 in 1989, .64 in 2001, and .63 in 2009.

20. In constructing this measure of individualism, it was decided to create an additive index of responses to the four questions rather than to use the factor scores as the basis for classifying clergy along the continuum. Factors scores can be cut at different points to create arbitrarily a chosen number of categories that contain a specified portion of respondents. The use of an index is more intuitive in terms of its interpretation. Consequently, for purposes of analysis here, clergy who reported agreement with an item were given a score of +1 on that item, with uncertainty related to the statement scored a 0, and disagreement scored a −1. Then the scores for each of the three items were added together, with those clergy obtaining scores of either 2 or 3 being classified as "high" on individualism. In other words, to be scored "high" on individualism, one not only had to agree with at least two of these three items as well as not express disagreement with any of them.

21. Four questions were used to assess whether this composite measure of individualism truly captured differences along an individualism-communitarian continuum. As noted, earlier in the chapter, contemporary communitarianism can be viewed as a "more inclusive and sociologically informed successor to the social gospel," with its particular ties to liberation theology and minority rights. Hence, it was anticipated that, if the measure is a valid one, those who score high on the individualism measure should be far less prone than those who score low to agree with the statement that "the ideas of liberation theology really get at the heart of the Gospel" or the statement that "feminist theology provides valuable insights about being a Christian" Likewise, one would might expect that those high in individualism should be less likely to agree with the statement that Christianity requires a substantial redistribution of wealth and that, given the clearer biblical injunctions related to doing justice, a far weaker relationship should exist between individualism and agreement with the statement that social justice gets at the heart of the gospel. Analysis revealed that each of these expectations was clearly met by the measure.

Chapter 5

1. The first three paragraphs of this section draw heavily on the discussion found in Guth (2009).
2. The initial clergy surveys were actually collected in late fall of 1988 and the early spring of 1989—though the year 1989 is used to designate when these surveys were collected.
3. The first several paragraphs of this section draw heavily on the discussion found in Guth et al. (1997, 103).
4. For example, given the seven denominations surveyed, clergy are much more prone to classify themselves ideologically as conservatives as opposed to liberals, as approximately twice as many clergy choose to label themselves as political conservatives as political liberals. This is true despite the fact that these percentages are based on clergy drawn from four mainline denominations compared to only three evangelical denominations.
5. For example, among AOG pastors, the percentage of clergy who fall within the middle three ideological categories dropped from 47 percent in 1989 to 16 percent in 2009. Comparable figures for the remaining denominations are: 53 percent down to 17 percent among the SBC clergy; 88 percent down to 64 percent among CRC clergy; 84 percent down to 50 percent among RCA clergy; 71 percent down to 51 percent among UMC clergy; 86 down to 48 percent among PC USA clergy; and, 75 percent down to 38 percent among DOC clergy.
6. Among CRC clergy in 2009, the percentage of pastors who chose one of the three middle designations was 64 percent.
7. Such ideological gaps between the "elite" and the "mass" of a group are not necessarily limited to clergy. Various studies of nonreligious elites, such as political party leaders, have also shown that they often hold positions that are more extreme than those held by their followers (Bibby

1987, 111-13; Layman 2001). However, a number of scholars have contended that liberal Protestant leaders are more representative of their constituencies than these images would suggest (e.g., Hertzke 1988; Hofrenning 1995; Djupe and Gilbert 2003).

8. In order to make this combination of responses more manageable, responses to each of the two separate items were reduced first into one of three different responses: "more conservative," "about the same," and "more liberal."

9. Perhaps, for example, the candidacy of Barack Obama might have served to create a different perception between where clergy perceived themselves to stand in relationship to those who filled their pews on Sunday morning.

10. In the aftermath of the 2004 presidential election, a number of different studies revealed a rather strong relationship between attendance at worship services and vote choice (e.g., Campbell 2007; Rozell and Whitney 2007, chs. 2–5; Smidt et al. 2010). Religiously observant voters were much more likely to vote for Republicans than Democrats. Thus, the term "God Gap" was born, a label used to describe the tendency of those who are highly religious to vote Republican and those who are less so to vote Democratic. Or, as political commentator Michael Barone had earlier noted (Carnes 2004): "Americans increasingly vote as they pray, or don't pray."

Chapter 6

1. Although encouraging one's congregation to register and vote does not reveal a particular partisan direction in terms of how to vote, it nevertheless constitutes a cue that suggests that the casting of a vote and the subsequent outcome of the election are important matters.

2. However, since most pastors who approved of clergy delivering sermons that addressed social and political issues of the day also approved of clergy taking pulpit stands on such issues, the action will continue to be treated as a cue-giving activity.

3. Djupe and Gilbert (2003, 53) report that 7 percent of the Episcopal priests and Evangelical Lutheran Church in American pastors they surveyed in 1998 indicated they approved of clergy endorsing candidates while preaching.

4. In the past, factor analysis has typically revealed two underlying dimensions of clergy norms: one related to cue-giving and one related to direct action. Factor analysis of the current data file also revealed two underlying dimensions related to cue-giving and direct action for each year when the eigenvalue was set at 1.2.

5. Each component item was assigned scores in the following manner: approval was coded +1, uncertainty was coded 0, and disapproval was coded −1, with the resultant scores added together. These scores were then recoded into three categories using a similar assignment procedure. Scores of 0 or less was scored "low" in terms of approval of such norms. Scores that constituted approval of all four cue-giving norms were coded "high" in terms of approval, while scores of +5 and +6 were coded "high" in terms of approval of direct political action. Scores that fell between these two categories were then were assigned to the "medium" category.

6. This is true whether or not cue-giving occurs on or off the pulpit. When the composite measure of cue-giving is divided into two separate components (using the first two items of the composite measure as being conducted from the pulpit and the last two items as being done off the pulpit), both measures exhibit a decline in high levels of approval. Although there was a modest decline in high levels of clergy approval for cue-giving from the pulpit (from 55 percent in 1989 to 48 percent in 2009), there was a noticeable decline over the same period of time in the percentage of clergy expressing high levels of approval for clergy giving political cues when off the pulpit (from 68 percent in 1989 to 50 percent in 2009).

7. In additional analyses of the data, I also broke down cue-giving into two separate variables (composed of cue-giving from the pulpit and cue-giving off the pulpit) as well as three separate direct action endeavors (composed of congregationally based, protest-related, and political campaigning actions). Each of the five variables consisted of responses to two items, with approval for both activities coded as "high level" of approval. Interestingly, though the overall level of approval for protest activity exhibited the lowest percentage of high approval in

each of the three surveys conducted, it was the only variable for which there was a consistent increase in high levels of clergy approval (from 38 percent in 1989 to 42 percent in 2009).

8. It appears that the most recent published findings related to this topic are found in Guth et al. (1997, 153–56).

9. Technically, the findings related to age were based on data collected from Southern Baptist Convention (SBC) clergy over time. Although not explicitly stated, it was largely assumed that SBC clergy were highly orthodox theologically (which had been demonstrated in table 3.1), and that the relationship between age and approval of direct political action was likely reflective of other clergy who were theologically orthodox.

10. Moreover, when direct action is broken down into three separate measures composed of two items each, theological orthodoxy is related to the three separate items in a similar fashion, with those low in theological orthodoxy exhibiting the largest percentages expressing high levels of approval (70 percent or greater) and with those high in theological orthodoxy exhibiting the lowest levels of approval (46 percent for congregationally based action, 48 percent for campaign-related action, and 30 percent for protest activities).

11. Clergy were able to indicate their level of political interest along a seven-point continuum in which the value of 1 was labeled "not very interested," the value of 4 "mildly interested," and 7 "very interested." Here, the two lowest values are combined to indicate "not very interested," while the two highest values are combined to indicate "very interested." The value of 3 was labeled "somewhat disinterested," while the value of 5 was labeled "somewhat interested."

12. Partisan identification has frequently been examined in terms of seven categories. However, for ease of presentation, weak identifiers with a party along with those who labeled themselves as independent but leaning toward that particular party are classified together as weak/leaning partisan identifiers, so that a total of five categories are employed when examining partisan identification along a continuum from strong Democrats to strong Republicans.

13. The one exception occurred in 1989, when 50 percent of both strong and weak Republicans reported a desire to be more involved politically.

14. Technically, given the strong correlations between and among religious tradition, theological orthodoxy, and partisan identifications, a series of MCAs were conducted adding and dropping the three variables to see the effects of interaction terms on the final result when all three variables are included.

Chapter 7

1. Portions of this chapter draw from material published in an earlier work. See Smidt and Schaap (2009).

2. It is also true, however, that this focus was partially shaped by the particular topics that some of the classic social scientific studies of clergy had previously examined.

3. Of course, it can be argued that even the lack of specific political cues of any kind during the worship context constitutes a specific kind of civic/political cue-giving—a cue that suggests to the worshipping community the relative unimportance or irrelevance of such considerations.

4. Technically, these survey items do not always inquire just where such urging or public praying may have occurred. It is possible that such urgings may have been done through a bulletin announcement or some church newsletter and some public prayers offered in contexts outside of congregational worship. However, most public prayers of clergy likely occur within the worship setting, and such urging may well occur during the portion of worship in which announcements are made. Hence, these items will be examined within the context of worship itself.

5. The survey items asked clergy to indicate whether they had done the specific activity within the past year, not specifically during the course of the presidential campaign. However, since the surveys were conducted in the early months of the year following a presidential election, it can be inferred that most such activities were done largely, if not totally, during the course of the presidential selection and election process.

6. Of course, not all such endorsements may have been done in the context of the presidential campaign; some endorsements could have been for candidates for local offices or even for candidates in nonpartisan elections.

7. Earlier clergy studies generally revealed that clergy who exhibited lower levels of theological orthodoxy were more likely than those higher in theological orthodoxy to deliver entire sermons on political issues, whereas more orthodox clergy preferred to insert political commentary through touching on political topics in sermons (Guth et al. 1997, 163-64). However, by 2009, this pattern has been largely reversed, as those low in orthodoxy were more likely than those high in orthodoxy to report that they had touched on a political issue in a sermon (82 versus 73 percent, respectively), whereas highly orthodox clergy were now slightly more likely than clergy low in orthodoxy to report that they had delivered a whole sermon on an issue—26 percent to 23 percent, respectively.

8. Even when one removes the two most common forms of political cue-giving activities (i.e., praying about an issue and urging congregants to register and vote) as well as the least reported form of cue-giving (i.e., endorsing a candidate while preaching), almost all clergy (88 percent) still reported that they had engaged in one of the remaining four cue-giving activities during the 2008 presidential election year, with more than one-third (37 percent) having engaged in at least three, if not all, of the four activities.

9. Technically speaking, these two items simply indicate that these actions did not occur "while preaching." For many pastors, however, the phrase "while preaching" is interpreted more broadly to mean any action done "from the pulpit."

10. It should be noted that these figures likely underestimate the actual level to which these particular topics were discussed. Pastors were given the list of nine topics and were simply asked to check those topics addressed. Given this format, it is therefore unclear from the data file whether the lack of noting the presence of such a class represents simply having not offered the class or the failure of some clergy to complete that section of the survey. The present figures are based on the assumptions that all clergy had completed this section of the questionnaire.

11. The lower level of reports of these classes within evangelical Protestant congregations is likely due, in part, to evangelical congregations offering relatively more Bible-study classes within their adult education programs.

Chapter 8

1. The portion of the questionnaire devoted to stands on political issues was found in a later section of the questionnaire.

2. Moreover, among those who did not address the topic with such frequency, approximately the same percentages were evident—with 39 percent agreeing with the statement and 51 percent disagreeing.

3. This latter finding reveals what Djupe and Gilbert (2003, 33) had noted earlier: talking about "gay rights" tends to be related to the social justice agenda, whereas talking about homosexuality is associated with the moral reform agenda.

4. Conventionally, this is done through exploratory factor analysis (e.g., Guth et al. 1997, 82; Djupe and Gilbert 2003, 33).

5. These particular items were selected in part because of their availability across all three surveys, as well as the particular scores each of the variables exhibited in terms of their factor loadings.

6. The content of clergy messages has also been found to be shaped by differences in the resources clergy possess and the particular opportunities they may enjoy (Guth et al. 1997; Olson 2000; Crawford and Olson 2001; Djupe and Gilbert 2003).

7. Pastors from the CRC and RCA were not asked these questions in 1989.

8. When comparing the percentages obtained for 2001 to those collected in 1999 from Episcopal priests and Evangelical Lutheran Church in America pastors (Djupe and Gilbert 2003, 59), the reported levels of activism across the two studies comport well with each other. A slightly higher percentage of clergy from the Djupe and Gilbert study reported they had contacted some public official over the course of the past year (40 percent did so) and

had contributed money to a candidate party or PAC (26 percent did so) than clergy from the seven denominations surveyed here, but otherwise the remaining percentages for identical items differ 2 percentage points or less across the two studies.

9. Conventionally, this seven-point scale moves along the following continuum: from strong Democrat on one end, to weak Democrat, then to Independent leaning Democrat, followed by Independent, then Independent leaning Republican, to weak Republican, to finally strong Republican.

10. Dealignment is understood to occur when a social group that typically votes in a particular partisan fashion (e.g., members of unions) abandons its long-standing loyalty to a party and becomes largely independent or nonvoting politically.

11. Realignments entail the switching of voting preferences among social groups from one party to the other. These shifts have been described in two different forms: the first being labeled a "critical realignment" in which a dramatic shift occurs in the alignment of voters with the two major parties over a very short period of time (Key 1955), with the second being labeled a "secular realignment" in which the shift in alignment occurs over the span of a number of elections before it completes its evolution (Key 1959). These realigning elections supposedly mobilize new voters to the polls, bring new issues to the forefront of political debate, and alter the distribution of voter alignments in a relatively durable fashion that serves to characterize American electoral politics for the next generation or two.

12. When denomination is used instead of religious tradition as a variable in the MCA, the beta value is somewhat higher for denomination than it is for religious tradition and the beta weight for theological orthodoxy diminishes several points. However, the overall explanatory value of the model hardly differs when denomination is used instead of religious tradition.

Conclusion

1. Gilligan's analysis has been criticized on a number of grounds. For a review of some these criticisms, see Robbins (1998, 75).

2. Some recent research (Niemela 2011), however, has shown that clergywomen have been important agents of religions change within the Evangelical Lutheran Church of Finland, as women clergy have moved the church in a more liberal direction by changing perceptions of faith and dogma, changing the policies of the church, and changing practices in the parishes.

3. It should be noted, however, that many do not work in congregations. They may work in denominational agencies, as chaplains in various capacities, as missionaries outside the country, as workers in nonprofit agencies, and so on.

4. As for the remaining three qualities, it is likely, first of all, that congregations will continue to serve as a moral community for those who regularly attend worship, a quality that fundamentally differentiates involvement in congregational life from that of involvement in other forms of voluntary associations. Likewise, the opportunities available to clergy within congregation life are not likely to change in any fundamental fashion, nor are the particular resources that clergy typically possess in terms of their typically higher levels of education and analytical ability, even though the relative advantages of possessing these resources have more recently diminished in relationship to the educational attainment of their congregants.

5. Of course, if, in the future, clergy would choose to diminish the extent to which they provide political cues, discuss public issues, or engage in political endeavors, this too would diminish their potential political significance.

6. Chaves and Anderson (2012, 215) report that, based on General Social Survey data, the percentage of Americans claiming a religion other than Christian or Jewish was about 1 percent in the 1970s, with that percentage increasing to 3 percent by 2008.

7. It should be noted, however, that many who are affiliated with some local congregation nonetheless report that they are religiously unaffiliated (Dougherty, Johnson, and Polson 2007; Johnson 2011). Consequently, one must take the seeming growth in the religiously unaffiliated somewhat cautiously when no follow-up questions are asked in relationship to affiliation with some local church.

8. This is also evident from the fact that clergy are the primary profession that older Americans rate more positively than younger Americans, with an 18-point difference between those under age 35 and those 55 and older (Jones 2013).

9. It should be noted, however, that this comparison over time among regular church attenders was one that compared the resultant data for 2009 with those for 2008. Hence, this assertion is based on very limited across-time data.

REFERENCES

Abramowitz, Alan, and Kyle Saunders. 2006. "Exploring the Bases of Partisanship in the American Electorate: Social Identity vs. Ideology." *Political Research Quarterly* 59 (June): 175–87.

Ammerman, Nancy Tatom. 1997. *Congregation & Community*. New Brunswick, NJ: Rutgers University Press.

Ammerman, Nancy Tatom. 2005. *Pillars of Faith: American Congregations and their Partners*. Berkeley: University of California Press.

Bade, Rachael. 2014. "Rogue Pastors Endorse Candidates, but IRS Looks Away." *Politico*, November 3. http://www.politico.com/story/2014/11/2014-elections-pastors-endorsing-candidates-irs-112434.html.

Baldassarri, Delia, and Andrew Gelman. 2008. "Partisans without Constraint: Political Polarization and Trends in American Public Opinion." *American Journal of Sociology* 114 (September): 408–46.

Barker, David, Jon Hurwitz, and Traci Nelsen. 2008. "Of Crusades and Culture Wars: 'Messianic' Militarism and Political Conflict in the United States." *Journal of Politics* 70 (2): 307–22.

Barnes, Samuel, and Max Kaase. 1979. *Political Action: Mass Participation in Five Western Democracies*. Beverly Hills, CA: Sage.

Bartels, Larry. 1996. "Uninformed Votes: Information Effects on Presidential Elections." *American Journal of Political Science* 40 (1): 194–230.

Beatty, Kathleen, and Oliver Walter. 1989. "A Group Theory of Religion and Politics: The Clergy as Group Leaders." *Western Political Quarterly* 42: 129–46.

Beck, Paul Allen, and M. Kent Jennings. 1991. "Family Traditions, Political Periods, and the Development of Partisan Orientations." *Journal of Politics* 53: 742–63.

Bellah, Robert, Richard Madsen, William Sullivan, Ann Swindler, and Steven Tipton. 2007. *Habits of the Heart: Individualism and Commitment in American Life*. 3rd ed. Berkeley: University of California Press.

Berelson, Bernard, Paul Lazarsfeld, and William McPhee. 1954. *Voting*. Chicago: University of Chicago Press.

Bibby, John. 1987. *Politics, Parties, and Elections in America*. Chicago: Nelson Hall.

Bjarnason, Thoroddur, and Michael Welch. 2004. "Father Knows Best: Parishes, Priests, and American Catholic Parishioners' Attitudes toward Capital Punishment." *Journal for the Scientific Study of Religion* 43: 103–18.

Breen, Tom. 2011. "Duke University Expert: America's Religious Faith is Waning." *The Grand Rapids Press*, August 27, C5.

Brewer, Mark, Rogan Kersh, and R. Eric Petersen. 2003. "Assessing Conventional Wisdom about Religion and Politics: A Preliminary View from the Pews." *Journal for the Scientific Study of Religion* 42 (1): 125–36.

Briggs, David. 2014. "For Better or Worse, Clergy Key Reason Worshipers Switch Congregations." *Beyond the Ordinary: Insights into U.S. Congregational Life*. http://presbyterian.typepad.com/beyondordinary/2014/02/for-better-or-worse-clergy-key-reason-worshipers-switch-congregations.html.

Brown, Don, and Corwin E. Smidt. 2003. "Media and Clergy: Influencing the Influential?" *Journal of Media and Religion* 2 (2): 75–92.

Buddenbaum, Judith. 2001. "The Media, Religion, and Public Opinion: Toward a Unified Theory of Influence." In *Religion and Popular Culture: Studies on the Interaction of Worldviews*, edited by Daniel Stout and Judith Buddenbaum, 19–38. Ames: Iowa State University Press.

Burnham, Walter Dean. 1970. *Critical Elections and the Mainsprings of American Politics*. New York: Norton.

Burns, Nancy, Kay Schlozman, and Sidney Verba. 2001. *The Private Roots of Public Action: Gender, Equality, and Political Participation*. Cambridge, MA: Harvard University Press.

Buzzard, Samuel. 1956. "The Minister's Dilemma." *Christian Century* 73: 508–9.

Calfano, Brian. 2009. "Choosing Constituent Cues: Reference Group Influence on Clergy Political Speech." *Social Science Quarterly* 90: 88–102.

Calfano, Brian. 2010. "Prophetic at Any Price? Clergy Political Behavior and Utility Maximization." *Social Science Quarterly* 91: 649–68.

Calfano, Brian, Elizabeth Oldmixon, and Mark Gray. 2014. "Strategically Prophetic Priests: An Analysis of Competing Principal Influence on Clergy Political Action." *Review of Religious Research* 56 (March): 1–22.

Campbell, Angus, Philip Converse, Warren Miller, and Donald Stokes. 1960. *The American Voter*. New York: John Wiley.

Campbell, Angus, Gerald Gurin, and Warren Miller. 1954. *The Voter Decides*. Evanston, IL: Row, Peterson, and Co.

Campbell, David E. 2004. "Community Heterogeneity and Participation." Paper presented at the annual meeting of the American Political Science Association, September 2–5.

Campbell, David E., ed. 2007. *A Matter of Faith: Religion in the 2004 Presidential Election*. Washington, DC: Brookings Institution Press.

Campbell, Ernest Q., and Thomas F. Pettigrew. 1959. *Christians in Racial Crisis: A Study of Little Rock's Ministry*. Washington, DC: Public Affairs Press.

Carmines, Edward, and Geoffrey Layman. 1997. "Issue Evolution in Postwar American Politics: Old Certainties and Fresh Tensions." In *Present Discontents: American Politics in the Very Late Twenties Century*, ed. Byron Shafer, 90–134. Chatham, NJ: Chatham House Publishers.

Carnes, Tony. 2004. " 'Swing Evangelicals': Democrats Seek to Show That They Also Have Faith-based Values." *Christianity Today*. February 1. http://www.christianitytoday.com/ct/2004/february/11.15.html.

Carroll, Jackson. 2006. *God's Potters: Pastoral Leadership in the Shaping of Congregations*. Grand Rapids, MI: William B. Eerdmans.

Carroll, Jackson, and Penny Long Marler. 1995. "Culture Wars? Insights from Ethnographies of Two Protestant Seminaries." *Sociology of Religion* 56: 1–20.

Carter, Stephen L. 1993. *The Culture of Disbelief: How American Law and Politics Trivialize Religious Devotion*. New York: Basic Books.

Casanova, Jose. 1994. *Public Religions in the Modern World*. Chicago: University of Chicago Press.

Chaves, Mark. 1997. *Ordaining Women: Culture and Conflict in Religious Organizations*. Cambridge, MA: Harvard University Press.

Chaves, Mark. 2004. *Congregations in America*. Cambridge, MA: Harvard University Press.

Chaves, Mark. 2011. *American Religion: Contemporary Trends*. Princeton, NJ: Princeton University Press.

Chaves, Mark, and Shawna Anderson. 2012. "Continuity and Change in American Religion, 1972–2008." In *Social Trends in American Life: Findings from the General Social Surveys since 1972*, edited by Peter V. Martsden, 212–39. Princeton, NJ: Princeton University Press.

Cnaan, Ram, Stephanie Boddie, Charlene McGrew, and Jennifer Kang. 2006. *The Other Philadelphia Story: How Local Congregations Support Quality of Life in Urban America*. Philadelphia: University of Pennsylvania Press.

Cochran, Clarke. 1990. *Religion in Public and Private Life*. New York: Routledge.

Coffin, Brent. 2005. "Moral Deliberation in Congregations." In *Taking Faith Seriously*, edited by Mary Jo Bane, Brent Coffin, and Richard Higgins, 113–45. Cambridge, MA: Harvard University Press.

Converse, Philip. 1964. "The Nature of Belief Systems in Mass Publics." In *Ideology and Discontent*, edited by David Apter, 206–61. New York: Free Press.

Cox, Harvey. 1967. "The 'New Breed' in American Churches: Sources of Social Activism in American Religion." *Daedalus* 96: 135–50.

Crawford, Sue, and Laura Olson, eds. 2001. *Christian Clergy in American Politics*. Baltimore, MD: Johns Hopkins University Press.

Dalton, Russell, Paul Allen Beck, and Robert Huckfeldt. 1998. "Partisan Cues and the Media: Information Flows in the 1992 Presidential Election." *American Political Science Review* 92 (March): 111–26.

Dart, John. 2013. "Evangelical Body Supports Politicking in the Pulpit." *Christian Century* 130 (19): 15.

Deckman, Melissa, Sue Crawford, Laura Olson, and John Green. 2003. "Clergy and the Politics of Gender: Women and Politics Opportunity in Mainline Protestant Churches." *Journal for the Scientific Study of Religion* 42 (December): 621–32.

Djupe, Paul A., and Brian R. Calfano. 2012. "The Deliberative Pulpit: The Democratic Norms and Practices of the PCUSA." *Journal for the Scientific Study of Religion* 51: 90–109.

Djupe, Paul A., and Brian R. Calfano. 2014. *God Talk: Experimenting with the Religious Causes of Public Opinion*. Philadelphia, PA: Temple University Press.

Djupe, Paul, and Christopher Gilbert. 2002. "The Political Voice of Clergy." *Journal of Politics* 64: 596–609.

Djupe, Paul, and Christopher Gilbert. 2003. *The Prophetic Pulpit: Clergy, Churches, and Communities in American Politics*. Lanham, MD: Rowman & Littlefield.

Djupe, Paul, and Christopher Gilbert. 2006. "The Resourceful Believer: Generating Civic Skills in Church." *Journal of Politics* 68 (February): 116–27.

Djupe, Paul, and Christopher Gilbert. 2008. "Politics and Church: Byproduct or Central Mission?" *Journal for the Scientific Study of Religion* 47: 45–62.

Djupe, Paul, and Christopher Gilbert. 2009. *The Political Influence of Churches*. New York: Cambridge University Press.

Djupe, Paul, and Jacob Neiheisel. 2008. "Clergy Deliberation on Gay Rights and Homosexuality." *Polity* 40 (October): 411–35.

Dougherty, Kevin, Byron Johnson, and Clay Polson. 2007. "Recovering the Lost: Remeasuring U.S. Religious Affiliation." *Journal for the Scientific Study of Religion* 46 (December): 483–99.

Downs, Anthony. 1957. *An Economic Theory of Democracy*. New York: Harper and Row.

Ellison, Christopher, and Linda George. 1994. "Religious Involvement, Social Ties, and Social Support in a Southeastern Community." *Journal for the Scientific Study of Religion* 33 (1): 46–61.

Emerson, Michael. 2006. *People of the Dream: Multiracial Congregations in the United States*. Princeton, NJ: Princeton University Press.

Federico, Christopher. 2012. "Ideology and Public Opinion." In *New Directions in Public Opinion*, edited by Adam Berinksy, 79–100. New York: Routledge.

Fetzer, Joel. 2001. "Shaping Pacifism: The Role of the Local Anabaptist Pastor." In *Christian Clergy in American Politics*, edited by Sue Crawford and Laura Olson, 177–87. Baltimore, MD: Johns Hopkins University Press.

Finnemore, Martha. 1996. *National Interests in International Society*. Ithaca, NY: Cornell University Press, 1996.

Fiorina, Morris, Samuel Abrams, and Jeremy Pope. 2005. *Culture War? The Myth of Polarized America*. New York: Pearson Longman.

Free, Lloyd, and Hadley Cantril. 1967. *The Political Beliefs of Americans*. New Brunswick, NJ: Rutgers University Press.

Gallup, George. 1998. "Pharmacists, Clergy Are Most Highly Rated Occupations." *Emerging Trends* 20 (January): 4.

Gallup Poll. 2014. "Honesty/Ethics in Professions." http://www.gallup.com/poll/1654/honesty-ethics-professions.aspx.

Garrett, William. 1973. "Politicized Clergy: A Sociological Interpretation of the 'New Breed.'" *Journal for the Scientific Study of Religion* 12: 384–99.

Gaustad, Edwin. 1990. "The Pulpit and the Pews." In *Between the Times: The Travail of the Protestant Establishment in America, 1900–1960*, edited by William R. Hutchison, 21–47. New York: Cambridge University Press.

Gilbert, Christopher. 1989. "The Political Influence of Church Discussion Partners." Paper presented at the annual meeting of the American Political Science Association, Atlanta.

Gilbert, Christopher. 1990. "Religious Environments and Political Attitudes." Paper presented at the annual meeting of the American Political Science Association, San Francisco.

Gilbert, Christopher. 1993. *The Impact of Churches on Political Behavior*. Westport, CT: Greenwood.

Gilligan, Carol. 1982. *In a Different Voice: Psychological Theory and Women's Development*. Cambridge, MA: Harvard University Press.

Gray, Donald. 2008. "Beyond Orthodoxy: Social Theology and the Views of Protestant Clergy on Social Issues." *Review of Religious Research* 50 (2): 221–40.

Green, Donald, Bradley Palmquist, and Erik Schickler. 2002. *Partisan Hearts & Minds*. New Haven, CT: Yale University Press.

Greenstein, Fred. 1965. *Children and Politics*. New Haven, CT: Yale University Press.

Guth, James L. 1983. "Southern Baptist Clergy: Vanguard of the Christian Right?" In *The New Christian Right: Mobilization and Legitimation*, edited by Robert Liebman and Robert Wuthnow, 117–30. Hawthorne, NY: Aldine.

Guth, James L. 1984. "The Politics of Preachers: Southern Baptist Ministers and Christian Right Activism." In *New Christian Politics*, edited by David Bromley and Anson Shupe, 235–49. Macon, GA: Mercer University Press.

Guth, James L. 2001. "Clergy in Politics; Reflections on the Status of Research in the Field." In *Christian Clergy in American Politics*, edited by Sue Crawford and Laura Olson, 30–43. Baltimore, MD: Johns Hopkins University Press.

Guth, James L. 2009. "Religion and American Public Opinion: Foreign Policy Issues." In *The Oxford Handbook of Religion and American Politics*, edited by Corwin Smidt, Lyman Kellstedt, and James Guth, 243–65. New York: Oxford University Press.

Guth, James L., John Green, Corwin Smidt, Lyman Kellstedt, and Margaret Poloma. 1997. *The Bully Pulpit: The Politics of Protestant Clergy*. Lawrence: University Press of Kansas.

Gutmann, Amy, and Dennis Thompson. 1996. *Democracy and Disagreement*. Cambridge, MA: Harvard University Press.

Hadaway, Kirk, Penny Marler, and Mark Chaves. 1993. "What the Polls Don't Show: A Closer Look at Church Attendance." *American Sociological Review* 58 (December): 741–52.

Hadden, Jeffrey. 1969. *The Gathering Storm in the Churches*. Garden City, NY: Doubleday.

Hagen, Michael, and William Mayer. 2000. "The Modern Politics of Presidential Selection." In *In Pursuit of the White House 2000*, edited by William Mayer, 3–44. New York: Chatham House.

Hero, Alfred. 1973. *American Religious Groups View Foreign Policy: Trends in Rank-and-File Opinion, 1937–1969*. Durham, NC: Duke University Press.

Hershey, Marjorie Randon. 2013. *Party Politics in America*, 15th ed. Boston: Pearson.

Hertzke, Allen. 1988. *Representing God in Washington: The Role of Religious Lobbies in the American Polity*. Knoxville: University of Tennessee Press.

Hofrenning, Daniel. 1995. *In Washington but Not of It*. Philadelphia, PA: Temple University Press.

Hoge, Dean. 1976. *Division in the Protestant House*. Philadelphia: Westminster Press.

Hoge, Dean, Benton Johnson, and Donald Luidens. 1994. *Vanishing Boundaries: The Religion of Mainline Protestant Baby Boomers*. Louisville, KY: Westminster/John Knox Press.

Hout, Michael, Andrew Greeley, and Melissa Wilde. 2001."The Demographic Imperative in Religious Change in the United States." *American Journal of Sociology* 107 (2): 468–500.

Huckfeldt, Robert, and John Sprague. 1995. *Citizens, Politics, and Social Communications: Information and Influence in an Election Campaign.* Cambridge: Cambridge University Press.

Hunter. James Davison. 1991. *Culture Wars: The Struggle to Define America.* New York: Basic Books.

Hunter, James Davison. 1994. *Before the Shooting Begins: Searching for Democracy in America's Culture War.* New York: Free Press.

Iyengar, Shanto. 1991. *Is Anyone Responsible? How Television Frames Political Issues.* Chicago: University of Chicago Press.

Iyengar, Shanto, and Donald Kinder. 1987. *News That Matters: Television and American Public Opinion.* Chicago: University of Chicago Press.

Jeffries, Vincent, and Clarence Tygart. 1974. "The Influence of Theology, Denomination, and Values upon the Position of Clergy on Social Issues." *Journal for the Scientific Study of Religion* 13: 309–24.

Jelen, Ted. 1993. *The Political World of the Clergy.* Westport, CT: Praeger.

Jelen, Ted. 2001. "Notes for a Theory of Clergy as Political Leaders." In *Christian Clergy in American Politics,* edited by Sue Crawford and Laura Olson, 15–29. Baltimore, MD: Johns Hopkins University Press.

Jelen, Ted, and Clyde Wilcox. 1993. "Preaching to the Converted: The Causes and Consequences of Viewing Religious Television." In *Rediscovering the Religious Factor in American Politics,* edited by David Leege and Lyman Kellstedt, 255–69. Armonk, NY: M. E. Sharpe.

Johnson, Benton. 1966. "Theology and Party Preference among Protestant Clergy." *American Sociological Review* 31: 200–208.

Johnson, Benton. 1967. "Theology and the Position of Pastor on Public Issues." *American Sociological Review* 32: 433–42.

Johnson, Benton. 1998. "Theology and the Position of Pastors on Public Issues: Continuity and Change since the 1960s." *Review of Religious Research* 39: 293–308.

Johnson, Bryon. 2011. "The Good News about Evangelicalism." *First Things* 210 (February): 12–14.

Johnson, Janet Buttolph, and H. T. Reynolds, with Jason Mycoff. 2008. *Political Science Research Methods.* Washington, DC: CQ Press.

Jones, Jeffrey. 2009. "U.S. Clergy, Bankers See New Lows in Honesty/Ethics Ratings." http:// www.gallup.com/poll/124628/clergy-bankers-new-lows-honesty-ethics-ratings.aspx.

Jones, Jeffrey. 2013. "Honesty Ratings of Police, Clergy Differ Most by Party." http://www.gallup. com/poll/166487/honesty-ratings-police-clergy-differ-party.aspx.

Kelly, Harold. 1979. *Personal Relationships: Their Structures and Processes.* Hillsdale, NJ: Erlbaum.

Key, V. O. 1955. "A Theory of Critical Elections." *Journal of Politics* 17 (1): 3–18.

Key, V. O. 1959. "Secular Realignment and the Party System." *Journal of Politics* 21 (2): 198–210.

Kohut, Andrew, and Bruce Stokes. 2006. *America against the World.* New York: Henry Holt.

Koller, Norman B., and Joseph D. Retzer. 1980. "The Sounds of Silence Revisited." *Sociological Analysis* 21 (2): 155–61.

Krosnick, Jon, and Laura Brannon. 1993. "The Media and Foundations of Presidential Support: George Bush and the Persian Gulf Conflict." *Journal of Social Issues* 49 (4): 167–82.

Kumar, Anugrah. 2014. "Over 1,800 Pastors Take Part in Pulpit Freedom Sunday." October 11. http://www.christianpost.com/news/over-1800-pastors-take-part-in-pulpit-freedom-sunday-127914/.

Kurtz, Lester, and Kelly Gordon Fulton. 2002. "Love Your Enemies? Protestants and United States Foreign Policy." In *The Quiet Hand of God: Faith-Based Activism and the Public Role of Mainline Protestantism,* edited by Robert Wuthnow and John H. Evans, 364–80. Berkeley: University of California Press.

Lawrence, David. 1997. *The Collapse of the Democratic Presidential Majority: Realignment, Dealignment, and Electoral Changes from Franklin Roosevelt to Bill Clinton.* Boulder, CO: Westview Press.

Layman, Geoffrey. 2001. *The Great Divide: Religious and Cultural Conflict in American Party Politics.* New York: Columbia University Press.

Layman, Geoffrey, and Thomas Carsey. 2002. "Party Polarization and 'Conflict Extension' in the American Electorate." *American Journal of Political Science* 46 (4): 786–802.

Leege, David, Lyman Kellstedt, and Kenneth Wald. 1990. "Religion and Politics: A Report on Measures of Religiosity in the 1989 NES Pilot Study." Paper presented at the annual meeting of the Midwest Political Science Association, Chicago.

Lenski, Gerhard. 1961. *The Religious Factor*. Garden City, NY: Doubleday Anchor.

Markoe, Lauren. 2014. "Houston Withdraws Pastors' Subpoenas." Religious News Service, October 29. http://www.religionnews.com/2014/10/29/houston-withdraws-pastors-subpoenas/.

Marler, Penny, and Kirk Hadaway. 1999. "Testing the Attendance Gap in a Conservative Church." *Sociology of Religion* 60 (2): 175–86.

Marsden, George. 1980. *Fundamentalism and American Culture: The Shaping of Twentieth-Century Evangelicalism 1870–1925*. New York: Oxford University Press.

Marshall, Paul. 2002. *God and the Constitution: Christianity and American Politics*. Lanham, MD: Rowman and Littlefield.

Marti, Gerardo. 2005. *A Mosaic of Believers: Diversity and Innovation in a Multiethnic Church*. Bloomington: Indiana University Press.

Marty, Martin E. 1989. "Introduction: Religion in America 1935–1985." In *Altered Landscapes: Christianity in America 1935–85*, edited by David W. Lutz, 1–16. Grand Rapids, MI: Eerdmans Publishing Company.

McCarty, Nolan, Keith Poole, and Howard Rosenthal. 2006. *Polarized America: The Dance of Ideology and Unequal Riches*. Cambridge, MA: MIT Press.

McClosky, Herbert, Paul Hoffman, and Rosemary O'Hara. 1960. "Issue Conflict and Consensus among Party Leaders and Followers." *American Political Science Review* 54: 406–27.

McKelvey, Richard, and Peter Ordeshook. 1986. "Information, Electoral Equilibria, and the Democratic Ideal." *Journal of Politics* 48 (4): 909–37.

Merritt, Jonathan. 2013. "What Southern Baptists Must Do to Slow Their Decline." http://jonathanmerritt.religionnews.com/2013/06/11/what-southern-baptists-must-do-to-slow-their-decline/.

Metaxas, Eric. 2014. "Hand Over Your Sermon or Else: Intimidating the Faithful." October 17. http://www.breakpoint.org/bpcommentaries/entry/13/26252.

Monsma, Stephen. 1984. *Pursuing Justice in a Sinful World*. Grand Rapids, MI: Eerdmans.

Morris, Alden. 1984. *The Origins of the Civic Rights Movement: Black Communities Organizing for Change*. New York: Free Press.

Mutz, Diana, and Jeffrey Mondak. 2006. "The Workplace as a Context for Cross-Cutting Political Discourse." *Journal of Politics* 68: 145–55.

Neiheisel, Jacob R., and Paul A. Djupe. 2008. "Intra-Organizational Constraints on Churches' Public Witness." *Journal for the Scientific Study of Religion* 47 (3): 427–41.

Neiheisel, Jacob R., Paul A. Djupe, and Anand E. Sokhey. 2009. "Veni, Vidi, Disseri: Churches and the Promise of Democratic Deliberation." *American Politics Research* 37 (4): 614–43.

Nelsen, Hart, and Sandra Baxter. 1981. "Ministers Speak on Watergate: Effects of Clergy Role during Political Crisis." *Review of Religious Research* 23 (December): 150–66.

Nesbitt, Paula. 1997. *Feminization of Clergy in America: Occupational and Organizational Perspectives*. New York: Oxford University Press.

Nesbitt, Paula. 2007. "Keepers of the Tradition: Religious Professionals and their Careers." In *The Sage Handbook of the Sociology of Religion*, edited by James Beckford and N. J. Demerath III, 295–322. Thousand Oaks, CA: Sage Publications.

Niemela, Kati. 2011. "Female Clergy as Agents of Religious Change?" *Religions* 2: 358–71.

Nteta, Tatishe, and Kevin Wallsten. 2012. "Preaching to the Choice? Religious Leaders and American Opinion on Immigration Reform." *Social Science Quarterly* 93 (4): 891–910.

Olson, Laura. 2000. *Filled with Spirit and Power: Protestant Clergy in Politics*. Albany: State University of New York Press.

Olson, Laura. 2009. "Clergy and American Politics." In *The Oxford Handbook of Religion and American Politics*, edited by Corwin E. Smidt, Lyman A. Kellstedt, and James L. Guth, 371–93. New York: Oxford University Press.

Olson, Laura, Sue Crawford, and Melissa Deckman. 2005. *Women with a Mission: Religion, Gender, and the Politics of Women Clergy.* Tuscaloosa: University of Alabama Press.

Page, Benjamin, with Marshall Bouton. 2006. *The Foreign Policy Disconnect: What Americans Want from Our Leaders But Don't Get.* Chicago: University of Chicago Press.

Penning, James. 2009. "Change and Continuity in the Political Norms of Protestant Clergy." Paper presented at the annual meeting of the Society for the Scientific Study of Religion. Denver, CO.

Peterson, Steven. 1992. "Church Participation and Political Participation: The Spillover Effect." *American Politics Quarterly* 20 (1): 123–39.

Petrocik, John. 1981. *Party Coalitions: Realignments and the Decline of the New Deal Party System.* Chicago: University of Chicago Press.

Pew Research Center. 2015. "America's Changing Religious Landscape." http://www.pewforum.org/2015/05/12/americas-changing-religious-landscape/.

Popkin, Samuel. 1991. *The Reasoning Voter: Communication and Persuasion in Presidential Campaigns.* Chicago: University of Chicago Press.

Price, Matthew. 2001. "Fear of Falling: Male Clergy in Economic Crisis." *Christian Century* 118 (23): 18–21.

Putnam, Robert. 2000. *Bowling Alone: The Collapse and Revival of American Community.* New York: Simon & Schuster.

Putnam, Robert, and David Campbell. 2010. *American Grace: How Religion Divides and Unites Us.* New York: Simon & Schuster.

Quinley, Harold E. 1974. *The Prophetic Clergy: Social Activism among Protestant Ministers.* New York: Wiley.

Richey, Russell E. 1994. "Denominations and Denominationalism: An American Morphology." In *Reimagining Denominationalism: Interpretive Essays*, edited by Robert B. Mullin and Russell E. Richey, 74–98. New York: Oxford University Press.

Robbins, Mandy. 1998. "A Different Voice: A Different View." *Review of Religious Research* 40 (September): 75–80.

Roof, Wade Clark, and William McKinney. 1987. *American Mainline Religion: Its Changing Shape and Future.* New Brunswick, NJ: Rutgers University Press.

Rosenof, Theodore. 2003. *Realignment: The Theory that Changed the Way We Think about American Politics.* Lanham, MD: Rowman & Littlefield.

Rosenstone, Steven, and John Hansen. 1993. *Mobilization, Participation, and Democracy in America.* New York: Macmillan.

Rozell, Mark, and Gleaves Whitney, eds. 2007. *Religion and the Bush Presidency.* Boulder, CO: Palgrave MacMillan.

Scammon, Richard, and Ben Wattenberg. 1970. *The Real Majority.* New York: Coward-McCann.

Scheufele, Dietram, M. C. Nisbet, D. Brossard, and E. C. Nisbet. 2004. "Social Structure and Citizenship: Examining the Impacts of Social Setting, Network Heterogeneity, and Information Variables on Political Participation." *Political Communication* 21: 315–38.

Scheufele, Dietram, and David Tewksbury. 2007. "Framing, Agenda Setting, and Priming: The Evolution of Three Media Effects Models." *Journal of Communication* 57: 9–20.

Shafer, Byron, ed. 1991. *The End of Realignment: Interpreting American Electoral Eras.* Madison: University of Wisconsin Press.

Smidt, Corwin E., ed. 2004. *Pulpit and Politics: Clergy in American Politics at the Advent of the Millennium.* Waco, TX: Baylor University Press.

Smidt, Corwin E., Kevin denDulk, Bryan Froehle, James Penning, Stephen Monsma, and Douglas Koopman. 2010. *The Disappearing God Gap? Religion in the 2008 Presidential Election.* New York: Oxford University Press.

Smidt, Corwin E., Kevin R. denDulk, James M. Penning, Stephen V. Monsma, and Douglas L. Koopman. 2008. *Pews, Prayers & Participation: Religion & Civic Responsibility in America.* Washington, DC: Georgetown University Press.

Smidt, Corwin E., and Brian Schaap. 2009. "Public Worship and Public Engagement: Pastoral Cues within the Context of Worship Services." *Review of Religious Research* 50 (June 2009): 441–62.

Smietana, Bob. 2013. "IRS Shouldn't Ban Clergy Endorsements, Panel Says. *USAToday*, August 14. http://www.usatoday.com/story/news/nation/2013/08/14/irs-shouldnt-ban-clergy-endorsements-panel-says/2657817/.

Smietana, Bob. 2014. "LifeWay Research: Pastors Believe Religious Liberty on Decline." February 20. http://www.lifewayresearch.com/2014/02/20/lifeway-research-pastors-believe-religious-liberty-on-decline-in-u-s.

Smith, Christian, and Melissa Lindquist Denton. 2005. *Soul Searching: The Religious and Spiritual Lives of American Teenagers*. New York: Oxford University Press.

Smith, Gregory. 2008. *Politics in the Parish: The Political Influence of Catholic Priests*. Washington, DC: Georgetown University Press.

Smith, Tom. 2012. "Trends in Confidence in Institutions: 1973–2006." In *Social Trends in American Life: Findings from the General Social Surveys since 1972*, edited by Peter V. Marsden, 177–211. Princeton, NJ: Princeton University Press.

Smith, Tom, and Seokho Kim. 2005. "The Vanishing Protestant Majority." *Journal for the Scientific Study of Religion* 44: 211–23.

Sniderman, Paul, Richard Brody, and Phillip Tetlock, eds. 1993. *Reasoning and Choice: Explorations in Political Psychology*. New York: Cambridge University Press.

Stanley, Erik. 2014. "Houston, We Have a Problem." Alliance Defending Freedom, October 13. http://www.adfmedia.org/News/PRDetail/9349.

Stark, Rodney. 1996. "Religion as Context: Hellfire and Delinquency One More Time. *Sociology of Religion* 57: 163–73.

Stark, Rodney, and Bruce Foster. 1970. "In Defense of Orthodoxy: Notes on the Validity of an Index." *Social Forces* 48 (March): 383–93.

Stark, Rodney, Bruce Foster, Charles Glock, and Harold Quinley. 1970. "Sounds of Silence." *Psychology Today*, April 11.

Stark, Rodney, Bruce Foster, Charles Glock, and Harold Quinley. 1971. *Wayward Shepherds: Prejudice and the Protestant Clergy*. New York: Harper & Row.

Stetzer, Ed. 2010. "Life in Those Old Bones." www.christianitytoday.com/ct/2010/june/11.24.html.

Stimson, James. 2004. *Tides of Consent: How Public Opinion Shapes American Politics*. New York: Cambridge University Press.

Tipton, Steven. 2007. *Public Pulpits: Methodists and Mainline Churches in the Moral Argument of Public Life*. Chicago: University of Chicago Press.

Verba, Sidney, Kay Schlozman, and Henry Brady. 1995. *Voice and Equality: Civic Voluntarism in American Politics*. Cambridge, MA: Harvard University Press.

Verba, Sidney, Kay Schlozman, Henry Brady, and Norman Nie. 1993. "Citizen Activity: Who Participates? What Do They Say?" *American Political Science Review* 87 (June): 303–19.

Verbrugge, Lois. 1977. "The Structure of Adult Friendship Choices." *Social Forces* 56: 576–79.

Vidich, Arthur, and Joseph Bensman. 1958. *Small Town in Mass Society*. Garden City, NY: Doubleday.

Wald, Kenneth D., Dennis E. Owen, and Samuel S. Hill, Jr. 1988. "Churches as Political Communities." *American Political Science Review* 82: 531–48.

Wald, Kenneth D., Dennis E. Owen, and Samuel S. Hill, Jr. 1990. "Political Cohesion in Churches." *Journal of Politics* 52: 197–215.

Warner, R. Stephen. 1994. "The Place of the Congregation in the Contemporary Religious Configuration." In *American Congregations: New Perspectives in the Study of Congregations*, Vol. 2, edited by James Wind and James W. Lewis, 54–99. Chicago: University of Chicago Press.

Weems, Lovett, Jr. 2010. "No Shows: The Decline in Worship Attendance." http://www.christian-century.org/article/2010–09/no-shows.

Welch, Michael R., David C. Leege, Kenneth D. Wald, and Lyman Kellstedt. 1993. "Are The Sheep Hearing the Shepards? Cue Perceptions, Congregational Responses and Political Communication Processes." In *Rediscovering the Religious Factor in American Politics*, edited by David Leege and Lyman Kellstedt, 235–54. Armonk, NY: M. E. Sharpe.

Wheeler, Barbara. 2010. "The Problem with Lay Pastors: Ready to Lead?" *Christian Century* 127 (14): 28–33.

Wheeler, Barbara, Sharon Miller, and Daniel Aleshire. 2007. "How Are We Doing?" The Effectiveness of Theological Schools as Measured by the Vocations and Views of Graduates." *Auburn Studies* 13 (December): 3-32.

Wilcox, Clyde. 1992. *God's Warriors: The Christian Right in 20th Century America*. Baltimore, MD: Johns Hopkins University Press.

Williams, Rhys. 1998. "Political Theology on the Right and Left." *Christian Century* 115 (21): 722–24.

Wilson, J. Matthew. 2009. "Religion and American Public Opinion: Economic Issues." In *The Oxford Handbook of Religion and American Politics*, edited by Corwin E. Smidt, Lyman A. Kellstedt, and James L. Guth, 191–216. New York: Oxford University Press.

Wittkopf, Eugene. 1990. *Faces of Internationalism: Public Opinion and Foreign Policy*. Durham, NC: Duke University Press.

Wood, Lawrence. 2010. "The Need for Lay Pastors: Called but not Ordained." *Christian Century* 127 (14): 22–27.

Woolfalk, Miya. 2012. "Sermons Aren't Explicitly Political but Clergy Are: Political Cue-Giving in Sermons by U.S. Christian Clergy." Unpublished paper available at http://miyawoolfalk. com/pages/mw-research/.

Woolfalk, Miya. 2014. "Activating Religious Thinking in Politics." Paper delivered at the annual meeting of the Midwest Political Science Association, Chicago, April.

Wuthnow, Robert. 1983. "The Political Rebirth of American Evangelicals." In *The New Christian Right: Mobilization and Legitimation*, edited by Robert C. Liebman and Robert Wuthnow, 165–85.

Wuthnow, Robert. 1999. "Democratic Liberalism and the Challenge of Diversity in Late-Twentieth Century America." In *Diversity and its Discontents: Cultural Conflict and Common Ground in Contemporary American Society*, edited by Neil Smelser and Jeffrey Alexander, 19–35. Princeton, NJ: Princeton University Press.

Wuthnow, Robert. 2005. *American and the Challenges of Religious Diversity*. Princeton, NJ: Princeton University Press.

Wuthnow, Robert. 2007. *After the Baby Boomers: How Twenty- and Thirty-Somethings Are Shaping the Future of American Religion*. Princeton, NJ: Princeton University Press.

Wuthnow, Robert. 2013. *Small-Town America: Finding Community, Shaping the Future*. Princeton, NJ: Princeton University Press.

Zaller, John. 1992. *The Nature and Origins of Mass Opinion*. New York: Cambridge University Press.

Zikmund, Barbara Brown, Adair Lumnis, and Patricia Chang. 1998. *Clergy Women: An Uphill Calling*. Louisville, KY: Westminster/John Knox.

INDEX

The letter *t* following a page number denotes a table.

redistribution of wealth, *90t*, 91, 102. *See also* free
   enterprise, compatibility with Christianity
religious freedom, restrictions on, 5, *93t*, 94,
   103, 202
religious persecution, *113t*, 114, 176, *177t*
Religious Right, 7, 140
religious tradition, of clergy
   and changing clergy presidential voting,
      195–96, *196t*
   and changing partisan identification, *190t*,
      191–93, *193t*
   and clergy forming small groups within
      church, 167–71, *167t*, *170t*
   and clergy use of political cue-giving, 159–64,
      160t, *162t*
   and ideological orientation, 121–22, *122t*,
      127–29, *127t*, *128t*
   and likelihood clergy will address particular
      issues, 179, 183
   as predictor of political behavior/interest, 141,
      141t, 149–51, *150t*

salvation through Jesus Christ alone, *60t*,
   60, 62–63
   as measure of theological orthodoxy, 64, *65t*
second coming of Jesus, *60t*, 60, 62, 86
   as measure of theological orthodoxy, 67,
      68t, 222n8
sex education programs, 109–11, *110t*
small groups, formation of in church setting, 11,
   165–71, *166t*
social issues
   clergy-laity gap on, 123–29
   clergy views on, 109–12, *110t*
social justice
   at heart of gospel, 71, 89–91, *90t*, 102, 201
   and theological orthodoxy of clergy, *77t*,
      78, *79t*
social justice agenda, 7, 179–84, *180t*, *181t*, *182t*,
   183t, 203
   issues addressed in, 179, *180t*, 228n3
social theology, 7
   of church and cultural change, 86–91, *90t*
   and clergy political ideology, 100–102, *101t*
   definition of, 85
   and nature of political life, 95–98, *96t*, *98t*

of religion's role in public life, 92–95, *93t*
and theological orthodoxy of clergy, 100, 103
social welfare issues, 106, 107–9, *108t*

theological orthodoxy, of clergy
   and absolute moral standards, 97–98, *98t*
   and changing clergy presidential voting,
      195–96, *196t*
   and changing partisan identification, *190t*,
      191–93, *193t*
   and clergy demographics, 72–82, *73t*, *75t*, *76t*,
      77t, *81t*, 201
   and clergy forming small groups within
      church, 168–71, *168t*, *170t*
   and clergy-laity gap on political issues,
      126–29, *127t*, *128t*
   and clergy political ideology, 100–102,
      101t, 103
   and clergy use of political cue-giving,
      163, 228n7
   and contrast between mainline and
      evangelical, *73t*, 74–82, *76t*, *79t*, 83–84
   and ideological orientation, 121–22, *122t*,
      127–30, *127t*, *128t*
   and likelihood clergy will address particular
      issues, 181–84, *182t*, *183t*
   measures of, 63–68
   as predictor of political behavior/interest ,
      139–41, *141t*, 146–51, *147t*, *150t*
   and religious perspectives, 70–71, *70t*

unaffiliated, religiously, 205, 206, 229n7
unemployment, 108, *108t*, 176–78, *177t*
universalism, *60t*, 62–63, 222n4
urbanization, 37, 88. *See also* community size

virgin birth, 60, *60t*, 62
   as measure of theological orthodoxy, 64, *65t*
voting in elections
   by clergy, 26, *184t*, 185–87, *186t*
   and changing clergy presidential
      voting, 194–96
vouchers, *110t*, 111

women's rights, *110t*, 111